er Auf zug.
nd Printzen von Oesterreich Josephi, Benedicti, Ioannis, Augusti
güng, von der Pragerischen Judenschafft den 24. April A° 1741. gehalten worden.
f seine aigene Spesen in druck verfassen Lassen.

A HISTORY OF JEWISH COSTUME

A HISTORY OF JEWISH COSTUME

ALFRED RUBENS

Fellow of the Society of Antiquaries of London and Fellow of the Royal Historical Society

FOREWORD BY JAMES LAVER

PETER OWEN LIMITED

First published in Great Britain 1967
Revised and enlarged edition 1973; reissued 1981 by
PETER OWEN LIMITED
73 Kenway Road London SW5 ORE

Lay-out by Jan van de Watering
Printed in the Netherlands by Drukkerij de Lange/van Leer B.V., Deventer

ISBN 0 7206 0588 1

TO THE MEMORY OF MY MOTHER, HESTER RENA RUBENS 1867–1958

Frontispiece: Morocco: 1832. *'Mariée juive'.* Water colour by E. Delacroix. Musée du Louvre. The costume of a Moroccan Jewish bride was extremely elaborate. Each piece was strictly governed by tradition and the ceremony of dressing formed part of the marriage celebrations (see p. 74). The wedding at Tangier attended by Delacroix was the subject of the famous painting in the Louvre.

Contents

דבר אל בני ישראל ואמרת אלהם ועשו להם ציצת על כנפי בנדיהם לדרתם
ונתנו על ציצת הכנף פתיל תכלת

Speak unto the children of Israel and bid them to make a tassel on the corners of their
garments throughout their generations and to put on it a twined cord of blue

Numbers xv 38

במתא שמאי בלא מתא תותבאי

At home you know the name, abroad the costume

Talmud B. Shabbat 145b

Preface to the new and enlarged edition

This new edition in a larger format and with many colour plates, enables me to incorporate new material and to correct a number of mistakes.

An attempt has been made, I believe for the first time, to reconstruct the costume of the High Priest according to Josephus. His description has been faithfully followed by Miss Barbara Phillipson in a series of brilliant drawings which represent months of patient research and numerous conferences in which my wife played a valuable part.

I have been able to devote more space to the Talmudic period by drawing extensively on Dr Samuel Krauss' *Talmudische Archäologie* a large section of which was translated for me by Mrs L. R. Galandauer.

I again received much help from Dr Richard Barnett, Mr Sol Cohen, Mr Harold Levy and Mr Raphael Loewe. I am indebted to the latter, in particular, for the extensive notes on rabbinic literature and for translation from medieval Latin. Miss R. Lehmann, Dr J. Rosenwasser, Miss N. Rothstein and Mr A. Schischa helped in a number of ways. Mrs Paul Ortweiler, Mrs Charles Rubens and Mrs Henry Weil kindly undertook French and German translation.

From Israel has come most of my new material. Mrs Elisheva Cohen, chief curator of the Israel Museum and Mrs Aviva Müller-Lancet, curator of the Department of Ethnography have been lavish with help and advice. Dr Edith Varga-Biro, curator of the Ethnological Museum at Haifa and Dr D. Davidovitch director of the Museum of Ethnography, Tel-Aviv, have also encouraged me by their keen interest.

I am grateful to the following for their help in connection with photographic sources: Mr Felix Gluck, Mr M. R. Q. Henriques, Dr Michael Kauffmann, Mrs Irene Lewitt, Major P. I. C. Payne, Messrs Quaritch, Mr F. Schapira, Mrs R. K. Silverman and Mr O. R. M. Sebag-Montefiore. It was particularly kind of Dr Miriam Ayalon-Rosen to allow me to publish photographs of her important Qajar paintings. My thanks also go to Harvey and Elly Miller for the keen personal interest they have taken in the production of this book.

Alfred Rubens. London, 1973

Acknowledgment is also made to the following for permission to reproduce photographs:

Amsterdam: Rijksmuseum; Stedelijk Museum. Cincinnati: Hebrew Union College. Constance: Rosgarten Museum. Dublin: Chester Beatty Library. Edinburgh: The National Trust for Scotland. Istanbul: University Library. Jerusalem: Ben-Zvi Institute; Israel Museum; Jewish National and University Library. Lisbon: Museu Nacional de Arte Antiga. London: British Museum; Jewish Museum; Jews' College; National Trust; Public Record Office; The Spanish and Portuguese Synagogue. Munich: Bäyerisches Nationalmuseum. New York: Jewish Theological Seminary. Oxford: Bodleian Library. Paris: Bibliothèque Nationale; Musée du Louvre. Philadelphia: The Insurance Company of North America. Prague: Statni Zidovske Museum. Stratford-on-Avon: The Royal Shakespeare Theatre. Tel-Aviv Museum. Trier: Stadtisches Museum. Worms: Stadtarchiv. Yale University Press.

Foreword by James Laver

The vast majority of histories of costume are concerned with 'Fashion': that is, the changing styles worn by Western European women (for men hardly come into the picture) during the last six hundred years. It is only, after all, a very small part of the story.

'Fashion' is a function of the Renaissance, and it is no accident that Petrarch, 'the first modern man', should have entitled his most influential and popular work *The Triumph of Time*. For the greater part of human history, if you stayed where you were, your clothes never altered. But if you went into the next village, everything was different. This was to be subject to the tyranny of Place. But the whole meaning of the Renaissance, the whole meaning of modernity, the whole meaning of Fashion, is that we have substituted for the tyranny of Place the tyranny of Time. Go to the ends of the earth and everything is the same; but stay where you are in your little village for three months and all the women have different hats.

The Place-complex, if we may use the term, certainly fought a long rearguard action, in the sense that regional, that is to say national costumes were still recognizable as late as the seventeenth century. It was still possible to speak of French, English, Spanish, Italian and German costumes. But the immense prestige of Louis XIV brought it about that for the upper classes in Europe fashionable clothes henceforward meant French clothes. This dominance lasted, for both men and women, until the French Revolution, when the dictatorship of male attire passed to England. But Paris maintained its rule over women's clothes and, indeed, has kept it to this day.

Meanwhile, national and regional costume began to mean merely 'peasant' costume, which in some parts of Europe persisted until our own time. Up to a generation ago it was still possible when walking in the Tuileries Gardens to detect, from their costumes, which particular province of France the various nursemaids came from. Nowadays it would not be much of an exaggeration to say that in Western Europe at least, where regional costume persists it has been artificially preserved as a tourist attraction, although this is still not quite true of the Near East and the Balkans.

The final triumph of Time over Place means not only no distinction between the nations but no class distinction either, or so little that it would take an expert eye to detect it. There is not even a time-lag between the clothes of the upper and the lower classes. Everything is uniformly up-to-date.

That this represents a sad diminution in the variety and colour of life needs no stressing. Regional costume was often beautiful and redolent of the history of those who wore it. It is, in a sense, far more *interesting* than Fashion's vagaries, and it is, perhaps, surprising that the books which have been written about it are so few compared with the vast 'literature of Fashion'. Any new, authoritative book on the subject is worthy of welcome.

It is particularly welcome in the case of the Jewish people, for the problem of presentation is here immensely complex. The long period of time covered by its history and the fact that Jewish communities have been scattered all over the world and so have absorbed and reflected the costume of many different periods and places, add to the difficulty of presenting a coherent picture. And in addition to all this is the fact that Jews have frequently been *compelled* to adopt a special costume, often imposed as a mark of contempt but finally accepted as a badge of honour. The characteristic dress of the Polish Jew, for example, although not as common as it was fifty years ago, can be seen in certain parts of London even today.

Yet Jews, no more than Gentiles, have been able to escape the triumph of Time. All over the world they are losing their distinctive dress, and it was high time that a museum of Jewish costume should have been established in Israel. In another generation it might have been too late. It is therefore particularly appropriate at this time that Mr Alfred Rubens should have produced so learned and far-reaching a study as his *History of Jewish Costume* now presented in this enlarged edition with a wealth of colour illustrations, and all those who are interested not only in Jewish costume as such but in costume in general are deeply in his debt.

Introduction

Certain features of Jewish dress are as valid today as they were two thousand years ago but most of the peculiarities which have characterised it in the past can be attributed to the principle of *Hukkath Hagoyim*: 'You shall not copy the practices of the land of Egypt where you dwelt or of the land of Canaan to which I am taking you nor shall you follow their customs'. (Leviticus xviii:3). It drove Zephaniah to denounce 'all such as are clothed with strange apparel' (Zephaniah 1:8).

A completely different trend in distinctive dress arose from discriminatory laws first under Islam and later under the Church. In their different ways Synagogue and Church had the same aim and achieved more or less the same results: sometimes it took the form of a complete outfit, perhaps rather antique in appearance, otherwise the distinctive feature was a badge or a single garment such as a hat or a collar. Frequently, when a specifically Jewish item like the *tallith* was discarded for everyday use it was retained in the synagogue or home.

Distinctive dress was so much taken for granted that very little reference to it is made in Jewish literature and most of the evidence is pictorial. Where information is lacking, as it is for the early medieval period, one can be fairly certain that traditional influence remained consistent. For more recent times there is ample material from illuminated manuscripts, from books of Jewish customs (*Minhagim*), illustrated books of travel and portraits even though it is rare to find the feeling for history displayed by the Karaite rabbi who sat for his portrait expressly in order that future generations might know what he wore (see p. 161).

A great deal can be learnt from the Jewish Dress Regulations of which those of Fürth, published here for the first time in English, are of special interest because of the observations made by the Christian commentator.

Costume is defined as the mode or fashion of personal attire and dress (including the way of wearing the hair and personal adornment). *Custom*, the older form of the word, with its wider implication explains why dress was such an important feature in Jewish life. In the past it isolated Jews from their neighbours, Sephardim from Ashkenazim and Jews in different countries from one another. Even a custom like the covering of the head for men, regarded as fundamental in some countries, was considered unimportant in others and while in Germany Jews were being excommunicated for wearing wigs, in England and Holland the rabbis, themselves, regarded them as part of their normal dress. The pictures in this book have been chosen to illustrate all these features so that they show costume with Jewish characteristics as well as the dress worn by Jews in the western democracies where they were free to wear what they liked.

Virtually no examples of European Jewish costume other than Polish have survived. Until quite recently a Jewish family originating from Arles owned a yellow hat and before the last war several Ancona families still possessed the red hats worn in the past but all these have now disappeared. It is therefore encouraging to know that the importance of the subject is now realised and that the last surviving examples of costume from the ancient Jewish communities of North Africa and the Middle East are being collected and preserved in the museums of Israel.

1 Origins and distinctive features

ISRAEL AND JUDAH

There are many references to dress in the Old Testament and the chief difficulty is to identify the different garments. This is not only a matter of translation. In many instances the meaning of a word has been lost and although it may be explained by the context, by the Septuagint or by Josephus, there is sometimes complete disagreement between the authorities.[1]

The descriptions of Hebrew costume in the Bible supported by archaeological evidence lead to the conclusion that it did not differ to any material extent from that of the neighbouring peoples. The basic garments were known in Hebrew as the *simlah* or *salmah*, the *ezor* and the *kethoneth*.

The *simlah* was the long roll of cloth, rectangular or shaped, worn as an outer garment by most peoples of Western Asia. It was the Greek *himation* and the Roman *pallium*. It served as a blanket[2] and the Israelites used it in order to carry the dough for their bread and their kneading bowls.[3]

The *ezor* (Arabic: *izar*) was the simplest form of dress and although usually translated 'girdle' was a loin cloth. Jeremiah wore it on his loins.[4] When Isaiah removed his ezor he was naked[5] and a king is humbled by being made to wear one.[6]

The *kethoneth* or *me'il*, another garment in general use, was the Greek *chiton* and the Roman *tunica*. It was a shirt-like garment with long or short sleeves and came down below the knees sometimes to the ankles. It was usually made of wool or linen but sometimes of skins.[7]

An early example of the *simlah* is seen on a Sumerian priest-god (plate 1) of about 2250 B.C. from Ur of the Chaldees, the traditional birthplace of Abraham. It is fringed and worn wrapped round the body. The same garment is seen on a number of scarabs found in Palestine dating from the Hyksos period (*c.* 1670–1570 B.C.) corresponding approximately with the time of the Patriarchs and the period during which the Hebrews settled in Egypt.[8]

According to Deuteronomy xxvi: 5 'a wandering Aramaean was my father and he went down into Egypt and sojourned there few in number and

1   Sumer: Ur, *c.* 2250–2040 B.C.
Priest-god figure. Oriental Museum,
Istanbul. The *kethoneth* and fringed
simlah remained the basic costume of
the ancient Near East for fifteen
hundred years.

2   Egypt: *c.* 1450 B.C. *Tomb painting* (detail). British Museum. Foreigners
bearing gifts wearing Syrian dress. The standing figure holding his infant son
has the typical pointed Syrian beard and wears a long-sleeved *kethoneth* with
tassels attached to its hem, the centre ones being blue and brown.

3   Egypt: Thebes, *c.* 1450 B.C. *Tomb painting*. British Museum. Semitic
envoys from Retenu in Syria bringing gifts to Egypt. With one exception
they wear a long-sleeved *kethoneth* around which is wrapped the *simlah*. All
the garments are white and are edged with blue and red. Syrian style beards
and hair fillets.

there he became a nation, great mighty and prosperous'. If, as the Bible implies, the Hebrew and the Aramaeans (Syrians) were kinsmen it is probable that the Syrian dress shown on plates 2 and 3 was similar to that worn by the Hebrews. Plate 2 shows the *ezor*. In plate 3 most of the Semitic envoys from Syria appear to be wearing the *simlah* wrapped round the *kethoneth*. They have the usual pointed Syrian beards and a fillet round the hair. An unusual feature of their dress is the long sleeves.

The oldest monument on which Israelites are represented is the 'black obelisk' of Shalmaneser III (842 B.C.) in the British Museum. This is divided into five registers of which the second shows Jehu, King of Israel paying homage to the Assyrian King. He is followed by four Assyrian court officials after whom come thirteen Israelite porters bearing tribute. They wear over the *kethoneth* a fringed *simlah* draped over the left shoulder with the end flung over the right shoulder. Their dress is distinguished from that of the Assyrians by their pointed caps and sandals with upturned toes. Their beards trimmed to a point are also distinctive. Jehu himself wears the same cap and apparently a fringed *kethoneth* down to his ankles without a *simlah*. There are slight traces of a girdle and he probably had tassels hanging from his waist like those worn by the Assyrian official who follows him. The Assyrians are shown with the *simlah* draped in a different manner and the King wears a special head-dress and tassels attached to cords suspended from the waist (plate 4).

4 Assyria: 841 B.C. *Israelites carrying tribute*. Detail from 'Black Obelisk'. British Museum. Each wears a *kethoneth* with fringed hem over which is draped a *simlah* the tasseled end of which is thrown over the left shoulder. Pointed cap, sandals with upturned toes, and pointed beard.

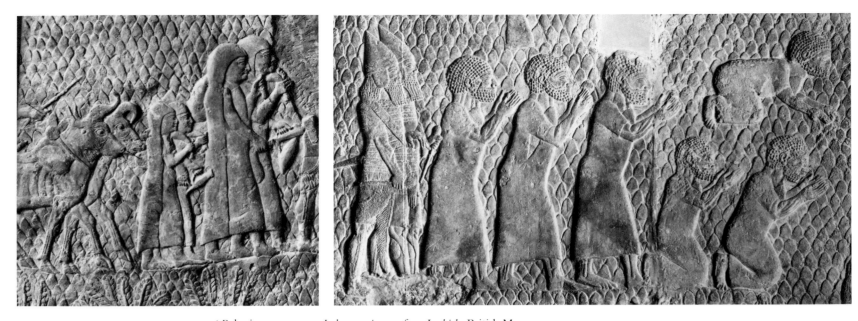

5–6 Palestine: *c.* 700 B.C. *Judaean prisoners from Lachish*. British Museum.
Details from reliefs showing the capture of the Judaean city of Lachish by
Sennacherib in 700 B.C. The Judaean men wear short-sleeved *kethoneth*, are
barefoot and have short trimmed beards. The women wear a *simlah* with a
plain border over a plain *kethoneth*.

These reliefs by themselves do not supply conclusive evidence of the
costume of the Israelites because the sculptor does not distinguish between
them and other peoples of Western Asia but as the same costume is seen on
prisoners from the Israelite city of Astartu (Ashtaroth?) after its capture by
Tiglath-Pileser III (745–727 B.C.)[9], there is a strong possibility that it is
authentic. It is different from the costume of the Judaean prisoners who are
seen being led away after the capture of Lachish by Sennacherib in 701 B.C.
(plates 5–6). These wear a short-sleeved full length *kethoneth*, are bare-
headed and have closely trimmed beards, while the beards of the Israelites
are more pointed in the Syrian manner.

There is no mention of head-dress in the Bible in pre-exilic times but there
are other Assyrian reliefs in the British Museum showing gangs of Semitic
prisoners wearing caps.

Women wore the *simlah* (plate 5) but theirs could be distinguished in some
way from the men's, possibly by its shape or colour.[10] They used cosmetics[11]
and there are many references to ornaments, bracelets, earrings and rings.
Isaiah indicates how wide was the choice: 'In that day the Lord will take
away all finery: anklets, discs, crescents, pendants, bangles, coronets,
head-bands, armlets, necklaces, lockets, charms, signets, nose-rings, fine
dresses, mantles, cloaks, flounced skirts, scarves of gauze, kerchiefs of linen,
turbans, and flowing veils'.[12]

Shoes are frequently mentioned in the Old Testament, the ordinary
Hebrew term being *nealim* which in the Septuagint is usually rendered
hupodemata but sometimes *sandalia*. *Hupodema* originally denoted a sandal

4

but was later applied to the Roman *calceus* (a shoe which covered the whole foot). The materials used for clothing were linen, wool and skins. The Hebrew word for cotton, *karpas*, from the Persian *kirpas* is found only in the Book of Esther.

Brides wore special dress and both bride and bridegroom wore jewels or ornaments.[13]

DISTINCTIVE FEATURES OF JEWISH DRESS

There are five distinctive features of Jewish dress of ancient origin. They are: *tsitsith* (tassels); *peoth* (hair locks); *shaatnez* (the ban on mixing wool and linen); *tefillin*; and the obligation for married women to cover their hair.

Tsitsith. There are two references in the Old Testament to the wearing of tassels. The more specific one is Numbers xv: 38: 'speak unto the children of Israel and bid them to make a tassel (*tsitsith*) on the corners of their garments throughout their generations and to put on it a twined cord of blue (*techeleth*)'. The other is Deuteronomy xxii: 12: 'you shall make for yourself twisted cords (*gedilim*)[14] on the four corners of your wrap (*kesuth*) with which you cover yourself'. Here the garment referred to is evidently the *simlah*, with which *kesuth* is synonymous, as opposed to general articles of clothing mentioned in Numbers, which would require a different kind of appendage; *gedilim* may have a different meaning from *tsitsith* a word which implies a flower-like form.[15] Another difference in the two texts is that the passage in Deuteronomy does not specify any colour.

According to tradition, *techeleth* represented sky-blue;[16] like Tyrian purple, it was derived from a mollusc (Heb. *hallazon*) similar to the *murex brandaris* which, by Talmudic times, had virtually been exterminated (see p. 24).

There were in fact two kinds of tassel in common use in Western Asia. One with three threads, which may be the *tsitsith*, is particularly associated with the Philistines but it is also found on Syrian dress in Egypt (plates 2 and 7) and is perhaps a stylized form of flower with the same magic properties as the lotus blossom. The other tassel, the *gedilim* or twisted cord, was probably similar to that seen in plate 8, attached to the corners of a *simlah*.

Among the Assyrians this type of tassel on cords suspended from the waist was a symbol of rank worn by the king and his chief officers and it probably had some religious significance.[17] In the palace at Khorsabad built by the Assyrian King Sargon II (721–705 B.C.) there were reliefs showing subject people, believed to be Anatolians or Phrygians, with various kinds of tassel attached to the corners of their tunics (plate 9).

In Talmudic times there were two schools of thought as to the correct

7 Egypt: *c.* 1180 B.C. *Philistine.* Foreign prisoner tile. Cairo Museum. He has a tassel in the shape of a trefoil attached to the projecting edge of his tunic.

number and colour of the threads forming the *tsitsith*, Beth Shammai maintaining that there should be four of white wool and four of blue, Beth Hillel that there should be two of each colour. This difference of opinion may be a clue to the original distinction between *tsitsith* and *gedilim*, while the lack of any absolute rule about colour can be attributed to the disappearance of the *hallazon*.[18]

Although according to the Talmud, *tsitsith* were a means of identifying a Jew[19] it seems that in early Christian times Jews and Christians were indistinguishable and Justin, one of the fathers of the Church, in a dialogue with Trypho the Jew, written in the middle of the second century, says: 'You are not recognized among the rest of men by any other marks than your fleshly circumcision'.[20] Jesus wore *tsitsith* (see p. 22) and the Ravenna mosaics provide evidence that some of the early Christians did so. Examples

8   Palestine: *c.* 750 B.C. *Statuette.* Jordan Archaeological Museum. Aramaean deity (?) holding in his left hand a lotus stalk. Over a short-sleeved *kethoneth* with girdle he wears a fringed *simlah* the corners of which are bound and terminate in tassels. He has side locks, a short square beard and his hair is worn in a fillet (p. 5). *Illustrated London News* 18 February 1950. R. D. Barnett, 'Four Sculptures from Amman' in *Annual of Department of Antiquities of Jordan*, I, Amman, 1951.

9   Assyria: 722–705 B.C. *Prisoners of Sargon II.* From a relief at the Palace of Khorsabad built by Sargon II King of Assyria. From Botta. The tailored tunics with double tassels on the corners are not found in Syria or Palestine and the figures probably represent Anatolians or Phrygians (p. 5).

6

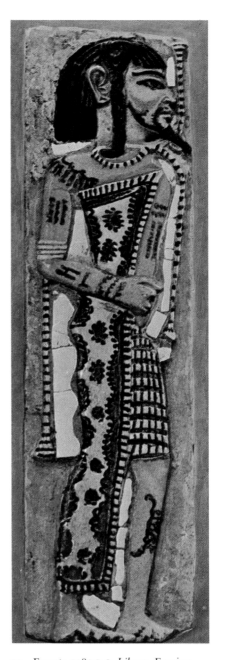

10 Egypt: 1180 B.C. *Libyan*. Foreign prisoner tile. Cairo Museum. He wears side-locks and his body is tattooed.

11 Persia: 600–500 B.C. *Lydians or Syrians*. From a stone relief at Persepolis. The characteristic features of their dress include side locks (*peoth*).

are to be found on the cupola of the sixth-century baptistery of the Arians, and in the groups of Christian martyrs in the sixth-century basilica of S. Apollinare Nuovo. They are also worn by the Apostle Matthew on a mosaic of the same period in the church of S. Vitale.[21]

Peoth. The special treatment of the hair and the wearing of side locks (*peoth*) is based on Leviticus xix:27: 'ye shall not round the corners (*peoth*) of your heads neither shalt thou mar the corners of thy beard'.

There is no evidence from antiquity that side locks were worn by Jews and they were, in fact, the characteristic feature of certain other peoples, particularly the Libyans, Syrians (see plates 10–11) and Cretans. The Hebrews shown on the Assyrian reliefs have neither *peoth* nor *tsitsith* which may be due to the fact that they came into use at a later date or because the sculptor did not take his figures from life. Nevertheless, *peoth* have been a Jewish distinctive feature in most countries in historical times and are still obligatory in certain orthodox circles.

Shaatnez. The law of *shaatnez* found in Deuteronomy xxii:11, is a prohibition against the mixture of wool and linen, but as it did not apply to the high priest's girdle nor to *tsitsith*[22] the objection does not seem to have been on moral grounds and one sees in it an early example of a sumptuary law comparable with Inca law whereby vicuna wool was reserved for the ruling classes.[23] It is still observed by orthodox Jews.

Tefillin consist of two small leather boxes attached by leather thongs, one to the forehead the other to the left arm (see plate 12). Each contains four passages from the Pentateuch. They are now worn by orthodox Jews for morning prayers, but in Talmudic times scholars wore them throughout the day in accordance with rabbinical precept. Their use is based on Exodus xiii: 9, 16 and Deuteronomy vi: 8, xi: 18 but the critical view is that these passages merely prove that the Hebrews originally wore amulets or tattoo marks on the forehead and hands and that in this respect they followed the practices of certain other Mediterranean peoples.[24] For this reason they are rejected by Reform Jews. They are not mentioned in the Old Testament and the supposed reference in Matthew xxiii: 5 has been questioned for the reasons given below. They are however referred to by Josephus.[25]

As we know that early Christians attached *tsitsith* to their *pallia* it is not surprising to learn that at the beginning of the sixth century there were some who also wore *tefillin* in church.[26]

Hair covering for married women. The custom for Jewish married women to have their head covered is of considerable antiquity. In the Mishnah it is described as a 'Jewish ordinance'[27] but its Biblical origin based on Numbers v: 18 is questionable. In Talmudic times it was considered immodest for a married woman to stir outside the house without a covering on her head although even a work basket was considered sufficient,[28] and if a Jewish woman wore her hair uncovered it was assumed that she was a virgin.[29] To the outside world a woman with her head completely covered was stamped as a Jewess. For this we have the authority of Tertullian (*c.* A.D. 155–222), one of the fathers of the Christian Church, who wrote: 'Among the Jews, it is so usual for their women to have the head veiled that this is the means by which they may be recognized'.[30]

Jewish women also wore wigs in Talmudic times[31] as a feminine aid to beauty. In time they came to be treated as a substitute for a head-covering

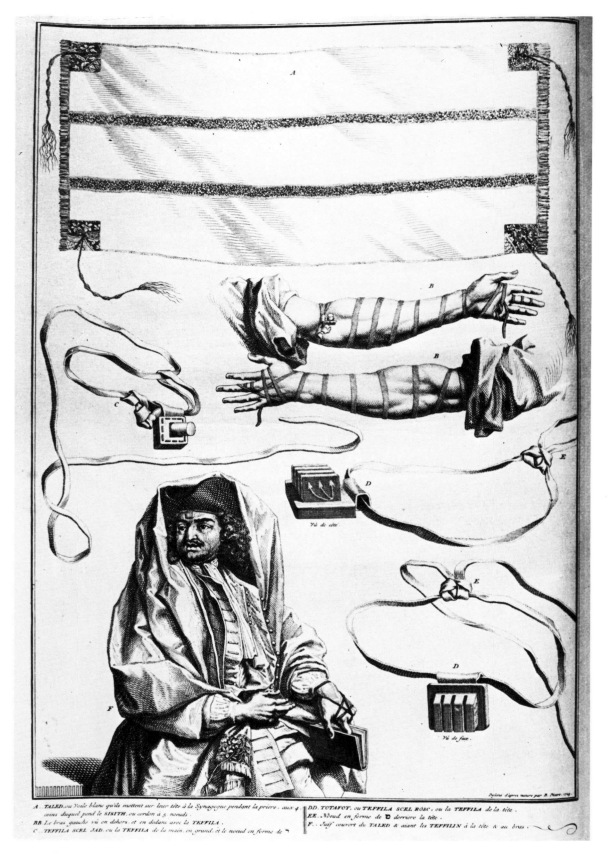

A. *TALED, ou Voile blanc qu'ils mettent sur leur tête à la Synagogue pendant la priere, aux 4 coins duquel pend le SISITH, ou cordon à 5 nœuds.*
BB. *Le bras gauche vû en dehors, et en dedans avec la TEFFILA.*
C. *TEFFILA SCEL JAD, ou la TEFFILA de la main, en grand, et le nœud en forme de ה.*
DD. *TOTAFOT, ou TEFFILA SCEL ROSC, ou la TEFFILA de la tête.*
EE. *Nœud en forme de ד derriere la tête.*
F. *Juif couvert du TALED & aiant les TEFFILIN à la tête & au bras.*

12   Holland: 1725. *Tallith and Tefillin*. Engraving. From Picart. Rubens (ii)
1196. The *tallith* has embroidered corners from which hang the *tsitsith*
consisting of eight threads and five knots. The engraving also shows the two
types of *tefillin*, one for the head, the other for the hand and arm.

14 Russia: Nineteenth century. *Karaite tallith and bag*. From the *Jewish Encyclopaedia* (see p. 108).

13 England (?): *c.* 1860. *Arba Kanfoth*. By kind permission of The Royal Shakespeare Theatre. Presented by Alfred de Rothschild to Sir Henry Irving (1838–1905) and worn by him for the role of Shylock. Jacquard woven red silk lined with purple silk and cotton. The *tsitsith* attached to each corner are knotted like those on the *tallith*.

and thereby the custom became established, chiefly in Eastern Europe, for Jewish women after marriage to cover their hair with a wig known as a *sheitel*. The custom was already well established by the sixteenth century as we learn from Leon of Modena (see p. 114). Beneath the *sheitel* the hair was shaved although in the Bible a woman's hair was cut only as a punishment[32] and in ancient Greece it was done so that the bride's hair could be dedicated to the goddess. The same custom existed in South-East Russia, Prussia and Sicily.[33]

The *Shulhan Aruch* requires married women to keep their hair covered at all times but makes no reference to the *sheitel*. There is, in fact, no religious authority for it, all the evidence being to the contrary. Objection to the *sheitel* started in the sixteenth-seventeenth centuries on the grounds that it was being used as a substitute for a hair covering and Moses Sofer of Presburg (1763–1839), a great authority on Jewish law, expressly banned it for the women of his family being supported in this by Akiba Joseph Schlessinger in his book *Lev Ha-ivri*.

Head covering for men. In the Bible no particular importance seems to have been attached to the covering of the head except for the priests and even they only did so when performing their priestly duties. The Mishnah[34] takes it for granted that men go bare-headed and only women and children cover their heads. In the Dura synagogue frescoes all the men except for the High Priest are shown bare-headed.

On the other hand one of the essential garments mentioned in the Talmud is the *kovha sheberosho* (head covering) and the benediction was recited when it was donned: 'Blessed is He who crowns Israel with glory'.[35] Krauss explains that like the *tallith* and *tefillin* a head covering was a privilege limited to scribes, Pharisees and rabbis.

Probably the best exposition of Jewish practice is that given by St Paul:

A man who keeps his head covered when he prays or prophesies brings shame on his head; a woman, on the contrary, brings shame on her head if she prays or prophesies bare-headed: it is as bad as if her head were shaved. If a woman is not to wear a veil she might as well have her hair cut off; but if it is a disgrace for her to be cropped and shaved, then she should wear a veil. A man has no need to cover his head, because man is the image of God, and the mirror of his glory, whereas woman reflects the glory of man.[36]

Rabbi Isaac ben Moses of Vienna (1200–1270) placed it on record that French rabbis in his time uttered the benedictions bare-headed. Rabbi Isserlein, a noted fifteenth-century rabbi, expressed the view that there was no explicit prohibition against Jews taking an oath bare-headed and Solomon Lurya (1510–1583), a great rabbinic authority, expressly stated that he knew of no prohibition against praying with uncovered head.

The rigid rules embodied in the Shulhan Aruch requiring the head to be covered on all occasions probably grew up during medieval times following the imposition of a special form of hat which Jews were obliged to wear whenever they appeared in public and it is clear that there is no religious significance in what was undoubtedly a purely regional custom. The situation has been summed up by Lauterbach and Israel Abrahams:

The oriental code of manners showed respect by covering the head and uncovering the feet in exact contradiction to the prevailing custom of Europe. The practice of covering the head when entering a synagogue and when reciting prayers or performing any other religious ceremony is not based upon any Talmudic law and cannot be supported by any express statement in the Talmud.

During the past fifty years the custom among Western Jews of wearing a head covering as a sign of orthodoxy has noticeably grown. What was originally a *minhag* (custom) restricted almost entirely to Jews from Eastern Europe has developed into a moral obligation and in time the skull-cap is likely to become as essential a part of the ordinary orthodox Jew's wardrobe as is the *caftan* for the Hasid.[37]

THE COSTUME OF THE HIGH PRIEST

The costume of the high priest is described at some length in Exodus 28. Apart from the head-dress it was similar to that worn by the Assyrian King, Ashur-Bani-Pal (668–624 B.C.) as seen on two reliefs in the British Museum (plates 15–16). The head-dress is like that found on an Elamite figurine of the second millennium B.C.[38]

For more detail of the vestments we have to rely on Josephus who, as a member of the priestly family, was an eye-witness of the ritual on the most sacred occasions just before the destruction of the temple in A.D. 70 and is therefore a reliable source. His account is particularly valuable because of the details he gives of the size and shape of the *ephod* which are not found in the Bible and for which Rashi drew on his imagination.

15–16 Assyria: *c. 650 B.C. Ashur-bani-pal.* Stone relief. British Museum. The costume of the Assyrian king worn for the lion hunt has strong affinities with that of the Jewish High Priest.

One item not mentioned in Exodus 28 is the gold crown which Josephus obviously regarded as of immense importance and describes in minute detail. Presumably it was a fairly late addition to the costume and signifies the supreme political authority invested in the high-priesthood under the Hasmonean kings. There is no doubt as to its authenticity since it is confirmed from independent sources: in the book of Ecclesiasticus, which dates from the second century B.C., where we are told that the glories of the high priest's costume included 'the gold crown upon his turban'[39] and in I Maccabees 10:20 where we learn that when Jonathan Maccabaeus was appointed high priest in 152 B.C. he was invested with a purple robe and a gold crown. This presumably was a new crown since 'the crowns' were included in the temple treasures seized and removed by Alexander Epiphanes in 169 B.C.[40]

The drawings representing the various vestments listed below follow the description given by Josephus in Jewish Antiquities iii: 150–174 and Jewish War v: 231–236 (see Appendix 1). Where details are lacking the artist has followed the styles adopted by the neo-Assyrian kings (plates 17, 18, 19).[41]

Breeches[42] (Heb. *mechnesayim*) made of fine spun linen worn low on the waist and terminating at the loins around which they were tightly drawn.

A linen robe or *chiton*[43] of double texture fine byssus enveloping the body and reaching to the ankles with long sleeves tightly laced round the arms. There was a loose opening at the neck. The garment was held over the shoulders by means of strings attached to its front and back.

A sash[44] for the *chiton* four fingers (8 cms) wide with an open texture like snakeskin and woven of flowers of crimson, purple, blue and fine linen but the warp was purely of fine linen. It was wound twice round the body at the breast and above; at the second winding it was carried up in front almost to the neck, where it was tied. The ends hung down to the ankles so that its full beauty could be seen and admired. When the priest was performing his duties, the ends of the sash were thrown over the priest's left shoulder so as not to impede his movements.

A mantle for the ephod[45] made of blue (or violet) woven material. It reached the feet and 'is called in our tongue *meeir*' (Heb. *me'il*). It was in one piece with hemmed slits for the head and arms but the slit for the head ran from back to front not crosswise. To the bottom edge were attached alternately gold bells and tassels coloured to resemble pomegranates. It had a sash similar in colour to the sash of the *chiton* but with gold added to the weave.

The ephod[46] made of woven fabric of many colours including gold embroidery and a cubit (about 55 cms) in length. It had sleeves and looked like a tunic. It resembled the Greek *epomis*.[47] On each shoulder there was a

17 Palestine: *c.* 500 B.C.–A.D. 70. *The High Priest*. Drawing by Barbara Phillipson.
The High Priest in his ceremonial robes as described by Josephus. His beard and
hair have been stylized and his *orant* attitude is based on early examples of Jewish art.

18   Palestine: *c.* 500 B.C.–A.D. 70. *Ordinary Priest*. Drawing by Barbara Phillipson.
He wears a white *kethoneth* with ornamental sash.

19   Palestine: *c.* 500 B.C.–A.D. 70. *The High Priest's vestments*. Drawing by Barbara Phillipson. 1. The mantle of the
High Priest's *ephod* with its sash. 2. The High Priest's *ephod*. 3. The buckles of the *ephod* with sardonyxes and
pins. 4. The High Priest's breastplate or pouch with gold chains and cords, blue ribbons to tie it in place and girdle.
5. The linen coronet. 6. The muslin head-dress covering the coronet. 7. The blue head-dress of the High Priest
with embroidery. 8. The High Priest's gold crown. 9. The gold plate engraved in ancient Hebrew characters worn
by the High Priest on his forehead.

brooch set with a sardonyx. The two stones were engraved with the names
of the sons of Jacob in Hebrew, six on each stone, in order of seniority
starting from the right shoulder. There was a cut-out in front which formed
a place for the breastplate.

Breastplate or pouch,[48] made of cloth. The colours were the same as
the *ephod* but mixed with gold. It was set with twelve stones 'of extraordinary
size and beauty—ornament not procurable by man by reasons of its surpassing value . . . all the stones have letters graven upon them forming the
names of the sons of Jacob . . . according to the order in which each of them
was born'.

Josephus describes in great detail how the breastplate was attached tó the *ephod* to prevent it slipping. Finally a band attached to the breastplate and of the same material with tassels at the ends was wound round the body.

For the gems on the breastplate it is impossible to follow either the Bible or Josephus since none of the English translations are in agreement. I have therefore fallen back on Jewish tradition and used the colours assigned to the twelve sons of Jacob in Midrash Numbers R.2:7. I have assumed that the arrangement would start from the wearer's right side as they would on a coat of arms and as they did on the shoulder pieces according to Josephus.

The colours are as follows:

Reuben	: red		Dan	: sapphire
Simeon	: green		Gad	: grey
Levi	: white, black and red		Naphtali	: rose
Judah	: azure		Asher	: beryl
Isaachar	: black		Joseph	: black
Zebulun	: white		Benjamin	: 12 colours

Head-dress.[49] A turban of woven linen over which was stitched a cover of blue embroidery. This was encircled by a crown of gold wrought in three tiers from which sprouted a golden calyx described by Josephus as being similar in shape to the plant known as *saccharon*. The crown extended from the nape of the neck to the two temples. The forehead was covered by a gold plate bearing the name of God.

GRECO-ROMAN AND PERSIAN INFLUENCES

General Effect. A change in the traditional costume of the Bible must have occurred in the time of Zephaniah (*c.* 630 B.C.) to produce his outburst: 'I will punish the princes and the king's children and all such as are clothed with strange apparel'.[50] This probably marks a trend towards Iranian costume which was similar to that worn by the Lydians and Phrygians, its chief characteristics being sewed garments, a coat of varying length with sleeves, riding trousers and as a rule, boots, leggings, cloak and a high cap of felt.

The principle invoked by Zephaniah was that of *Hukkath Hagoyim*: 'You shall not copy the practices of the land of Egypt where you dwelt or of the land of Canaan to which I am taking you nor shall you follow their customs'.[51] It was to have an important influence on dress throughout Jewish history. An example is the resistance to Jason when he seized power in Jerusalem as high priest in 175 B.C. and attempted to introduce the *petasos*, the Greek broad-brimmed hat associated with Hermes.[52]

This was an objection to a pagan symbol and not to Greek dress which was already accepted as the regulation Jewish costume. The Dura frescoes show that Persian styles were also in vogue under Sassanid rule but any influences other than Greek were usually opposed and a distinctive Roman garment like the toga was not worn by the Jews.

In the highly developed Jewish society of the Talmudic period clothes played an important role hence the saying 'without a shirt to one's name life is not worth living', or 'one should sell the beams of one's house to buy shoes'. Everyone was expected to dress according to his station in life from the high priest downwards and each rank and occupation: the shepherd, the peasant, the merchant, the scholar no less than the prostitute could thus be identified.

At the top of the scale there was great luxury. On the Day of Atonement the High Priest wore the finest materials imported from Pelusium in Egypt and India and in the household of the Babylonian exilarchs a certain weave of Indian linen as fine as muslin was used.

Rabbi Judah II had a state robe called *golyan* or *madda*.

The rich wore the *tunica talaris* the long *chiton* reaching to the ankles and several shirts might be worn one on top of another as a sign of wealth while the poor and particularly scholars sometimes possessed only one shawl (*tallith*) and one shirt (*haluk*).

Some idea of the social importance of dress can be drawn from the fact that shortly before the fall of Jerusalem the Levites persuaded King Agrippa to go to the length of calling a sanhedrin to authorise them to wear the same linen garments as priests.[53]

A change of clothes was obligatory for Sabbaths and festivals. This applied particularly to a white under-garment known as *sadin*.

Apart from the special cases mentioned, Greek styles for men were so simple that probably the only opportunities for display and ostentation were provided by the length of *tsitsith*, the width of *clavi* and the size of *tefillin* (see p. 23). With women it was different. A bride had no less than twenty-four pieces of jewellery and St. Paul was expressing Jewish teaching when he wrote: 'women again must dress in becoming manner, modestly and soberly, avoiding elaborate hair styles and should not deck themselves out with gold or pearls or expensive clothes'.[54]

There are no pre-Christian illustrations of Jewish costume. Examples of Jewish costume are found on the Greco-Roman mosaic of the Sacrifice of Isaac from the Beth-Alpha synagogue (plate 20) and in scenes from early Christian art some of which are believed to be of Jewish origin particularly those based on Old Testament stories of Abraham, Isaac and of Joseph, the Three Children in the Furnace, Jonah and the Whale and Daniel in the Den of Lions (plates 21–3).

20 Palestine: Sixth century A.D. *The sacrifice of Isaac.* Mosaic detail. Beth-Alpha Synagogue, Israel. Abraham wearing shoes is in a *colobium* with *clavi* and long sleeves with bands round the cuffs (p. 17).

21 Italy: Ravenna, sixth century A.D. *Alexandrian Jews.* Mosaic. S. Vitale. A group of Alexandrian Jews of the first or second century B.C. representing Aaron and the twelve tribes of Israel (p. 17).

22 Egypt: Sixth century A.D. *The Three Children in the Furnace.* Wall painting. From Wadi Sarga, Egypt. British Museum. The three children wear a Persian hat (*kyrbasia*), a cloak fastened in front, belted tunic with roundels near the lower edge and long Persian leggings.

23 Italy: Rome A.D. 432–440. *Abraham and Sarah*. S. Maria Maggiore, Rome.
From Wilpert. Part of a mosaic illustrating the story of Abraham and the Three
Angels (Genesis xviii: 1–3). Abraham wears pale yellow *colobium* with clavi and
a *pallium* decorated with *gams*. Sarah has a white under-tunic of which only the
tight white sleeves are visible from the elbows downwards; an orange *dalmatica*
with *clavi* and on her head a white coif indicating her married status (p. 17).

Other pictures are believed to originate from illustrated pre-Christian
versions of the Septuagint. A fourth-century drawing from Egypt (plate 22)
interprets the Persian dress of the Three Children in the Furnace so well that
it might have been based on a contemporary illustration of the text: 'then
they were bound in their cloaks (*sarbalehon*), their breeches (*pateshehon*) and
their hats (*karbelathehon*) and other garments'.[55]

The three obscure Aramaic words used to describe the garments of the
Three Children have been translated in a number of ways but the interpretation given by the drawing seems the most likely. The *sarbal* as a cloak is
mentioned in the Talmud[56] and was still worn during the seventeenth
century by which time it had acquired special importance for use during
prayers (see p. 115). The word *patesh* is used in the Talmud to mean a leg
covering fastened at the hips. *Karbela* literally means a cock's comb in
reference, presumably, to the Persian hat of that shape, the *kyrbasia*, which
came into fashion during the Achaemenid period (546–330 B.C.).

The most important early illustrations of Jewish costume come from the frescoes of the third-century synagogue at Dura Europos (plates 24–6). Dura, a Roman fortress on the Euphrates frontier, was totally destroyed by the Sassanians in A.D. 256. Before being incorporated in the Roman Empire it had been a Parthian city and before that had been held by the Seleucids, and its costume as well as its art and architecture display the joint Iranian and Greco-Roman influences which were the feature of Palmyran culture. The remarkable series of paintings illustrating the Old Testament displays all these elements. There are two distinct types of dress: the Greco-Roman, consisting of *chiton* (*dalmatica* or *colobium*) with *clavi*, *himation* (*pallium*) and sandals; and the Persian, consisting of tunic, trousers and boots or shoes.

In one or two cases there are *tsitsith* attached to the corners of the *himation*. It is difficult to draw any conclusions from the costume. Kings are given Persian royal costume while the simple Persian style is applied to persons of different status regardless of rank. Jewish prophets and priests wear a *chiton* with *clavi* and *himation* with *gams*. In pagan and Christian art this is the costume assigned to holy men and philosophers and many examples are to be seen in the early Christian mosaics at Ravenna and at S. Maria Maggiore in Rome.

24 Mesopotamia: Third century A.D. *The High Priest and his Attendants.*
Fresco. Dura Europos Synagogue. The High Priest is labelled 'Aaron' in Greek but his costume bears little relation to that described in Exodus or the later version given by Josephus and is the costume of Persian royalty. The attendants are dressed in belted tunics and Persian trousers. Kraeling, plate 60. Reproduced by kind permission of Yale University Press.

25 Mesopotamia: Third century A.D. *Samuel anoints David*. Fresco. Dura Europos Synagogue. The dress assigned to prophets and priests in the synagogue frescoes: *chiton* with *clavi* over which was worn the *himation* decorated with *gams*. Kraeling, plate 66.
Reproduced by kind permission of Yale University Press.

26 Mesopotamia: Third century A.D. *Moses and the miraculous well of Be'er*. Fresco. Dura Europos synagogue. Moses wears a yellow chiton with gams. The feature of his dress is the amount of purple decoration, an attribute of royalty. Kraeling, plate 59.
Reproduced by kind permission of Yale University Press.

THE GARMENTS OF THE MIDRASH, MISHNAH AND TALMUD

In the Midrash, the Mishnah and the Talmud the words used to describe dress are almost entirely Greek or Latin terms transliterated into Hebrew and most of the garments are of Greek, Roman or Iranian origin. We learn for instance that 'Raba went out in a new Roman red tunic'[57] (Heb. *himmutsatha*).

The garment most frequently mentioned in rabbinic writings is the *tallith* (Gr. *stole*; Lat. *stola*) a shawl worn by all classes which became a Jewish garment only when *tsitsith* were attached to it otherwise it cannot be distinguished from the *pallium* or *himation*.

This is because the *tsitsith* had religious significance, not the garment to which they were attached.

The morning benedictions[58] show that the girdle (Heb. *hagorah*) and the *sudarium* or kerchief (Heb. *sudar*) although not of equal importance come into the same category. The two types of *sudarium* mentioned in the Talmud correspond with those worn by the Romans, one on the neck, the other on the shoulder or forearm.

The *haluk*, a kind of shirt, was in general use. Examples found in the caves of Bar–Kokhba show that they were made by joining two squares of material together hence the name (Heb.=divided).[59]

The *colobium* served the same purpose as the *haluk* but was more luxurious being woven in one piece. Both the *haluk* and the *colobium* were usually adorned with *clavi*, two vertical strips of purple material.

The *buros*, a large cloak with cape attached, was a popular and important garment. The *liburnica* was similar.

Sandals are mentioned more frequently than shoes (*Heb. minalim*) and as a sign of humility, were favoured by scholars.

In the following list of the principal garments mentioned in these works, the first sixteen are designated in the Talmud as essential.[60] They are Hellenistic except for the *haluk* and the *hagorah*. The Babylonian Talmud omits the *bracae* and the Jerusalem Talmud the *paragauda*.

	Greek	Latin	Description
Miktorin		*amictorium*	wrapped garment, cloak or scarf
Unkelai	*anacholos*		under-tunic
Funda		*funda*	money belt
Kolob	*kolobus*	*colobium*	linen tunic
Haluk			shirt
Appilion		*pallium*	*pallium*
Maaporeth		*mappa*	napkin; apron
Savrikin	*subrichion*	*subucula*	woman's tunic
Minalim			shoes
Impilayoth		*impilia*	socks; felt shoes
Afrikin		*bracae*	trousers or breeches
Pargod		*paragauda*	bordered garment
Hagorah			girdle
Kova Sheberosho			head covering
Sudar Shebetsavaro	*soudarion*	*sudarium*	kerchief for the neck
Sudar Sheal Zero-othav	*soudarion*	*sudarium*	kerchief for the arm
Isticharion	*sticharion*		short-sleeved jacket
Itstela; Istela	*stole*	*stola*	shawl; *tallith*
Buros		*birrus*	rectangular cloak or cape with hood attached
Balneri		*balnearia*	bath clothes
Dalmatikon		*dalmatica*	
Toga		*toga*	
Kalmus	*chlamus*	*chlamys*	cloak
Sagos; sagum	*sagos*	*sagum*	coarse woollen blanket or mantle
Sandal	*sandalon*	*sandalium*	sandal
Pilion	*pilos*	*pileus*	felt cap
Falnis	*phainoles*	*paenula*	cloak or mantle; *cucullus*
Famalniya		*feminalia*	leggings

THE COSTUME OF THE NEW TESTAMENT

The usual garments worn by Jesus consisted of *colobium*,[61] *sudarium*[62] and *himation* with *tsitsith* (Gr. *kraspeda*) attached to its four corners. It was by touching these that the woman suffering from a haemorrhage was cured.

Jesus attacked the scribes and Pharisees for wearing *tsitsith* and coats which were too long[63] and phylacteries which were too wide or too large.[64] According to Epiphanius (c. 315–402), one of the Church fathers, by *phylacteries*, Jesus meant *clavi*, the vertical purple stripes attached to the colobium. Epiphanius is not very reliable but is worth quoting:

They (the scribes) had certain 'borders' (*kraspeda*)[65] as tokens of their citizenship, alike to show their pride and to win the commendation of those who saw them. And they put 'phylacteries' upon their himations, that is broad purple stripes (or marks, *sēmata*). Now one must not think, because in the Gospel they are given this name, that the reference is to amulets (*periapta*: literally, amulets of the type bound around) since some people are used to understanding 'phylacteries' (in the Gospel) as amulets of this kind. The account has no reference to this sort of thing. But since these people dressed in outer garments of the type of *ampechonai*[66] and dalmatics of the type of *colobia*, adorned with broad stripes (*platusēma*, the word most used in Greek for the *latus clavus*) of purple made of purple cloth, those who were most accurate were accustomed to call the stripes of purple 'phylacteries', and for this reason the Lord called them 'phylacteries' as worn by these men. What follows makes clear the meaning of the words 'and the borders of their cloaks'. For he (the Lord) said 'borders' (*kraspeda*) in the definite sense of fringes (*krossoi*), and 'phylacteries' in the sense of stripes of purple, when he said, 'Ye make broad your phylacteries and deep the fringes on your cloaks'.[67]

Until Goodenough drew attention to the writing of Epiphanius on this subject it was assumed that the *phylacteries* referred to in the New Testament were *tefillin*. Goodenough was inclined to accept Epiphanius' theory on the grounds that *tefillin* are limited in size because they are worn on the forehead. This is not in fact the case and even today the size provides opportunities for a display of piety. The customary interpretation of Matthew xxiii:5 should not therefore readily be discarded.

DYES AND COLOURS[68]

The Jews acquired the art of dyeing from the Phoenicians. Tyre was a great centre for the industry but Serepta, Neapolis (Sichem), Lydda and Jerusalem are also mentioned. The inhabitants of whole villages in the 'Darom', i.e. the south, were occupied in purple-dyeing, from which their hands became coloured while a place called 'Castle of Dyers', which also contained weaving mills, obtained its name from its dyeing industry.

The many references to dyeing in the Talmud indicate the large number of Jews engaged in it. The dyer (Heb. *tsabba*; Lat. *infector*), whether Jew or heathen, belonged to the best social class and worked on his own premises 'by the piece' or was self-employed. In the street he wore the sign of his trade, a piece of dyed material behind his ear, though he was also known by his coloured hands.

From antiquity only basic colours are known: white, black, red and green sometimes in different shades; to these a considerable number were added during the Talmudic period and in the Bar-Kokhba caves thirty-four varieties were found. The concept of 'colour' (Heb. *tseva*), indicates a certain variety but in former times and especially in the Orient there was a preference for white garments as the natural property of linen and wool and thus the Jews distinguished between two main groups, viz. white (*begadim levanim*) and coloured clothes (*bigdai tsivonim*), here mainly referring to red. White clothes constituted the dress for happy events contrasting with black for mourning. Their attribute was purity as well as aristocracy and grandeur so that important people tended to dress in white[69] leaving colours to people of lower status and to women. Purple, the only exception, remained the privilege of the highest ranks.

The dyes were mainly derived from vegetable or animal substances. Among vegetable dyes there were 'woad' (Heb. *isatis*; Gr. *isatis*; Lat. *isatis tinctorum*) for blue dyes; the saffron (Heb. *kotsa*; Gr. *crocus*) for yellow; the red dye, also called madder (Heb. *pu'ah*; Gr. *eruthrodanon*; Lat. *rubia tinctorum*) and the litanus (Heb. *pikas*; Gr. *fucus*), a red dye more beautiful but less durable than purple. Other materials used included nutshells, pomegranate peel, sumach (*rhus coriaria*; Heb. *alai og*), a kind of onion (Heb. *richpa*) and wine. The wool dyed with the scarlet-red dye is the Biblical *argaman*. Purple (Heb. *purpurea*; Gr. *porphura*) the most prized and the most expensive of all dyes, was obtained from two kinds of snail, the trumpet snail (*bucinum* or *murex*) and the purple snail (Gr. *purpura*; Lat. *purpura* or *pelagia*); the Jews called both *hallazon*.

The purple snail used by the Jews was found on the coast of the 'Tyrian Ladder' up to Haifa. From it was obtained the *techeleth* colour of the Bible, a blue with a reddish iridescence, of the utmost importance for dyeing the *tsitsith*. The purple industry was based mainly in Tyre but the Rabbis also mention the ancient Luz in this connection. The snails which were thrown onto the land in large numbers after heavy rain produced a coloured slime which was boiled in oven-pits and cleaned. From the combined juice of both types of snail, the blackish tint of the purple-snail with the reddish one of the trumpet-snail one obtained the hyacinth or janthin purple (Heb. *tinun*), the most beautiful and precious purple product while the so-called Tyrian and Laconian purple was dyed twice (Gr. *dibaphos*), at first in half-boiled *pelagium* and then in *bucinum*. If the fabric saturated in *coccum* was then dyed Tyrian, one obtained the Hysgin purple (Heb. *sasgona*). Owing to the high prices of genuine purple there were many imitations. The genuine purple was to be found only among the rich. To own a purple gown was, for Jews as well as for Romans, the privilege of kings. Jewish sources refer to the dye only in connection with wool but the Greeks and Romans also used it to dye byssus and silk.

By Talmudic times the *hallazon* had become a legend. The distinction between real and imitation blue dye for *tsitsith* depended on the colour not fading so that the *tsitsith* should be bought only from an expert.[70]

ORNAMENTS AND DECORATION

There was a great variety of decorative marks and bands for clothing. Of these the most common were the two bands of material, usually purple in colour, the *clavi*, attached to the *tunica* or *haluk*, the *colobium* and the *dalmatica*. They were applied vertically on each side of the garment front and back. Among the Romans the *clavus* was originally a badge of rank but by the first century A.D. it had become purely a decorative feature.

27   Egypt: Sixth century A.D. *The story of Joseph.* Wool on linen. Städtisches
Museum, Trier, West Germany. Roundel from a tunic presumably worn by a
Jew on account of the two Hebrew letters which form part of the design (p. 26).

It was so usual for the *haluk* to have *clavi*, as well as decorative bands round the hem, the neck opening and the sleeves, that the Hebrew word, *immera*, used to describe the decoration was also used to apply to the garment itself (plate 26). Due to Greek influence the purple decoration was also called *periphuros* or *purpurea* for which the corresponding Hebrew word was *hativah* (=*immera*).

Segmentae. The decorative square and round patches applied to the *haluk* or tunic usually known as *segmentae* were called in Hebrew *tavlin* (Gr. *tablion*). They are seen in the form of roundels on Jewish dress on plate 22 and in the fourth-century Exodus paintings at Bagawat in Egypt.[71]

Roundels are said to have originated in Syria but most of those which have survived come from Coptic tombs of the sixth–seventh century in Egypt and they usually carry Christian motifs. Some, however, have designs based on Old Testament themes and one example at least may have come from a garment worn by a Jew (plate 27). This has on it the story of Joseph with two Hebrew letters in the centre. The design is fairly common but the feature of this one is that the narrative runs from right to left which would seem to indicate a Jewish prototype while in the more common examples it is reversed.[72]

Gams. Certain marks known in Christian tradition as *gams* or *gammadiae* are a conspicuous feature on much of the dress seen in the early Christian mosaics dating from the fifth and sixth centuries B.C. in the church of Santa Maria Maggiore at Rome (plate 23), and at Ravenna. They vary in shape and size but the most common is like the Greek letter *gamma*.

The frescoes at Dura Europos show two kinds of *gam* on Jewish dress: type *b* for men and type *a* for women (see drawing). Outside the synagogue area many fragments of material were found with *gams* attached corresponding to types *a*, *b*, and *c*.

Final proof that *gams* were worn by Jews came from the caves of Bar-Kokhba where types *a* and *b* were discovered.[73] The only reference to a *gamma* shape in the Talmud[74] is not in connection with a woman's garment and the name itself seems to indicate the original shape as it appears on male dress in early Christian mosaics not only at Ravenna and Rome but also at Naples (San Restituta) and Milan (San Lorenzo) all of which point to a much earlier, possibly pagan, prototype. Goodenough, who examined the subject in depth (but before the discoveries in the Bar-Kokhba caves), discusses similar marks in hellenized Egypt, Palmyra and pagan Dura and concluded that they originally had some symbolic meaning which in the course of time had been lost.[75]

Distinctive marks. Distinct from *segmentae* and *gams* are those marks on

a

b

c　　d

clothing, indicating the wearer's occupation, which are mentioned in the Talmud.[76] Scholars carried a sign on their head-covering, slaves on their clothes; the tailor carried a needle, the scribe a pen at his ear, the money-changer a coin, the carpenter a chip of wood, the weaver and comber a woollen thread and so on. This was perhaps the means whereby the different trades were identified in the Great Synagogue at Alexandria where, we are told, they remained in separate groups.[77]

THE TALLITH

Among the Romans, the *pallium* or *himation* had by the third century A.D. ceased to be used as a garment but was regarded as the attribute of learned men. It was also used for official purposes when it was worn folded two or three times, reducing its width to about eighteen inches. The removal of the surplus material finally reduced it to a scarf or stole and the ecclesiastical *pallium*, ultimately reduced to a single strip of cloth or silk, is still worn by high dignitaries of the Christian church.

By a somewhat similar sequence of events the *pallium* or *himation* worn by Jews developed into the modern *tallith*. It was probably made of wool or linen, usually white but sometimes black or red. With *tsitsith* attached to its corners it was as characteristic for Jews as the *toga* was for Romans. Out of doors the two sides were thrown over the shoulder or wound round several times. In Talmudic times the *tallith* was still essentially an attribute of scholars who wore it over a long *haluk*. The religious significance of the *tsitsith* was recognized by the special benediction recited over them as part of the ordinary routine of dressing[78] but the *tallith* is not one of the essential garments listed in the Talmud (see p. 22). Etymologically it seems to be the same word as *stole* and it is the stole rather than the *pallium* which is its counterpart in the Christian church.[79]

The modern *tallith* (see plates 12 and 14), a prayer shawl for males who have reached the age of thirteen,[80] is woven of wool or silk, in white, with black or blue stripes at the ends. The silk ones vary in size from fifty-four to ninety-six inches in length and from thirty-six to seventy-two inches in width; the woollen *tallith* is larger, sometimes reaching to the ankle, and is made of two lengths sewed together, the stitching being covered with a narrow silk ribbon. A ribbon or band woven with silver or gold thread is sometimes sewn along the top edge where it touches the neck. This is usually called the *ata* and according to Goldstein and Dresdner, who reproduce a number of examples, the traditional design is Spanish and of Sephardi origin. This would account for its alternative name, *spania*. In modern times they were manufactured at Sassow in Poland. From each of the four corners of the *tallith* hang the *tsitsith* consisting of four threads looped to form eight which may be blue or white in colour.[81]

Arba Kanfoth. The *arba kanfoth* (four corners) or *tallith katan*, first mentioned in the code of Jacob ben Asher *c.* 1350 is designed to fulfil the requirements of Numbers xv:38 and Deuteronomy xxii:12. It normally consists of a rectangular piece of cloth usually of wool, about three feet long and one foot wide with an aperture for the head. To its four corners are attached *tsitsith*.

Among orthodox Jews it is still worn by males from childhood as an under-garment throughout the day but in the ghettos it was sometimes worn as an outer-garment and occasionally, perhaps for Sabbath use, it was richly embroidered (see plate 13).

Authorities: I. Abrahams; S. Bertman; M. P. E. Botta; F. G. Bratton; *Brit. Mus. Cat. of Ivory Carvings; Brit. Mus. Guide to early Christian Antiquities*; A. Brüll; E. A. W. Budge; P. Cintas; T. Ehrenstein; *Encyc. Biblica; Encyc. Judaica*; Ahmed Fakhry; P. R. Garrucci; E. R. Goodenough; C. H. Gordon; O. R. Gurney; L. & J. Heuzey; U. Hölscher; M. G. Houston; *International Standard Bible Encyc.; Interpreter's Bible*; M. Jastrow; *Jewish Encyc.*; A. F. Kendrick; E. G. Kraeling; S. Krauss; L. Kybalova; H. F. Lutz; C. F. Morey; *New Schaff-Herzog Encyc.*; H. Norris; A. Parrot; R. Pfister & L. Bellinger; J. S. Parkes; J. B. Pritchard; A. Rosenzweig; D. Talbot Rice; J. P. Richter & A. C. Taylor; S. Schemel; H. Seyrig; E. L. Sukenik; V. Tcherikover; R. de Vaux; J. Wilpert; C. L. Woolley; Y. Yadin. See Bibliography.

2 The Eastern world and the influence of Islam

CHINA

Jewish settlements in China were associated with the silk trade between China and Rome and there is every reason to believe that their origins go back at least to the first century of the Christian era. According to their own traditions the Jews entered China during the Han Dynasty (206 B.C.–A.D. 221) or more exactly during the reign of Han Ming-Ti (A.D. 58–76). Graetz connects their arrival with the persecution of the Jews in Persia in A.D. 231. The original communities were probably continually recruiting new members from Persia, Turkestan and India and Elkan Adler found that their customs were similar to those observed by the Jews of Bokhara. The community at K'ai-Fêng the capital of Honan was the last to disappear. Some of their religious practices, such as the observance of the New Moon Festival, indicate a pre-Talmudic origin. In the synagogue during the reading of the Law the minister covered his face with a transparent veil of gauze in memory of Moses, who came down from the mountain with his face covered—a custom unknown elsewhere but mentioned by St Paul as being well established in his time.[1] The *tallith* was not worn, but for *Simchat Torah* (Feast of Tabernacles) a red silk scarf was draped over the right shoulder and tied under the left arm. As was customary in the East shoes were removed before entering the synagogue, except by the rabbi who alone wore blue shoes and sat on an elevated position beneath a large red satin umbrella. The men wore blue caps in synagogue and the women had to remove their headscarves.

The Jesuit priest, Matteo Ricci, who talked to one of the Chinese Jews in 1605, described him as a Jew in religion, race and features, but the sketches made at K'ai-Fêng a century later by Jean Domenge, another Jesuit, show that the Jews he met were indistinguishable from the Chinese (see plate 28).

Renewed interest in the Chinese Jews has been aroused in recent years following the discovery of clay tomb figures of the T'ang Dynasty (A.D. 618–907) with semitic features. These figures form part of the *Ming Chi* which were buried with the dead in accordance with Chinese practice to provide the deceased with the services to which he was accustomed in his

28   China: 1723. *Chinese Jews reading from the Torah*. From a sketch by J. Domenge made in 1723. From Tobar. By this period all differences in dress to distinguish them from the native Chinese had disappeared. In the original drawing the men are barefoot.

29

29   China: *c. 618–907. Pottery tomb figure.* C. T. Loo Collection.
Pedlar in Persian hat and *caftan.*

30   China: *c. 618–907. Pottery tomb figure.* Author's collection.
Pedlar in Persian hat and *caftan* with girdle.

lifetime. Most of them come from around Ch'ang-An, the Western capital, an important centre for foreign trade and situated close to the Jewish settlement at K'ai-Fêng. The tombs in which they were found date between A.D. 683 and 728.

William Charles White, formerly Bishop of Honan and later Professor of Chinese Studies at the University of Toronto, who lived for twenty-five years at K'ai-Fêng and devoted much of his life to the study of the Chinese Jews and the careful documentation of their history, was convinced that some of these figures represented Jews. This view is supported by Mrs Mahler and Signore Prodan. After examining photographs of figurines in the collections of Mr Frank Caro (C. T. Loo Collection), The Royal

Ontario Museum, The Seattle Art Museum and the late Mrs Brenda Seligman, I have selected, as most likely to represent Jews, the figures with long pointed hats(see plates 29–30). This hat appears to be the Persian *kalansuwa* and when accompanied by a *caftan* and a corded belt the costume seems to correspond with that worn by Persian Jews (see below). The pedlar with his pack bears a striking resemblance to the Jewish pedlars of more modern times carrying on their age-old occupation.

UNDER ISLAM

From the rise of Islam during the seventh century a great deal of material emerges, much of it confusing, about the special clothing which the *Dhimmis*, the non-Believers, had to wear under Moslem rule. The need to distinguish non-Moslems did not arise until the Arabs with their lower cultural background began to adopt the fashions of the newly converted townspeople, and the first restrictions are believed to have been introduced during the eighth century under the Caliph Umar II—although the 'covenant of Umar' often cited is now regarded as spurious.

The frequent repetition and the lack of uniformity in the Dress Regulations reflect the weakness of the Caliphate after the ninth century and the degree of enforcement probably varied in different parts of the empire.

In 849 the Caliph al-Mutawakkil ordered Christians and other non-Believers to wear a yellow Persian mantle (*tailasân*), a belt of cord (*zunnâr*),[2] to fix two balls behind their saddles and to use wooden stirrups only. If they wore the Persian hat, the *kalansuwa* (*qalasuva*), they were restricted to certain colours and two buttons of a different colour had to be attached to it; if they wore a turban it had to be yellow. This is the first mention of special colours for non-Moslems or of a badge, although at first this last mark of distinction applied only to their slaves, who were required to fix two patches of cloth on their outer garment and of a different colour to it. Four years later all non-Believers were ordered to wear the badge in the form of two patches of yellow cloth. These patches were perhaps the roundels commonly worn on tunics in the Eastern Mediterranean and already referred to above.

In 1004 the mad Caliph of Egypt, al-Hakim, in order to annoy his enemies, the Abbasids, ordered non-Moslems to wear black turbans like theirs and later he decreed that all their clothing should be black. He also required Jews to wear suspended from their neck a block of wood carved to represent the golden calf while Christians were obliged to display an enormous iron cross.

At the end of the twelfth century A.D. Jewish converts to Islam were required to wear blue clothes[3] with very wide long sleeves and long veils instead of turbans.

By the fourteenth century, under the Mameluks, the distinctive colours were yellow for Jews, blue for Christians and red for Samaritans. Non-Moslems, men and women, wore the corded girdle (*zunnâr*) and a badge. According to some authorities one of these distinctions was sufficient. Women, besides wearing the appropriate colour, had to wear non-matching shoes: red and black or black and white. Christians were treated with greater severity than Jews and it was not unknown for them to borrow yellow turbans from Jews when feeling ran high against them.

There was no prohibition against non-Moslems wearing a turban provided it conformed to the prescribed colour and did not exceed a certain length. Nevertheless, the turban was the symbol of Mahomed and the distinctive head-dress for non-Moslems was the *kalansuwa*, a hat of Persian origin which went out of fashion among Moslems in the eighth century and when worn by them was usually draped with a scarf to form a turban.

In its later form the *kalansuwa* was tall and cone-shaped probably like that worn by Chinese Jews and it may have inspired the *hennin*, the steeple-shaped hat worn by women in Western Europe during the fifteenth century.

Under Ottoman rule Jews were on the whole favourably treated and in many parts of the empire developed their own national costume. The further they were removed from the seat of central government the greater were the restrictions, and in the case of North Africa these were not relaxed until after the French occupation during the nineteenth century. Turkey, Syria, Palestine and the countries of North Africa which had important Jewish communities are dealt with separately below.

TURKISH EMPIRE

The privileged status which the Jews enjoyed when they first came under Turkish rule was reflected in their dress; such distinctions as existed were retained voluntarily and there were no humiliating restrictions like those suffered in Christian countries. Thus, in 1454, Isaac Zarfati, a Jew of Constantinople, is able to write to the Jews of the Rhineland:

Is it not better for you to live under Moslems than under Christians? Here every man may dwell at peace under his own vine and his own fig tree. In Christendom on the contrary, ye dare not even venture to clothe your children in red or in blue according to your taste without exposing them to insult and yourself to extortion; and therefore are ye condemned to go about meanly clad in sad-coloured raiment.[4]

The Jews who fled from Spain in the fifteenth century settled chiefly in Constantinople, Salonica, Adrianople, Brusa, Jerusalem, Safed, Syria and Egypt. Their dress differed from that worn by the native Jews, many of whom were Ashkenazim, and the distinction continued for at least two centuries. Hans Dernschwam, about the middle of the sixteenth century, writes:

The Jews of Turkey wear clothes according to the language they speak. Usually the garments are long like a *caftan* which is a long tunic tied about the waist over which is a sort of skirt made of cloth of good quality and silk. Just as Turks wear white turbans, the Jews wear yellow. Some foreign Jews still wear the black Italian birettas. Some who pretend to be physicians wear the red pointed elongated birettas.[5]

George Sandys (1578–1644), who travelled through Turkey at the beginning of the seventeenth century, noted various peculiarities about Jewish costume. At Zycanthus in Greece the Jews wore a blue ribbon on their hats. He was struck by the fact that while in Christendom they were obliged to wear different clothing, in Turkey they did so voluntarily and he described their dress:

Their undergarments, differing little from the Turks in fashion, are of purple cloth, over that they wear gowns of the same colour with large wide sleeves and clasped beneath the chin without band or collar; on their heads high brimless caps of purple . . . they shave their heads all over . . . their familiar language is Spanish . . . to speak a word or two of their women: the elder mabble (i.e. muffle) their heads in linnen with the knots hanging down behind. Others do wear high caps of plate whereof some I have seen of beaten gold. They wear long quilted waistcoats with breeches underneath; in winter of cloth, in summer of linnen, and over all, when they stir abroad, loose gowns of purple flowing from the shoulders.[6]

Sumptuary laws existed in Turkey as they did in Europe. In 1554 the rabbis of Salonica passed the following law which was to run for ten years and was renewed in 1564: 'women who have reached puberty and especially married women are forbidden to wear in the streets any jewels of gold or silver except for one plain ring on the finger. Jewels may be worn only inside the house.'

Michel Febre, a Capuchin monk who lived for eighteen years in Turkey during the middle of the seventeenth century, observed that the Spanish and Portuguese Jews wore a peculiar head-dress 'like a brimless Spanish hat' while the 'native' Jews had coloured turbans and could be distinguished from the Christians only by the colour of their shoes which were black or violet.[7] De Thevenot, who travelled in the Levant in the seventeenth century, writes:

The Jews in Turkey dress like the Turks except that they may not wear green, nor a white turban, nor a red jacket. They are usually dressed in violet but they are obliged to wear a violet bonnet (*bonnet*) made in the shape of and the same height as a hat (*chapeau*), and those who have the means to own a turban wear it round the base of their bonnet. They must also wear socks (*mest*) and violet slippers (*paboudj*). Jewish and Christian subjects of the Grand Seigneur pay an annual tribute. Those who are not his subjects, in order to prove their exemption wear a hat (*chapeau*) and carry a certificate from a Consul proving their nationality.[8]

Dandini, another seventeenth century writer, observed that there were at least 500 Jews living at Tripoli in Syria, mostly Spanish or Portuguese, and that they normally wore 'a red bonnet, half a foot high, flat and round'.[9]

M. de Ferriol, French ambassador to Turkey, writing in 1714, describes the Jews as being dressed in black and wearing a round violet turban with a checkered border, a compromise between the tall brimless hat formerly worn by the Sephardim and the turban of the native Jews. In its typical form, with the two lobes of the turban padded out on each side and twisted so as to leave the base of the hat exposed above the forehead, it remained the characteristic Jewish headgear for men in most parts of the Turkish empire until the end of the nineteenth century. Hamdy-Bey calls it a *kaveze* (plates 31, 41, 52).

Lt-Col. Charles Hamilton Smith (1776–1859), who lived in Turkey in the 1820's and was a careful observer of costume, makes this comment:

Christians and Jews are not allowed to wear brilliant colours. They are obliged to choose such as are dull even in painting the outside of their houses. In Egypt, however, little thought is given this order and excepting green all colours may be worn. With the Turks green is a sacred colour and is only worn by themselves though they also have all other colours. Europeans are indulged with permission to have yellow slippers but Oriental Christians and Jews are confined to red, blue or black.[10]

Another reliable eye-witness was an Englishwoman, Lucy M. J. Garnett, who, in 1891, published a study of the women of Turkey in which she gives this description of the costume of the Jewish women:

The ancient costumes which all the native Jews continue to wear are, on the whole, exceedingly picturesque and curious. They vary slightly according to locality, the head-dress at Smyrna being different in style and material from that worn at Salonica where the costume is particularly ornate. Here the married women put away their back hair in a rectangular bag of silk or stuff about twelve inches in length and three to four in width, the extremity being ornamented with embroidery and terminated by a fringe frequently of seed pearls. This bag is attached to a kind of cap which covers the top of the head, round which fine muslin handkerchiefs are twisted, one of them passing under the chin, strings of seed pearls and gold coins being added for full dress. The costume consists chiefly of two or three gowns, or rather long tight jackets, open from the hip downwards, worn one over the other, and full Turkish trousers. None of these garments meet at the throat but leave the chest bare, or at most only partially covered by the gauze vests worn by the wealthy, or the coarse cotton gown which forms the under-garment of the poor. The materials vary from printed cotton to the richest brocaded silk damask, but the designs are always similar—namely wide contrasting stripes with flower patterns stamped over them. For outdoor wear, a long pelisse of dark red cloth, lined and trimmed with fur is added and over the head a fine white Turkish towel, with fringed ends, which does not, however, conceal the face. Handsome gold bracelets and a necklace of pearls complete the costume. Pearls are indeed a passion with Salonica Jewesses who, whatever their rank, spend all the money at their command in these ornaments for their heads and necks.

The costume of the Jewish women of Constantinople differs chiefly from that of Salonica in

31–32   Turkey: *c.* 1800. *Bridal couple*. Paintings. Istanbul University Library.
Their clothes are in the distinctive Jewish blue or violet colour and his turban
is the Jewish *kaveze*. He also wears *peoth*.

the substitution for outdoor wear of a short loose jacket, lined and faced with lambskin, swansdown or squirrel for the long red pelisse. The coiffure is also much more simple being merely a *yemeni*, or large square kerchief of coloured muslin painted with large flowers and bordered, like the outer gown, with white *oya* lace. This lace border, though rather expensive—or perhaps for that reason—is indispensable. One side of the kerchief is brought low over the forehead, completely concealing the hair, and two of the corners fall over the shoulders behind. This head-dress, however, has only been adopted since the interdiction of the preposterous *chalebi* formerly worn by the Jewesses of the Turkish capital. It consisted of a large ball of cotton wool, or linen rags, tightly compressed, which was placed on the crown of the head and held there by one person while another wound round it, in complicated folds, a shawl or scarf, until it attained monstrous proportions and completely covered the head of the wearer, whom it not only frightfully disfigured but at the same time exposed to the derisive remarks of both Moslems and Christians. (At the request of the Vizier the *chalebi* was prohibited by the Chief Rabbi, to the great indignation of the women.)

The coiffure of the Jewish women of Aleppo is a high dome-shaped cap, made of silk striped in different colours and worn low on the forehead. From under it depends a quantity of false hair, either plaited in tresses or hanging loose over the shoulders. The *fotoz* affected by the Israelite ladies of Broussa, like that formerly worn in the capital, is an enormous cushion of parti-coloured stuffs covered with jewels and strings of pearls some of which hang in festoons over the cheeks. A veil of white muslin is worn over this out of doors and the remainder of the dress is concealed by a *feradjé* or cloak differing in colour and also in shape from that worn by Moslem women.[11]

The earliest illustrations of Turkish Jews appear in N. de Nicolay's *Les Quatre Premiers Livres Des Navigations . . . Orientales* published at Lyons in 1568. Numerous other editions followed and the plates were pirated for books of costume during the next two centuries. Nicolay's 'Medecin Juif' (plate 33) who can be identified as Moses Hamon, physician to Sulaiman the Magnificent (1520–66), is bearded and reveals his Sephardi ancestry by wearing 'a high topped cappe' of red scarlet. The 'Marchant Juif' (plate 34) who, we are told, wears a yellow turban as a mark of distinction, is presumably a native Jew. The 'Femme Juifve' of Adrianople (plate 35) does not appear to be wearing distinctive dress, but has her head 'mabbled' in linen as described by Sandys.

Other illustrations of Turkish Jews are seen in a Turkish miniature (plate 36) where the red hats of the men are the outstanding feature.

All these illustrations are consistent with the descriptions of Jewish costume quoted above, but the traditional *mest* and *paboudj* mentioned by De Thevenot are not heard of again until the nineteenth century when they were noticed by Hamdy-Bey (see plate 48).

The richness and variety of Jewish costume in different parts of the Turkish empire may be judged by the accompanying illustrations (plates 31–66 etc.).

Women in particular developed the most elaborate wardrobes which usually had special characteristics to distinguish them from Moslem dress.

The picture of a Jewish wedding (plate 45), published in 1862, was sketched by an American missionary, the Rev. Henry J. Van Lennep, who attended the ceremony after having had the bride's dress sent to his lodgings so that he could faithfully represent in colours the minutest details; in addition to this he supplies the following description:

The bridegroom was twenty and the bride twelve. They stood up in their bridal garments under a tentlike structure supported by poles and made of cloths belonging to the bride's dowry, erected in the largest apartment in her parent's house. The remainder of the dowry besides what she wore, was contained in two green chests which stood behind them and were used as seats by the pair. The bride's pasteboard horn was the same as the Armenian bride with this difference, that no veil was thrown over it in the present case. Natural and artificial flowers and sprigs of wormwood adorned her head like a crown. Her veil was of gauze and perfectly transparent and her eyes remained closed during the whole ceremony. Two tall candlesticks stood before them on which tallow candles burned all the while. . . . The mothers of the parties stood by them closely veiled during the ceremony soon after the conclusion of which the bride's peculiar ornaments were removed from her and she was allowed freely to mingle with the company.

In Syria, the Lebanon, Baghdad and Rhodes the Jews wore regional dress with certain characteristics (plates 53–7).

33 Turkey: 1568. '*Medico Giudeo*'. Etching. From the Italian edition of De Nicolay. Rubens (ii) 1871. Portrait of Moses Hamon, physician to Sulaiman The Magnificent (1520–66), in the tall hat worn by the Sephardim and short-sleeved *caftan*. According to the author 'insteede of a yeallow Tulbant very neere like unto the Jewish nation (he wore) a high topped cappe died of redde scarlet'.

34 Turkey: 1568. '*Mercante Giudeo*'. (Cloth Merchant). Etching. From the Italian edition of De Nicolay. Rubens (ii) 1874. In the turban worn by the native Jews. According to the author the Jews of Turkey wore long garments like those of the other people of the Levant and as a distinction, a yellow turban.

35 Turkey: Adrianople 1568. '*Donna Giudea d' Andrinopoli*'. Etching. From the Italian edition of De Nicolay. Rubens (ii) 1003. She is heavily veiled but a small portion of her hair is uncovered.

36 Turkey: 1594. *Jews and Jewesses*. Miniature. Chester Beatty Library
Ms. 419. f.308A. Minorsky, 37. Twelve women from the Jewish Banū
Qaynuqa tribe are converted to Islam after seeing Fatima's cloak. Three of
them produce a sleeve to the sages of Israel most of whom are distinguished
by their red head-dress (p. 36).

37 Turkey: Seventeenth century.
'*Dona Ebrea in casa*'. Drawing. British
Museum. Sloane 5255. Tall hat with veil.

38 Turkey: 1768. '*A Jewish girl dressed for her marriage ceremony*'. Engraving.
Rubens (ii) 1879. Her head-dress is made up of a copper plate (see plate 46).

39   Turkey: *c.* 1800. '*Un Juif Turqueois avec sa famille à Vienne*'. Aquatint.
Rubens (ii) 1887. They are in Turkish costume and the man does not wear the
kaveze, the typical head–dress of Turkish Jews. Many Turkish Jews took
advantage of the Treaty of Passarowitz 1718, which permitted them to live in
Vienna as Turkish subjects.

40   Turkey: 1821. '*Femme juive dans la maison*'. Lithograph.
From Lachaise *Costumes de l'Empire Turc*, Paris, 1821. The
author tells us that her rich costume is worn exclusively
indoors so as not to excite the envy of the Turks.

41   Turkey: Smyrna, *c.* 1830. '*Habillement des Juifs de Smyrne*'.
Lithograph. Rubens (ii) 1777. His *kaveze* is slightly different
to the one worn at Constantinople. He wears a striped *entari*
with girdle under a *djubba*.

42 Turkey: Smyrna, *c. 1830*. *'Femme juive dans la maison'*. Lithograph. Rubens (ii) 1775. The head-dress is probably the distinctive feature of her costume.

43 Turkey: Constantinople, *1842*. *'Juive de Constantinople'*. Lithograph. Rubens (ii) 1371 b. Her head-dress appears to be the only distinctively Jewish feature of her costume.

44 Turkey: *c. 1890*. *'Jüdinnen aus der Türkei'*. Engraving. Their head-dress is the traditional Jewish *fotoz* with a white sheet and over their backs they wear a *feradjé* of a special design.

45 Turkey: 1862. *'Jewish marriage'*. Lithograph. From Van Lennep. The bride's
fantastic costume is authentic having been sketched from life by an American
missionary (see p. 37).

46 Turkey: Smyrna, 1719. *'Juifve de Smyrne femme qui sort'*. Engraving. From M. Guerdeville, *Atlas Historique*, Amsterdam, 1719. The distinctive feature is the head-dress consisting of a tin or copper plate covered in white satin embroidered in gold and silver as was the kerchief attached, the hair, tied in a knot, being held in a bag of coloured silk. Also distinctive of the Jewish women were the numerous rows of pearls tightly strung round the neck. In the street like the other women of Smyrna they wore a long white sheet and a black veil completely covering the face.

48 Turkey: Smyrna, 1873. *'Haham de Smyrne'*. Photograph. From Hamdy-Bey. The leader of the Smyrna community wears a dignified costume in keeping with his office. His *bonneto*, a kind of turban, is different from that worn by Moslems but somewhat resembles the turban worn by doctors and divines. He carries a long cane and wears a grey cashmere scarf with fringes round his waist, a long *entari* of striped silk over which is a dark-coloured *binich* with long hanging sleeves, *mest* (socks) and *paboudj* (slippers). (Hamdy-Bey's description).

47 Turkey: Constantinople, 1846. *'Jewish woman of Pera'*. Lithograph. From Sir David Wilkie's *Sketches in Spain* etc., 1846. 'A Jewess dressed with the Smyrna cap who gave me a sitting; she was a handsome and elegant person'. (From the artist's Journal) She wear European style dress and her hair is only partly covered.

49 Turkey: Salonica, 1873. 'Haham Bachi de Selanik'. Photograph. From Hamdy-Bey. The head of the Salonica community has side locks (peoth). He wears an entari of striped silk under a djubba of fine cloth. The colours are dark and the whole costume is quiet and restrained so as to set a good example. His footwear is the traditional mest (socks) and paboudj (slippers) in black leather. (Hamdy-Bey's description).

50 Turkey: Constantinople, 1873. 'Juive de Constantinople'. Photograph. From Hamdy-Bey. A yemeni painted with large flowers with a white fringe is bound round the forehead completely covering the hair. This, particularly the fringe (oya), was worn by all married Jewish women. In other respects there is nothing unusual about the costume: a silk entari striped or checked hemmed with gold braid with a belt and a coloured hyrka lined and hemmed with white astrakhan. (Hamdy-Bey's description).

51 Turkey: Salonica, 1873. 'Dame juive de Selanik'. Photograph. From Hamdy-Bey. The chief characteristic of the costume is the head-dress, a net made of pearls resting on an avlou, a square of cotton, designed to cover the hair completely. She wears a long entari which trails behind; over it, a fistan and over all a djubba of fine cloth lined with silk and ornamented with fur. Her shoes are European in style. (Hamdy-Bey's description).

52 Turkey: Brusa, 1873. *'Juif et juives de Brousse'*. Photograph. From Hamdy-Bey. The man's head-dress, called *kaveze*, consists of a high crown of cardboard covered with black material around which is rolled a piece of light-colour cotton. The only other distinctive feature of his dress is the lining of his *djubba* which is white on top and black at the bottom. Moslems and Christians wear a lining all of one colour. The women, like all the Jewish women of the East, have different dress for the house and the street. The woman on the left is dressed in the peculiar *fotoz* in which they bury their hair so that it cannot be seen after they are married. She wears an *entari*, open in front, of rich flowered silk with a scarf tied round the waist, a *hyrka* without sleeves, lined and edged with fur and *paboudj* (slippers) of yellow morocco. The woman on the right, dressed for the street, wears a *fotoz* covered with a *yachmak* to which are attached jewels which hang down in front of her nose and cheeks. The *feradjé* which is of a special shape, distinguishes the Jewish from the Moslem women. It is a piece of silk worn like a scarf from above the breast and down the back. (Hamdy-Bey's description).

53 Rhodes: 1873. *'Juif de Rhôdes; Juive de Rhôdes'*. Photograph. From Hamdy-Bey. The man is dressed very simply. His head-dress is a *fez* encircled by a *yemeni* (painted handkerchief). He wears a long *entari* of silk or cotton, a *djubba* of cloth and black shoes. The woman is dressed even more simply; a good *entari* of cotton, a *chalwar* and over all an excellent *djubba* of silk or fine cloth through which pass the sleeves of the *entari*. Her head-dress is a cotton bonnet (*takke*) under two *yemeni* kerchiefs designed to conceal the hair which no good Jewish woman wears uncovered from the day of her marriage. Her shoes are black *paboudj* (slippers). (Hamdy-Bey's description).

44

55   56

54   Mesopotamia: *c.* 1900. *'Jewish merchant of Baghdad'.*
Photograph. Ben-Zvi Institute. He wears traditional dress.

55   Syria: 1590. *'Hebrea'.* Woodcut. From Vecellio, *Abiti Antici*, Venice 1590.
According to the author the Jewish women wore a tall coiffure covered by a
silk veil with a silk band underneath cunningly arranged to cover the hair. The
skirt is short and is of silk with bands round the hem.

56   Syria: Aleppo 1873. *'Dame juive d'Halep'.* Photograph. From Hamdy-Bey.
The head-dress is peculiar to Aleppo. The author remarks that in many parts
of the Orient when Jewish women cut off their hair after marriage, it was the
practice to ornament their head-dress with cock's feathers or white fringes.
Only in Aleppo, apparently, did they wear a wig. This woman wears a kind of
mitre of striped silk to which is attached a trimming of false hair and long
tresses. The long *entari* of silk with wide red and yellow stripes has no sleeves.
She also wears a *chalwar* which cannot be seen, a *mintan* of the same material
as the *entari* with excessively long sleeves fitting tightly round the arms and
opening out past the hands, a *hyrka* of light colour closed up to the neck, the
tight sleeves of which finish above the elbows. A scarf of silk and cotton is
worn round the waist. The skirt of the *entari* is gathered in little pleats round
the hips and falls stiffly covering the shoes which are either *tchédik* (soft boots)
or yellow *paboudj* (slippers). (Hamdy-Bey's description).

57   Lebanon: 1880. *'Israélites de Beyrouth'.* Engraving. From L. Lortet, *La Syrie*
D'aujourdhui. Voyages dans La Phénicie, Le Liban et La Judée, 1875–1880, Paris,
1884. They appear to be wearing regional dress.

The dress of Palestinian Jews under Turkish rule was similar to that in other parts of the empire (plates 58–66). There was the same distinction between the oriental Jews and the Sephardim whose tongue was Spanish. According to Eugene Roger, a seventeenth century French missionary, many of these practised as physicians or farmed the customs and they all dressed alike (plate 58).

Bartlett devotes a considerable amount of space to the family seen in plate 59, the head of which he describes as the wealthiest Jew of Jerusalem, although not a native of the city. He continues:

We found him seated on the low divan fondling his youngest child and on our expressing a wish to draw the costume of the female members of his family he commanded their attendance. . . . Their costume (as represented in the illustration) was chastely elegant.

The prominent figure in the sketch is the married daughter, whose little husband, a boy of fourteen or fifteen, as he seemed, wanted nearly a head of the stature of his wife, but was already chargeable with the onerous duties of a father. An oval head-dress of peculiar shape, from which is slung a long veil of embroidered muslin, shown as hanging, in the sketch, from the back of another figure, admirably sets off the brow and eyes; the neck is ornamented with bracelets, and the bosom with a profusion of gold coins, partly concealed by folds of muslin; a graceful robe of striped silk, with long open sleeves, half-laced under the bosom, invests the whole person, over which is worn a jacket of green silk with short sleeves, leaving the white arm and braceleted hand at liberty. The elder person on the sofa is the mother, whose dress was more grave, her turban less oval, and of blue shawl, and the breast covered, entirely to the neck, with a kind of ornamented gold tissue, above which is seen a jacket of fur: she was engaged in knitting, while her younger daughter bent over her in conversation: her dress is similar to that of her sister, but with no gold coins or tight muslin folds; and instead of large earrings, the vermilion blossom of the pomegranate formed an exquisite pendant, reflecting its glow upon the dazzling whiteness of her skin.

We were surprised at the fairness and delicacy of their complexions, and the vivacity of their manner. Unlike the wives of oriental Christians, who respectfully attend at a distance till invited to approach, these pretty Jewesses seemed on a perfect footing of equality, and chatted and laughed without intermission.[12]

Mrs Finn makes several observations about Jewish costume in Jerusalem between 1846 and 1863 when her husband, James Finn, was British consul. The Jewish women of Jerusalem wore a white sheet, but not a coloured handkerchief over the face like the Moslem and Christian women. The oriental rabbis she met wore full trousers of crimson cloth, a vest of light Damascus silk and a cloth robe with ample gray turban most carefully folded. Mrs Finn also visited the Jewish family on Mount Zion mentioned by Bartlett and gives this description:

A servant conducted us into an upper room, which I at once recognized as the room in the frontispiece of 'Bartlett's Walks'. The lady of the house came forward and greeted us with much cordiality. She was small, slight, and very fair in complexion, and did not look more than forty. Her dress was rich: a sky-blue jacket, and white silk skirt embroidered with silver, just below

58   Palestine: 1664. '*Juif de la Terre Sainte*'. Etching. From F. E. Roger, *La Terre Sainte*,
Paris, 1664. Rubens (ii) 1729. He wears a tall Sephardi hat and a fur lined pelisse.

59   Palestine: Jerusalem, 1842. '*Jewish family on Mount Zion*'. Engraving. From Bartlett.

which peeped full trousers of pale yellow silk and little green Morocco slippers. The head-dress
was a turban, projecting forwards in a halfmoon shape, and down the back hung a white muslin
veil spangled with gold.

Two pretty daughters, dressed in the same manner as their mother, stood ready to make their
salaam, as soon as she had done greeting her guests. They led us to the divan, and then repeated the
salaams. Mr Andersen spoke with them in Spanish, and Mary in Arabic.

Meanwhile I observed the gold necklaces and bracelets which the ladies wore. The necklaces
were a sort of fringe, composed of separate little pointed ornaments of gold, something like
sharks' teeth. The bracelets were much handsomer, and composed of a multitude of beautifully-
wrought flexible chains. The long clasps were thickly set with diamonds.

Small chains of gold and festoons of pearls were attached to the turban, and one wore a large
emerald depending on her forehead.

The mother had a variety of diamond ornaments set on her turban, and they all wore fresh
flowers intermingled with the jewellery. Two pretty little boys sat shyly at the lower end of the
divan. Their red caps were ornamented with gold coins; but, like all other children that we had
seen, they were spoiled in appearance by the old-fashioned, clumsy look of their clothes; jackets
and full trousers, such as men wore, sat awkwardly upon these little fellows . . .[13]

Mrs Finn's brother, Walter, made a sketch of the two daughters called
'Spanish Jewesses wearing the moon-shaped turban' which is the turban
seen in plate 44.

The late Israel Abrahams, in a letter to his wife dated 10 April 1898 from
Jerusalem, describes the Jewish promenade on the Jaffa road on a Saturday
evening. He writes:

The people pass and repass in all costumes—(by the way again, many here also wear European
dress all the week, but revert to Oriental costume on Sabbaths and Festivals). There is nothing in
the world, I should think, quite like the Jerusalem costumes. There is more variety, less brilliancy

than in Cairo. It is an idealized East End of London. The people bring all the costumes of the world here, then borrow from each other, and thus in the end I have no doubt that a Jerusalem type of costume will evolve itself. Each man plays several parts. I have just given you one instance. Now I meet the same people on the same day at different houses (I pay lots of visits) and find them differently dressed. Especially does this apply to the head-dress. A man wears different styles to suit his hosts. This is not a common thing, but it occurs often enough to excite one's notice.[14]

The Rev. W. J. Woodcock who visited Palestine in 1848 accompanied by the Rev. M. Margoliouth has this to say about the Sephardim of Jerusalem:

They are a very handsome race with black eyes and hair and the younger women are often of great beauty. Their dress is very much like that of the Moslems, though somewhat less gay, a turban, an under-surtout or tunic with sleeves, bound round the waist with a silk or shawl girdle and extending nearly down to the feet, a loose overcoat, lined with silk or fur, with red or yellow sleeves. This is the every-day garb. The learned, the rabbis, and some of the students, wear a high dark-blue cap, having a black and white scarf or turban wound round the lower part—a singular head-dress peculiar to the Jewish people. They pretend that the whole of this dress is very ancient . . .

I took, in Jerusalem, the likeness of a youth about fourteen years of age, the son of Rabbi D. S. Majahr, a lad of studious habits and considerable intelligence . . . [see plate 60].

60 Palestine: Jerusalem, 1849. '*David, son of Rabbi Samuel Majha 2nd Chief Rabbi of Jerusalem*'. Lithograph. From W. J. Woodcock *Scripture Lands*, London, 1849. He wears the traditional *kaveze* with a striped *entari* under a *djubba*.

61 Palestine: Jerusalem, 1854. '*Costume and likeness of a native Jew and Jewess of Jerusalem*'. Lithograph. From *Jerusalem and the Holy Land . . . from drawings taken on the spot by Mrs Ewald*, London, 1854. Both in traditional Jewish dress; the man wearing *kaveze*, striped *entari* with girdle under a *djubba*; the woman in characteristic head-dress (*fotoz*).

62 Palestine: 1840. '*A Jew dragoman of the British Consul teaching children*'. Drawing by David Wilkie inscribed 'A Jew Dragoman at Jerusalem, 1840'. National Trust for Scotland. He wears a *fez* and a fur-trimmed *djubba*.

63 Palestine: 1840. '*Hebrew woman and child*'. Lithograph by David Wilkie. From his Sketches in Turkey, Syria and Egypt, 1843. Rubens (ii) 1644. The artist comments: 'In their girlhood the Jewish women generally take great pride in the adornment of their hair; but from the time of their marriage it is commonly hidden and for its better concealment a second handkerchief is attached to the turban behind which it descends very low and covers the whole more effectually than the simpler head-dress.'

All of the women, both Sephardim and Ashcanazim, have a beautiful head-dress, consisting of a turban, presenting in front over the forehead, semi-circular appearance, which, being often of a gay colour (lilac and scarlet very commonly), contrasts very well with the white drapery in which they enfold themselves. . . .

Those Jewesses who come from the Austrian dominions and some particular parts of Germany, wear a strip of scarlet cloth or silk loosely folded over their forehead.[15]

Of the Jews of Damascus, Woodcock writes:

The Jews of Damascus seem, on the whole, more wealthy than any I saw in the East, and they are also a very good-looking people. They dress more like the inhabitants of the country than those of Constantinople or Jerusalem yet the women have the same white head-dress. I saw one Jewish lady with a very curious cap, like an inverted hen's nest on her head, from which hung down behind, for about a yard and a half, some thirty thin tails or plaits of hair giving the wearer a most singular appearance. The personal resemblance of these Asiatic Jews (or rather Spanish Jews living in Asia) is quite extraordinary, and in Smyrna and Damascus it was generally sufficient for me to distinguish them from other people, though their dress did not indicate any difference.[16]

64 Palestine: Jerusalem, 1873. '*Juif de Jerusalem, Juive de Jerusalem*'.
Photograph. From Hamdy-Bey. The man has a dignified appearance. His
head-dress is a black *kaveze* widening out at the top to form a polygon,
surrounded by a turban of white muslin ribbed and divided in two lobes
stretched to the right and left of his head and padded out. The material is
folded so as to leave the base of the hat in front and behind uncovered. Round
his neck he wears a cashmere scarf with a border of *palmettes* arranged with
great neatness and his *djubba* of white cashmere is worn with the same
precision over a long *entari* of white silk with pink stripes. Round his waist he
wears a rich scarf of cashmere artistically tied which trails to the ground
covering his footwear which are *mest* (socks) and *paboudj* (slippers) of black
morocco. The woman's *fistan* is of dark green decorated with gold
embroidery. Its long open sleeves are brought through the narrow sleeves of
the *salta* which is of white cashmere. Her head-dress, the *fotoz*, is decorated
with a large number of *yemeni*, handkerchiefs painted with flowers, arranged
one on top of the other in the shape of a melon. To the borders are attached
sequins and gold pins which hang over the nose and cheeks producing a
strange effect. A *bach eurtussu* of white muslin fixed to the top of the *fotoz*
frames the face, crosses under the chin and hangs over the arms and back. The
footwear consists of *mest* (socks) and *paboudj* (slippers) of black morocco.
(Hamdy-Bey's description).

65 Palestine: Tiberias, *c.* 1880. '*Jewish woman and children, Tiberias*'. Engraving.
From J. L. Porter, *Through Samaria to Galilee and the Jordan*, London, 1889.
They appear to be wearing Arab dress.

66 Palestine: Jerusalem, 1880. '*Famille Israélite à Jerusalem*'. Engraving. From
L. Lortet, *La Syrie D'aujourdhui. Voyages dans La Phénicie, Le Liban et La Judée,
1875–1880*, Paris, 1884. They are all in Turkish dress.

67   Bokhara: *c.* 1900. *Jewish family*. Photograph. Jewish National and
University Library, Jerusalem. The traditional dress of the Bokharan Jews.

TURKESTAN

An English traveller who visited Bokhara at the beginning of the nineteenth
century found the Jews wearing distinctive dress and a conical cap. The
women, who were remarkably handsome, wore their hair in ringlets
covering their cheeks and neck.[17] When Adler was in Bokhara in 1896 the
Jews were still wearing a badge and until the Soviet government was
established they were required to wear a special type of fur cap instead of a
turban and to tie a rope round their waist, a survival presumably of the
zunnâr imposed on Jews under Islam (see p. 31). They shaved their heads but
wore side locks (*peoth*).[18] The ornate Bokharan dress seen in Israel today
(plate 67) was probably adopted in fairly recent times.

   Krafft publishes some excellent photographs of Turkestan Jews (plate
68) accompanied by the following description:

Among the Jewish women the love of finery is even more developed than among the Sartes
women but it is displayed with less taste. The material of their gala dresses covered with braidings,
flowers and arabesques, with raised embroidery in too lively colours, the artificial flowers planted
in their hair on brightly coloured scarves, give a theatrical effect, too crude and vulgar. The jewels
they possess nevertheless have real beauty, particularly their diadems decorated with pendants of
pearls, rubies and cabuchon emeralds.

   The photographs of the Jewish women taken with the consent of their husbands were the only
ones of married women (of all races) I could get. Even the Moslem members of my party were not
allowed to enter their houses. I was the only person admitted and I had to promise to send direct
to the husbands proofs of the photographs.

   If the Sartes are jealous of their women, the Jews are no less so, certainly towards the Sartes.

The latent animosity between Moslems and Jews is even stronger in Central Asia than elsewhere because the Sartes, by their natural love of gain, can rival the commercial genius of the Jews.

The situation of the latter has in any case greatly improved under Russian rule and the numerous Jews of Tashkent and Samarkand have little to envy the Jews of other countries in this respect. They seem to be even more favoured than their brethren in Russia and are well acquainted with all modern progress.

In Bokhara the Jews were always very oppressed and even now their position is like that of the Jews of Europe in the middle ages. For instance their dress distinguishes them from the rest of the population. They are not allowed to wear a turban and they are obliged to wear round their waist a piece of common rope as a belt, a symbol, it is said, of the cord which will be used to hang them. They are also forbidden to ride on horseback.

From the point of view of type, the Jews of Turkestan are a great mixture because Jews are coming from Poland in increasing numbers.

The native Jews are Djougout originally from Persia and speaking the Persian dialect of the Tadjik. Generally they have fine features and many of them are handsome. The Jewish children are beautiful. They are easily recognised by the two locks of hair hanging above their ears while their head is always shaved.

Out of doors all the women, without distinction and even the Jews, are completely veiled. They hide themselves under a thick rigid veil woven from black horse-hair (*tchachband*), covering the forehead and reaching the waist. The veil is held in place by a large robe (*faranghi*) placed over the head. Richly adorned with black beading, the *faranghi* is of coloured silk and completely envelops the wearer. The sleeves hang down the back and the ends are joined. Thus concealed, the women can see everything without a trace of their features being exposed.[19]

68 a–c   Bokhara: *c.* 1900. Photographs from Krafft. (a). '*Un jeune juif de Tachkent portant le bonnet bordé de fourrure*'. (b). '*Un jeune juif de Tachkent*'. (c). '*Une femme juive de Samarkand en atours de cérémonie*'.

68d

68e

68 d–g: *c.* 1900. Photographs from Krafft. (d). '*Une femme de Samarkand coiffée d'un diadème de perles et d'emeraudes.*' (e). '*Une femme revêtue de son manteau et de son voile.*' (f). '*Jeunes juives de Samarkand.*' (g). '*Un vieux juif de Samarkand.*'

68f

68g

Adler, who visited the Caucasus at the end of the nineteenth century, found the Jews wearing a high black (or occasionally white) astrakhan fez, but otherwise in national costume with bandoliers (see plates 69–70). The Jews of Afghanistan still wear a fur hat as a mark of distinction.[20]

At the beginning of the twentieth century the Jews of Aden had *peoth* and wore *arba kanfoth*. Their *tallith*, which was called *mandil* (Arabic= kerchief or shawl), had green silk corners. The women wore trousers and a wig called *masr* and they were veiled like the Moslem women.

The costume of the Jewish women of the Yemen is extremely interesting and has received special study.[21] Here one can only refer to the magnificent costume of the Sa'ana bride (plates 71–2).

A great variety of Jewish costume from Turkestan, Kurdistan, Yemen and Aden is to be seen now in museums at Haifa, Tel-Aviv and Jerusalem.

69   Russia: Caucasus, *c.* 1930. *Jew of the Caucasus.* Photograph. From *Jüdisches Lexikon* III, 637. In typical fur hat and carrying bandolier as described by Adler.

70   Russia: Caucasus, *c.* 1900. *Coat.* Photograph. Israel Museum. Man's coat worn for synagogue and ceremonial occasions.

55

71 Yemen: Sa'ana, *c.* 1900. *Hood.*
Photograph. Israel Museum.
Hood worn exclusively by Jewish
women for ceremonial occasions.

72 Yemen: Sa'ana, Twentieth century.
Jewish bride. Photograph. Israel Museum.
During the two week wedding celebrations different prescribed costumes
are worn of which this is the richest.

PERSIA

In Persia by edict of Abbas I (*c.* 1557–1628) all Jews of the empire were ordered to wear a felt hat like that worn by slaves.

A traveller who visited Persia towards the end of the seventeenth century observed that the Jews wore a hat of special colour and also a square patch of cloth on their coats.[22]

According to Benjamin, in the middle of the nineteenth century the Jews no longer had a distinctive dress but the women were obliged to wear black veils instead of white ones when they appeared in public and at the end of the century Curzon still found a badge being worn in certain parts of the country. A nineteenth-century drawing of a Persian Jew displays no obvious characteristics (plate 73).

Little is known about the social life of Persian Jews as prior to the reign of the present Shah's father they were restricted to ghettos under intolerable conditions and most of them in abject poverty. It is therefore surprising to find pictures of the Qajar period apparently representing a Jewish bridal couple wearing expensive clothes (plates 75–6). Possibly behind the ghetto walls the few rich Jews mentioned by Benjamin lived a more colourful life than has hitherto been suspected. Another version of the male portrait with the same Hebrew inscription is in the author's possession.

EGYPT

At the end of the fifteenth century the distinctive dress of the Jews of Cairo was a yellow turban while Christians and Moslems wore blue and white turbans respectively.[23] Two centuries later, according to De Bruyn, the Jews had to wear a turban of blue stripes and violet coloured clothing. The women

73   Persia: *c.* 1850. '*A Persian an Israelite*'. Drawing.
In turban and *caftan* with girdle.

74   Egypt: 1698. '*Femme juive*'. Engraving. From C. de Bruyn, *Reizen*, Delft, 1698. She wears a very long black hat covered with a white or brown kerchief striped with gold and silver. The clothes of the Jewish women were usually of striped silk.

תארין עריס בן
שלמו

רחל דר חאל וסמה כשידן

75–76 Persia: *c.* 1840. '*The bridegroom Ben Shlomo playing the tar. Rachel making up her eyes*'. Paintings. Reproduced by kind permission of Mrs Miriam Ayalon-Rosen. A remarkable pair of pictures presumably painted on the occasion of a wedding. The dress is that worn by Persian aristocracy. The Hebrew titles are in Judaeo-Persian.

wore long black hats with a white or brown kerchief striped with gold and silver (plate 74).

When Lane was in Egypt between 1825 and 1849 there was very little distinction in dress between Jews and Moslems but Jews and Christians wore turbans of the same colour. The women veiled themselves and in public dressed like the Egyptian women.

Benjamin, who visited Egypt in the course of his travels between 1846 and 1855, gives this description of Jewish costume:

The dress of the Egyptian Jews is like that worn by the Jews in Turkey. Many wear white turbans, and they often dress with great splendour. The women are also attired like those of Turkey; their head-dress alone differs from that of the Turkish Jewesses, for they wear a red fez, the tassel of which consists of long single silken threads, hanging down to the feet. At the end of each thread is attached a silver or some other coin, whereby this head-dress is made very heavy. I once had such a fez in my hand, and I should reckon its weight to have been about ten pounds. The long tassels with the coins attached to them cause quite a ringing sound when the women appear in the street.[24]

LIBYA

According to Lyon, who visited Tripoli between 1818 and 1820, the Jews wore blue turbans and black shoes. The women dressed like the Moslem women except that they were allowed only black or yellow shoes and when they went out they left both eyes uncovered instead of only one.

A rather different account is given by Benjamin:

Many dress in the same fashion as in Tunis, others in the fashion of Algiers, and many others wear a peculiar costume consisting of a long garment reaching to the knees, a short burnos, white trowsers reaching to the knees, and red shoes. The women wear for head-dress a red fez wound round with a silk kerchief, and beautifully ornamented in different ways. To this is added a long garment, and a wide shawl hanging from the head, thrown gracefully round the upper part of the body. They wear slippers but no stockings, their hands and feet are covered with gold and silver rings, the nails painted red and the eyebrows black.[25]

The chief feature of the women's costume was their parti-coloured dress (plate 77).

TUNISIA

The Jewish community goes back to Roman times and the normal restrictions on dress would have applied from the beginning of Arab rule. By the sixteenth century the special dress worn by men, like that of Jews in other parts of North Africa under Moslem rule, was a blue collarless tunic with loose sleeves, wide linen drawers, black slippers and a black skull cap.

Mordecai M. Noah who was the American consul at Tunis from 1813 to 1815 makes these comments about the Jews there:

The kingdom of Tunis contains about sixty thousand Jews, and whatever difference of opinion may exist as to their population in the city, I do not believe that it contains more than twenty thousand. These are divided into Italian and Barbary Jews, who are distinguished by their dress. The Barbary Jews wear a blue frock without a collar or sleeves, loose linen sleeves being substituted with wide drawers of the same article, no stockings, except in winter, and black slippers, a small black scull-cap on their head, which is shaved, and around which a blue silk handkerchief is bound; they are permitted to wear no colours. The Italian Jews dress like Christian residents, with the addition of a *haick*, or *bournouse*, thrown over their heads.

As it will readily be imagined in a country which is not civilized, the Jewish women, like the Turkish, are considered as an inferior race. They are fat and awkward, their dress consisting of a pettycoat of silk of two colours, principally yellow and purple, around which is thrown, in several folds, a thin gauze wrapper; the head is covered with a coloured silk handkerchief; those who are single, have their hair plaited in two or three rows, to the end of which they suspend coloured ribands; they wear no stockings, but slippers, with silver cinctures around their ankles; and the soles of their feet, their hands, nails, and eyebrows, tinged and coloured of a dark brown, from the juice of an herb called henna. When they walk they unloosen from their neck a piece of black crape, with which they cover their mouth and chin, leaving the upper part of their face bare. As to their living and domestic concerns, I can say no thing, never having visited any of them.

On the birth-night of General Washington, a ball was given at the American Consulate; the

77 Libya: Tripoli, 1842. *'Eine Jüdin von Tripolis'*. Engraving. From Ewald. She wears a head-scarf and a long belted dress the distinctive Jewish feature of which is the divided colours.

78 Tunis: Soliman, 1842. *'Eine Jüdenfrau in Soliman'*. Engraving. From Ewald. An unusual method of wearing the *çârma* covered by an enormous veil. The dress also is distinctive.

Jew brokers called to solicit the favour of permission to bring their women, as they call them, to see the company, which I granted; and one of the rooms was nearly filled with the Jewish beauty and *beau monde* of Tunis. They were all dressed magnificently, covered with jewels, gold brocades, tissue, lama and gauze, arranged without any taste, and crowded together without fancy; their feet bare, with embroidered slippers, and gold and silver bracelets around their ankles. Their complexions were fair, their eyes and teeth were good, but their figures were corpulent and unwieldy, which is considered a sign of beauty. The ladies of Tunis, who could speak Arabic, conversed with the Jewesses very courteously, and they appeared modest and well behaved.[26]

In January 1823 the British consul at Tunis reported to Downing Street that the government of Tunis 'whose maxim is constantly to oppress the Jews' had issued an order that all Jews who wore European dress must in future wear a red cap and he had been requested to inform all British Jews that they must comply with the order or leave the country. The consul had informed the Bey that it was incompatible with the dignity of a British subject to submit to such a humiliation and that it would not be tolerated whereupon, after a heated interview, the Bey had rescinded the order so far as it applied to British subjects.

Acknowledging the consul's letter the Earl of Bathurst expressed 'his entire approbation of the firmness and energy with which you resisted the

79 Tunis: *c.* 1840. *'Juifs Tunisiens'.* Wood engraving. Jewish Theological
Seminary. The man wears a turban and native costume; the women in
çârmas, ghlîlas and *djubbas* like the Algerian Jewesses.

unwarrantable attempt of the Bey of Tunis to oppress those of His Majesty's
subjects who are of the Jewish persuasion by subjecting them to a degrading
sign of humiliation'.[27]

The Livornese Jews living in Tunis did not fare so well and a treaty drawn
up at the same time between the Bey and the government of Tuscany
provided that Tuscan Jews should not retain the privileges granted to
Europeans after two years' residence in Tunis.[28]

The women's dress as seen in plates 78–9 is similar to that of Algeria but
later in the nineteenth century and in recent times the characteristic features
were the velvet *kufia*, tight pantaloons down to the ankle and white socks
(plate 80).

Benjamin, visiting the country on his travels (1846–55), gives this
description of the costume of the Jews in Tunis:

The men wear wide cloth trowsers, stockings, and shoes, an embroidered vest, and over this a
burnos. They shave their heads; the unmarried men wear a small black cap, and the married ones a
turban with a black fez. The women wear a folded garment and wide trowsers of silk or satin,
which are quite tight from the knee, and ornamented with rich embroideries of gold and silver.
Over all this they put on a kind of silk tunic, without sleeves, reaching as far as the knee, composed
generally of two different coloured kinds of stuff. They cover their head with a fez, round which is

62

wound a silk kerchief, with the ends hanging down. They likewise wear stockings and shoes. Upon their trowsers, in particular, great extravagance is lavished; and I was told that they often cost the rich 400 to 500 reals. The married women wear round their waist a kind of girdle. In the street they wrap themselves in a wide silk or fine woollen shawl; but leave their face uncovered, and hold up their garments as high as the knee, in order to display the embroidery on their trowsers. They are generally very beautiful, rather stout, and in their beauty resemble their sisters in Baghdad; except that the women in that town are more noble looking and graceful, while the ladies of Tunis are more corpulent. The Baghdad ladies are very industrious, while it is quite the contrary with those in Tunis. In Tunis as well as in Baghdad the girls marry from the age of thirteen and upwards.[29]

Hesse-Warteg, writing in 1882, states that the Jews of Tunis had not become emancipated as rapidly as those of Algeria and could still be distinguished at once by their appearance and dress which he describes thus:

Tall and strongly-built, with fine, noble features and long beards, they show still more to advantage in their peculiar, picturesque costumes. They are not bound to wear a certain dress, as formerly, but they seem desirous of their hereditary appearance. They have only changed their head-dress. Formerly they were forbidden to wear the red fez or sheshia of the Arab, but wore the prescribed black turban wound round a white fez—a kind of nightcap. They have now adopted the red fez, but keep to the black turban, while the younger generation has given up the turban altogether. They are allowed to wear the white turban of the Arabs, but they never make use of this permission. Their short jackets are of light colour, richly embroidered with gold and open in front; and while the old orthodox Jews still keep to the black trowsers, with many folds tied below the knee, the younger generation has adopted light-coloured ones. They all wear snow-white stockings; and the yellow or red leather slippers of the Arabs have been discarded by the Jewish swell in favour of the patent leather shoes imported from Europe, but which he treads down, so that his heel

80 Tunis: *c.* 1900. '*Young Jewish married couple*'. Photograph. From B. Fletcher, *Carthage and Tunis*, London, 1906. The man is in regional dress. The woman is dressed in white like the Arab women and the distinctive feature of her costume is the pointed velvet hat, *kufia*, embroidered in gold and tied by a red or yellow silk ribbon worn only by married women.

63

projects one or two inches beyond the shoe. A broad shawl, generally richly embroidered, is thrown round the loins, and while in winter their costume is completed by a long circular cloak of light-blue colour, they replace this in summer by a fine cloak of spotless whiteness, called the r'fara.

Neither they nor the Arabs carry arms; and they are scarcely necessary in Tunis, which is safer than European towns. Stately as a Jew's appearance is, and tasteful as is his dress, it is only so as long as he keeps his fez on his head. Like the Arabs, they are in the habit of shaving their heads, only leaving a small tuft of hair on the top which has a most ludicrous effect. . . .

The costume of the Jewesses is just as ugly as the dress of the Jews has been shown to be picturesque and beautiful. It is scarcely possible to imagine a toilet more tasteless and odd. Seen from a distance, Jewesses resemble ballet-girls, of whose body the upper part seems wrapped in a sack down to the hips. The stranger who meets such a figure for the first time fancies he sees a woman who has forgotten to dress herself, and is rather perplexed. The costume of a Jewess, whether a child or an old woman, consists of very few articles. Over the nether garment, made of white linen, they wear a small, gold-embroidered velvet jacket, a pair of white, very tight pantaloons, which reach to the ankle, and differ in nothing from the tights of ballet-girls. Short white socks cover, as a rule, their small feet, of which the points are covered by tiny, black kid slippers, scarcely protecting half the foot; or they wear high wooden sandals. Over the upper part of the body a baggy chemise falls down to the hips, made of red, yellow, or light-green silk, and their head is covered by the velvet 'kufia' embroidered in gold and shaped like a sugar-loaf, and is tied by a red or yellow silk ribbon. On their arms and necks they wear heavy gold chains and bracelets, and face and hands are uncovered.[30]

The same writer describes the costume of a Jewish bride as being of such splendour that it defied description. Her face was covered with a gold-embroidered veil and she wore a gold-brocaded upper garment, velvet pantaloons covered with gold braid, red silk stockings and gold-embroidered slippers. Her fingers were entirely covered with diamonds and dyed down to the second joint with henna.

In the 1930's the rabbis wore a caftan, short wide trousers and a mauve turban wound around a skull cap. The women were in white blouses, wide drawers under an ample top skirt fastened by a metal girdle, a silk kerchief around the head, a necklace of large gold coins, and slippers. In the street they wore a white silk cloak.[31]

ALGERIA

Jewish settlements in Algeria go back to the Roman era and there has been an important community there since medieval times. Under the Arabs the Jews suffered the same restrictions as they did in other parts of the Moslem Empire. In 1391 many Jewish refugees from Castile, Aragon, Andalusia and the Balearic Islands fled to Algeria. The new-comers were known as 'wearers of birettas' while the native Algerian Jews were called 'wearers of turbans'.

Native Algerian dress, which Jewish women gradually adopted, owed much of its attraction to Andalusian or Turkish influences.

The earliest description of the Jews is given by Diego De Haedo in a book published at Valladolid in Spain in 1612. He divides the Jews of Algiers into three categories: descendants of Spanish refugees; immigrants from Majorca, France and Italy; and the indigenous Jews of Africa. All carried on a trade of some kind, particularly tailoring and coral working; they were the only ones who coined money, the entire mint being in their hands, and most of the silversmiths were Jews. They traded with Tripoli, Gelves, Tunis, Bone, Constantine, Oran, Tlemcen, Tetuan, Fez, Marrakesh and Constantinople.

The Spanish Jews wore a round cap of Toledo needlework, the Jews from Majorca, France and Italy a black wool garment with half sleeves and a hood; those coming from Constantinople and Turkey wore turbans of choice materials but yellow in colour, and some had top-boots which had to be black. The native Jews wore a red cap around which was wrapped a *toca* (headcloth) of white canvas material. This was like the head-dress of the local Moors and as a distinction the Jews had to leave the forelock uncovered

81 Algeria: *c.* 1796. '*Ein Allgierischer Jüd*'. Etching. From A. M. Wolffgang, *Costumes Algériens c.* 1796. Jewish Theological Seminary. He is bearded and wears head scarf, belted tunic, shirt with voluminous sleeves, *burnous*, trousers and mules with heels.

82 Algeria: 1833. '*Juive d'Alger*'. Etching by E. Delacroix. Delacroix noted in his journal that he made a drawing of the Jewess, Dititia, in Algerian costume. Her dress, in fact, with its wrap-over skirt embroidered on one corner is more like the ceremonial dress of the Moroccan Jewesses but her head-dress is native Algerian.

83 Algeria: 1835. 'Festin Juif'. Lithograph. From *Voyage Pittoresque dans la Regence d'Alger*, Paris, 1835. Rubens (ii) 1708. Feast to celebrate a circumcision with the women all in their ceremonial dresses and *çârmas*; the men in turbans.

hanging down the centre of the forehead. In other respects all the Jews dressed alike in wide breeches, a shirt, and a long black coat over which was worn an *albornoz* (burnous), usually black but sometimes white. Jews were not allowed to wear proper shoes but were restricted to slippers which were always black in colour. Most of the Jewish women also wore slippers which were always black in colour. When they went out they covered their faces with a delicate white veil secured by a knot at the back of the head leaving the eyes and the forehead visible. They also wore a cloak called an *alhuyke* made of very fine white wool or woven silk and wool. There was little to distinguish their costume from that of the Moorish women.

Jewish brides did not paint their arms black like the Moorish women but used much colour and white cosmetics and adorned themselves with bracelets, rings, gold earrings and *aljofar* (a misshapen pearl). The wedding day was a day of *fête* set aside for music and dancing. The courtyard of the house where the ceremony was held was decorated with silk and the bride sat on a dais like a May Queen. Anyone, Moors and Christians included, could enter and watch.

The Chevalier d'Arvieux, in an account of his travels in Algeria in 1676 published in Paris in 1735, describes a visit to a Jewish wedding. He found nothing unusual about the costume of the Jewish women except that when they went out they were so completely covered from head to toe that only their eyes were visible. The distinctive feature of the men's dress was a kind of soutane, a long black robe pleated at the back over which they wore a burnous. Their cap was of black knitted wool. The Jews from Leghorn and Alexandria wore European hats and were dressed like Italians or Spaniards. Other foreign Jews wore a hood of black cloth to which was attached a tail a foot long (? liripipe).[32]

The most striking feature of Algerian Jewish married women's costume during the nineteenth century on gala occasions was the long cone-shaped head-dress on a metal frame known as the *çârma*, which is similar to the *tantoura* worn by Druse women and the fifteenth-century European *hennin*. It is not known in Algeria before the eighteenth-century and its use by Jewish women was first observed by Abraham Salamé, an Egyptian interpreter, who visited the country in 1816. At that period only Turkish or Moorish women were allowed to have *çârmas* made of silver or gold, the Jewish women being restricted to brass, except the wife of Jacob Bacri, banker to the Dey, who wore one of gold. They went out of fashion among Moslems towards the end of the nineteenth century.

The normal dress for Jewish women by the middle of the nineteenth century was the native *ghlîla* and *djubba*. The former was a décolletée vest reaching the knees with short sleeves brought through the armholes of the *djubba*, which was an ankle-length gown.

The following description of the Jews was given by an English traveller in 1835:

The Jews of Barbary shave the head close and allow the beard to grow. They are not permitted to use the turban but wear a small black woollen cap, which merely covers the back of the head, leaving the forehead and temples bare. The shirt is made with very wide sleeves, which hang loose as far as the elbows; over this is a vest of dark cloth, which fastens tight round the neck, and down the front, by means of small metal buttons or wire hooks. Loose drawers reaching to the knees and black leather slippers complete the dress; but when the weather is cold, they throw over all the burnoose or cloak, made of black wool. In winter they sometimes wear stockings but generally the legs are naked. Their girdle, like the rest of their dress, must be black, red is strictly forbidden.

The dress of the Jewish women consists of a fine linen chemise with long loose sleeves, over this a large robe, covering the body, but leaving the neck and breasts bare: it is made of cloth or velvet, according to the circumstances of the wearer, and is embroidered round the edges; their petticoat is commonly dark green superfine cloth, embroidered with gold, and reaching no farther than the knee; the legs are bare, and the feet thrust into little slippers, so small that they just cover the toes, and can scarcely be kept on in walking. Round the waist they wear a sash of silk and gold, the ends of which, adorned with little metallic plates, are suffered to hang loosely behind, so that when they move these make a tinkling noise. The unmarried women wear the hair plaited in different folds and flowing down the back; they have a very graceful methods of twining a wreath of wrought silk round the head and weaving it behind into a bow. The married women cover their heads with a flowing silk handkerchief, and occasionally use the sarmah or tiara, made of gold or silver, and set with precious stones, over which they throw a veil on going out, so managed as to draw across the

back of the head, shoulders, and lower part of the face, leaving uncovered their eyes, of which they make excellent use. They have an extravagant passion for ornaments; and every Jew who can afford it, tricks out his wife and daughters in the greatest profusion of earrings, bracelets, anklets, rings, chains and other trinkets. On Sabbaths and feast days, they appear in all their finery, the men putting on their best clothes, which, however, cannot vary in form and colour from the appointed standard, while the women, who are less restricted, set no bounds to the splendour of their attire. . . .

Their robes are generally of blue wool or silk, embroidered with gold; over this they place a spencer without sleeves, also ornamented with gold, and closed by golden buttons. The sarmah is festooned with a silk shawl enriched with pearls, and supplied with a long golden streamer, which, attached like a tail to its inferior parts, hangs as low as the ground. The slippers are velvet or Morocco leather, embroidered with gold wreaths, but the legs are always naked. Bracelets of gold or silver adorn their arms; finally necklaces of pearl, or coral, or golden chains, set off the snowy whiteness of the neck, which they take particular pains to expose as much as possible. The Jewish women do not paint figures on their faces and limbs, as the Moorish women do, but they stain with henna the nails, the palms of the hands and soles of the feet, and renew this once a week; they, some of them, blacken their eyebrows, and all use depilatories, which are applied in the form of a paste at the bath, and come off bringing with them superfluous hairs.

Bathing is a frequent practice; a Jewess, even in moderate circumstances, will go to the bath at least twice a month. The Jewish children are clothed in the same manner as their parents, but the girls are not allowed the sarmah and the golden tails until they are marriageable, that is when they have attained their ninth year. The boys wear their hair long up to the same period, and have it almost dyed red with henna. The children of the rich are dressed sufficiently well, and both sexes wear caps of blue velvet, adorned with a number of gold coins, proportionate to the wealth of the family. As many as a hundred gold sequins may be at times seen thus disposed.

Finally he gives this description of a Jewish bride:

In the afternoon her female friends congregate to pay their compliments to the bride, and dress her out in the finest clothes which she possesses. The inside of her hands, and the soles of her feet are stained red; red figures are traced on her forehead, on each cheek a triangle of the same colour with a gold leaf in the centre. Her eyebrows and the edges of the lids are blackened, her hands, from the bend of the wrist to the tips of the fingers, covered with black lines drawn zig-zag; her head-dress is tricked out with jewels and lace, finally they throw over her shoulder a kind of scarlet silk mantle, embroidered with gold.[33]

By the middle of the nineteenth century most of the restrictions on Jewish dress had disappeared. In some cases if a turban was worn it had a tassel attached to it as a distinction and old men still wore the traditional costume[34] (plates 81–7).

86 Algeria: 1842. '*Demoiselle juive d'Alger*'. Lithograph. Rubens (ii) 1709. She wears a blue and gold *djubba* over a blue *ghlîla* the short sleeves of which are tied behind her back. On her head is a *mharma*.

87 Algeria: 1842. '*Juif d'Alger*'. Lithograph. Rubens (ii) 1710. Black cap; black blouse and tunic; girdle; navy blue scarf; white breeches; *cobbât*.

As in most parts of North Africa where Jews are found, the Moroccan community is of ancient origin and dates back well before the Arab conquest. Its costume, which is particularly interesting, has been carefully studied and few travellers have failed to comment on the beauty of the Jewish women and the richness of their dress.

An early reference to the black clothing common to all Jews in North Africa is contained in a twelfth-century edict of the Sultan Moulay Ismaël from which it appears that all his subjects had hitherto worn black slippers; thenceforth they were to be worn only by Jews.

According to Leo Africanus (*c.* 1526) the Jews of Fez wore black turbans or a cap with a piece of red material attached and were not allowed shoes.

Lancelot Addison, who was chaplain at Tangier from 1662 until 1670 when it belonged to Charles II, has left the best account of the Moroccan Jews of that time. They wore, he said:

> little black brimless caps, as the Moors red which they seldom move in greeting one another. They likewise, as the Moors, go slipshod (i.e. in slippers) and wear linnen drawers and vest over which they put a loose garment called a *ganephe* which differs only in colour from the *mandilion* or *albornoz* which the Moors bestow upon the Christians when they are redeemed from slavery. This *ganephe* is a black square piece of coarse hairstuff closed at the cross corners and all round it is a large Thrum which at first sight looks like their Religious Fringes whereof we shall have occasion in due time and place to discourse. The Jews in this Continent much resemble the Spaniard and Portuguez in their stature and complexion . . .[35]

In a description of a wedding Addison mentions that it was a custom for the bride to send the bridegroom a girdle with a silver buckle and for him to send her one with a gold buckle. The wearing of a silk sash or girdle was a Moorish custom.

Another writer gives a very similar account of the men's dress at this period: 'The Jews wear a shirt, drawers, a black closecoat or Caffetan and over it a black or dark coloured kind of cloak which they call Albernous made with a cowl like a Fryers Frock but there hangs down strings at the end of the cowl and at the bottom. They have a black cap, black pumps and slippers.[36]

Höst supplies information about Jewish costume at the end of the eighteenth century (plate 88). All the men wore black caps, *burnous* and slippers. Only the *caftan* could be of a different colour. The rabbis had no special dress but wore, as a distinction, larger and wider sleeves, a red mark on their black *burnous* (as mentioned by Leo Africanus) and usually a navy handkerchief round the cap.

The women, who according to Höst were usually good-looking, did not

88 Morocco: 1781. Engraving. From Höst.
Fig. 1. *Moroccan Jew.* All Jews wore black caps,
burnous and slippers but the *caftan* could be of other
colours. The Jews had to drape the *burnous* over the
shoulder as shown. Fig. 2. *Rabbi.* He has no special
costume but wears larger and wider sleeves, a red
sign on the black *burnous* and usually a blue handkerchief around the cap. Figs. 3 and 4. *Jewess.* She
wears a wrap-over skirt of red or green material,
the outer pointed end of which is decorated with
gold or silk embroidery; belt; corselet; *plastron*
with long sleeves joined together on the back and
red or embroidered shoes with heels. An early
version of the *keswa el khira.*

differ much in their dress from the Moorish women. They wore an open
skirt of red or green material, the outer pointed end of which was embroidered in gold or silk; the skirt was held together by a belt above the
waist. The sleeves of the jacket were usually knotted behind the back. The
slippers were red or embroidered and had heels. In the streets half the face was
exposed to distinguish them from the Moorish women.

In 1789 William Lempriere, an army physician attached to the garrison
at Gibraltar, travelled through Morocco, where he had been invited in order
to attend the emperor's son. In the towns he usually stayed at a Jewish house
in the mellah (the only part of the town where a Christian was safe) and as
he was held almost as a prisoner long after he wished to leave he had plenty of
opportunity of studying the Jews. He was shocked at the way the Moors
treated them, particularly as they were the only mechanics and were
responsible for the whole of the commerce of the country including the
treasury and mint.

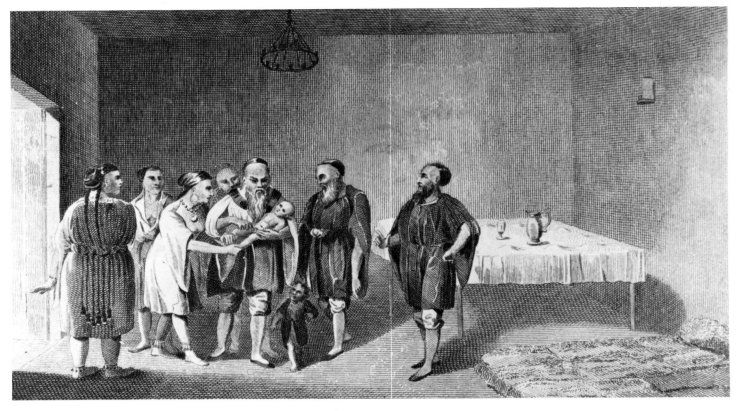

89   Morocco: *c. 1830. Circumcision.* Engraving. Jewish Theological Seminary.
The men bearded in black caps, belted tunics, *burnous* and breeches; the
women with false hair, the long tails of which hang down their backs.

The men shaved their heads close and wore their beards long. They were
dressed in a black cap, black slippers and instead of the Moorish *haick* an
alberoce (burnous), a cloak made of black wool. They were not allowed to
carry a sword or ride a horse (see plates 88–90).

Lempriere writes at length about the Jewish women:

The dress of the Jewish women consists of a fine linen shirt, with large and loose sleeves, which
hang almost to the ground; over the shirt is worn a *caftan*, a loose dress made of woollen cloth, or
velvet, of any colour, reaching as low as the hips, and covering the whole of the body, except the
neck and breast, which are left open, the edges of the caftan being embroidered with gold. In
addition to these is the *geraldito*, or petticoats, made of fine green woollen cloth, the edges and
corners of which have sometimes a gold ornament; this part of the dress is fastened by a broad
sash of silk and gold, which surrounds the waist, and the ends of it are suffered to hang down
behind, in an easy manner; when they go abroad, they cover the whole with the *haick*, the same as
used by the Moorish women. The unmarried Jewesses wear their hair plaited in different folds,
and hanging down behind; and to this they have a very graceful and becoming method of putting
a wreath of wrought silk round the head, and tying it behind in a bow. This dress sets off their
features to great advantage, and distinguishes them from the married women, who cover their
heads with a red silk handkerchief, which they tie behind, and over it place a silk sash, leaving
the ends to hang loose on their backs. None of the Jewish women have stockings, but use red slippers, curiously embroidered with gold. They wear very large gold ear-rings at the lower part of
the ears, and at the upper, three small ones set with pearls or precious stones; their necks are loaded
with beads, and their fingers with small gold or silver rings; round each wrist and ancle are fixed
large and solid silver bracelets; and the rich have gold and silver chains suspended from the sash
behind.

72

Their marriages are celebrated with much festivity for some time previous to the ceremony, and the intended bride, with all her female relations, go through the form of having their faces painted red and white, and their hands and feet stained yellow, with an herb named *henna*. A variety of figures are marked out with a needle, and this herb, which is powdered and mixed with water into a paste, is worked in, and these marks continue on the hands and feet for a long time.

The Jewesses of this empire in general are remarkably fair and beautiful. They marry very young, and when married, though they are not obliged to hide their faces in the street, yet at home they are frequently treated with the same severity as the Moorish women. Like the Moors, the Jewish men and women at Morocco eat separate; and the unmarried women are not permitted to go out, except on particular occasions.[37]

The most striking of the costumes worn by the Jewish women of Morocco is the dress described by Höst, the *keswa el kbira*, given to a bride by her father as part of her dowry and worn for special occasions like weddings and circumcisions. The best were produced by the Jewish women of Tetuan who were famous for their embroidery. The costume attracted the attention of many writers and artists. Delacroix has left an impression of the Jewish bride at Tangier whose wedding he attended in 1832 (frontispiece) and a

90 Morocco: c. 1830. '*Costume of the Barbary Jew hawker in Gibraltar*'. Drawing. Beard, cap, *burnous*, striped silk girdle, shirt with long sleeves, trousers, mules.

91 Morocco: 1878. '*Tangerienne Israélite*'. Drawing by Victor Eeckhout. A good example of the Jewish ceremonial dress the *keswa el kbira*.

Flemish artist, Victor Eeckhout, shows how the costume looked when worn on other occasions (plate 91). Goulven, writing in the 1920's, gives this description of the bride's dress:

The bride has to remain motionless as a doll while the maids hand her the *ktef*, a kind of velvet chemise worn over the breast and the *gonbaiz* which is a claret or green velvet corsage embossed with gold stripes and with silver buttons. She is then wrapped in a wide velvet skirt (*jelteta*) of the same colour, which usually is richly ornamented with gold braid. Under this skirt numerous petticoats (*saiat*) disguise the slender young figure. There is a choice of two belts: the *endema*, the same colour as the dress, embroidered with gold thread and fastened with a silver clasp (*lezim*) or the *hezam* a stiff, wide belt of gold embroidered velvet. Added to the principal articles of this curious costume are silk stockings and gold embroidered slippers called *kheaya el kebira* or *baboutcha*. There remain now such details as the wide separate sleeves of white voile, *lekmam detsmira*, which are stitched to the shoulders in such a way that the remainder of the material floats bell-shaped. The *dlalat* consist of two plaits of thick black thread which fall forward each side of the head. After being powdered and rouged the bride is given the *festoul*, a long sash of fine silk which is used like the *kah el ras* to tie up her hair leaving the ends hanging down her back. They then place on her head a kind of mitre called *sualef ez zoher* in Rabat and *khamar* in Salé, which is covered with pearls, precious stones, gold coins etc. Over this coiffure comes first the *sebnia*, a white or green silk foulard, then the *elbelo*, a thin white veil, lowered over the girl's face, softening the brilliance of the gilt and velvet, harmonising the warm and lively tones of this sumptuous costume. Finally, for the actual marriage the bride's shoulders are covered with a white *haik* to hide the profusion of jewels, cosmetics and henna. Adjusting this *haik* is a little ceremony added to the long, complicated wedding ceremonial among rich Moroccan Jews.[38]

The traditional costumes of the Jewish women of Morocco are now museum pieces as are the wigs which replaced their own hair after marriage. Fortunately they have been well recorded by, among others, Mlle Jouin and Monsieur Besancenot to whom we owe the illustrations of the various regional style (plates 92–99) and many actual examples are preserved in the Israel Museum.

93 Morocco: Fez, *c.* 1940. *Married Jewess of Fez*. Drawing. Besancenot, plate 52. Another example of the ceremonial costume, *keswa el kbira*. It differs slightly in cut from the Rabat model, and the muslin sleeves, which are much shorter, are turned back below the elbow and pinned to the inside of the short sleeves of the corselet. The decoration, which is much simpler, includes the stylized *hmames* designed to ward off the evil eye. The coiffure is also simpler than that at Rabat. It comprises a frame, *sfifa*, to which are attached long strands of black silk imitating hair separated into two long bands falling behind on to the shoulders. Her chin and cheeks are painted with little white and red dots following an ancient Arab custom. This costume which was painted from authentic documents is now extremely rare as most of the examples were destroyed when the mellah was sacked in the 1912 riots.

94 Morocco: Goulmima, *c.* 1940. *Jewess of Goulmima*. Drawing. Besancenot, plate 57. This woman from the mellah of Goulmima close to Tafilelt wears a red dress. From the immense coiffure two corkscrews of wool can be seen hanging from the wig on to the shoulders.

95 Morocco: Tiznit, *c.* 1940. *Jewess of Tiznit*. Drawing. Besancenot, plate 53. This ceremonial dress is a compromise between that of the towns and the Anti-Atlas. It is also of velvet, red or green, but the flounced skirt, *jelteta*, retains the style of the *saya*. The corselet is called *qaftan*. The coiffure, *tijajin d-mahduh*, is particularly remarkable. It is like a coif made of silver thread with five grooves decorated with cloisonné enamel. The hair made from black cows' tails falls in two bands across the forehead. Attached to the hair is the *festul*, a red scarf with gold brocade.

92 Morocco: Rabat, *c.* 1940. *Married Jewess of Rabat.* Drawing. Besancenot, plate 51. She wears the ceremonial dress, *keswa el kbira*, reserved for weddings and special occasions. It is made entirely of velvet usually of green or blue for towns in the interior and claret for the coasts and south. The open skirt, *jelteta*, which is wound from left to right is heavily decorated with gold braid. A corselet, deeply scooped out, with short sleeves, *gonbaiz*, also loaded with gold braid has attached to it by silver filigree buttons the *plastron* (front) made of the same velvet and covered with gold embroidery. Long wide sleeves, *kmam tsmira*, are attached to the short sleeves of the *plastron* and the ends are pinned on the back. Her coiffure, the *sualef*, consists of two fringes of imitation hair made of black silk thread with two plaits, *dlalat*, which hang down in front. It is held in place by means of a tiara set with pearls and precious stones and has a silk scarf, *festul*, attached to it which hangs down behind as far as her heels. Her eyes are blacked with *khol* and she is heavily made up.

92

93

94

95

96

97

98

96 Morocco: Tafilelt, c. 1940. *Jewess of Tafilelt*. Drawing. Besancenot, plate 55. The Jewish women in the Mellahs of the Atlas Mountains and the oases of the south dress like their neighbours and this dress is similar to that worn by Berber women. It is only the coiffure which shows Jewish influence. It is called *grun* (horns) from its unusual shape and is made of two skeins of thick wool tightly bound with little plaits to form a horn on each side of the face. These are firmly held by bands of material and a bonnet. This woman is in her outdoor dress and her coiffure is covered with a large veil of white muslin decorated with little flowers.

97 Morocco: Todrha, c. 1940. *Jewess of Todrha*. Drawing. Besancenot, plate 58. Her wig, *sualef*, probably the most curious in Morocco contains 30 to 40 cows' tails made into two enormous headbands weighing nearly a kilo. Down the centre is a string of small silver ornaments and coloured stones crowned by a band of silver coins and a silk handkerchief. From the wig hang two long thick skeins of heavy wool on to the shoulders.

98 Morocco: Tililt, c. 1940. *Jewess of Tililt*. Drawing. Besancenot, plate 59. Her wig is covered by a diadem made of small silver plaques. The black and red designs on her face are similar to those of the Berber women.

99 Morocco: Beni-Sbih, c. 1940. *Jewess of Beni-sbih*. Drawing. Besancenot, plate 60. She is dressed like the Berber women. The Jewish women of the valley of the Dra do not wear wigs but have little curls of ostrich feathers on their temples.

100 Morocco: 1936. *Moroccan Jewish coiffures*. From Jouin.
1. Fez. Meknes. Séfrou;
2. Taroudant; 3. Tiznit. Talaint;
4. Rabat. Tetuan; 5. Midelt;
6. Tafilalet; 7. Dades. Todrha;
8. Figuig; 9. Ouarzazat;
10. Todrha.

INDIA

The Jews of India are divided into four main groups: the Bnei Israel, who are coloured, the White Jews originating from Baghdad, the Black Jews of Cochin and the White Jews of Cochin.

The earliest known drawing of a man and woman of the Bnei Israel (plate 101) dates from about 1830. The man is clean shaven but has side locks (*peoth*) and wears a black skull cap and Moslem-style white cotton trousers. The woman's upper garment is Western in style and she has a rather unusual sarong type of skirt. Her hair is not completely covered and the married women were apparently allowed to show their hair. Later in the nineteenth century it seems that the men wore turbans. Elderly men wore beards; young men, side locks (see plate 102). At the beginning of the present century the men had abandoned turbans and were wearing a round embroidered cap (plate 103).

The Baghdadi Jews, some of whom came from other parts of the Levant besides Baghdad, wore the Turkish *djubba* and *entari* with a turban. They all had long rounded beards (plate 105).

The following description of the White Jews of Cochin was written in

101 India: *c.* 1830. *'Jew'*. Drawing. Man and woman of the Bnei-Israel. Rubens (ii) 1639. The man is clean shaven but has side locks and a black skull cap. He wears a waistcoat with long sleeves, jacket with short sleeves. Muslim-style white cotton trousers and Indian-type wooden shoes. The woman wears a white scarf over her hair, the front part of which is exposed. Her white upper garment is Western in style. Her red skirt is in the sarong style of Malaya and Indonesia which is occasionally seen in India where it is known as *mekhala*.

1860: 'their features are fine if not (especially with the elders) noble; broad and high forehead, roman nose, thick lips, generally however concealed by a most luxuriant, jet-black, curly beard'. For synagogue they wore fine clothing: 'robes of silk, velvet or satin of a scarlet, blue, green or amber tint with costly shawls wrapped around the head and waist and a lavish display of gold chains and buttons made of English sovereigns . . . their costume does not at all resemble that of the natives of India.' On ordinary occasions they wore a white cotton skull cap, jacket, waistcoat and trousers. The jacket had full sleeves, breast pockets and twelve silver buttons fastened by a fine silver chain attached to the topmost hole. The writer observes that the Jewish women had recently adopted gowns of silk, linen or chintz but that formerly their costume was very different and far more pleasing.[39]

The women's ceremonial dresses, which are made of silk and gold brocade are Western in cut, and have a strong affinity with the Spanish costumes of the Jewish women of Morocco (plate 104).

The weekday dress of the White Jews at the beginning of the present century was the same as that worn by the natives, but the Black Jews were covered only from the waist down, wore a red handkerchief on their heads, and had side locks (*peoth*). In the synagogue the White Jews wore a turban, a shirt, a jacket with twelve buttons (as described by Lawson) and over this a *djubba*, and trousers. All married women wore a gold chain with a peculiar coin in the middle called *tahli* (plate 104).

78

102 India: Bombay, 1842. *Bnei-Israel of Bombay*. Engraving. From Wilson. The author gives this description of the Bnei-Israel: 'The Bnei-Israel in their physiognomy resemble the Arabian Jews, though they view the name *Yehud*, when applied to them, as one of reproach. They are fairer than the other natives of India of the same rank of life with themselves; but they are not much to be distinguished from them with regard to dress. They have no *shendi*, like the Hindus, on the crown of their heads; but they preserve a tuft of hair above each of their ears. Their turbans, *angrakhâs*, and shoes are like those of the Hindus; and their trousers like those of the Musalmans. Their ornaments are the same as those worn by the middle class of natives in the Maratha country. Their houses do not differ from those of other natives of the same rank.'

103 India: Cochin, *c.* 1900. *Black Jews*. Photograph. From *Jewish Encyclopaedia* iv: 135. They wear regional dress.

104 India: Cochin, 1870. *White Jews of Cochin*. Photographs. From A. Grandidier, *Voyage dans les Provinces Méridionales de l'Inde*, Paris, 1870. The men are bearded and dressed in Indian Islamic style but the material which is silk would not be worn by Moslems. The women's dress is in Spanish style and has affinities with the ceremonial dress of the Jewish women of Morocco. The costume on the left is particularly fine being made entirely of gold brocade with lace sleeves. Both women wear a Tahli gold chain. Their hair is only partly covered.

105 India: *c.* 1864. '*David Sassoon*'. Engraving. Rubens (i) 344. David Sassoon (1792–1864) the founder of David Sassoon & Co., the Bombay banking house, was a native of Baghdad and wears the traditional Baghdadi costume.

3 The Western world–The effects of tradition and restrictive laws

EARLY MEDIEVAL PERIOD

Nothing is known about Jewish costume in Europe during Carolingian times and the earliest reference to Jewish dress is a complaint by Archbishop Agobar of Lyon in 826 about the lavishness of the clothing given to Jewish women by princesses and the wives of courtiers. In 839, Deacon Bodo, a German, became a convert to Judaism and to mark the occasion adopted the name of Eleazar, allowed his hair and beard to grow and put on a military belt. Whether the last item had any significance is not known but a belt or girdle later became a Jewish characteristic in certain countries, notably in Poland.

Fur-trimmed garments were a feature of Jewish dress, according to the ninth-century writer who reported that 'Pope Nicholas was so strongly opposed to Arsenius, Bishop of Orta, because of his effort to introduce Jewish fur garments (*judaicae peluciae*) that the Pope threatened to exclude him from the Palatine procession unless he vowed to discard the clothes of the superstitious race and agreed to walk in the procession wearing the priestly fillet'.[1]

In the absence of any real evidence of the nature of Jewish dress during this period it is reasonable to assume that the traditional aversion to change and to the adoption of gentile customs continued to have its effect and maintained a very conservative form of dress. The precepts regarding *tsitsith*, *peoth*, *shaatnez* and *tefillin* and the obligation for married women to cover their hair remained in force and the distinctive Jewish hat imported from the Orient probably came into use at an early date. It was presumably due to a weakening of these influences that the Church decided that legislation was needed to compel Jews to wear distinctive dress.

THE FOURTH GENERAL COUNCIL OF THE LATERAN

The Fourth General Council of the Lateran, which ruled that Jews should in future be distinguished by their clothing, was more important that any of the church councils which preceded it and remained for generations the authority on all disputed points of canon law. It was summoned by Innocent III, the Pope who supported King John of England against the barons over Magna Carta.

The Council opened on 1 November 1215 and the Pope announced that the two chief tasks before him were the recovery of the Holy Land and the reform of Catholic life. Of the seventy canons, No. 68 requires Jews to wear a distinctive dress:

In some Church provinces a difference in dress distinguishes the Jews and Saracens from the Christians, but in certain others there is great confusion and they cannot be distinguished. Thus it happens at times that through error Christians have relations with Jewish and Saracen women and Jews and Saracens with Christian women. Therefore, that they may not, under such pretext resort to excusing themselves in the future for the excesses of such accursed intercourse, we decree that such (Jews and Saracens) of both sexes in every Christian province and at all times shall be distinguished in the eyes of the public from other peoples by the character of their dress. Particularly, since it may be read (in Numbers xv: 37–41) that this very law has been enjoined upon them by Moses.[2]

The sixth canon ordered the bishops for each ecclesiastical province to meet annually in order to secure observance of the laws and to remedy abuses.

The Council did not specify what distinctions were required nor did it indicate where action had to be taken but presumably England, France and Spain were the chief countries it had in mind since it was in these countries that traditional dress was being abandoned.

THE BADGE

Although not specifically mentioned by the General Council of the Lateran, the badge owed its introduction in Europe to the legislation passed in 1215. It was presumably inspired by its much earlier Moslem counterpart and to the extent that it applied to Moslems it was a reprisal for the badge which they imposed on Christians as well as Jews. Jews had to endure it intermittently for four centuries in every Christian country and it was regarded as a mark of degradation which was always bitterly resented. At first it seems to have had little effect since to enforce its decisions the Church had to rely on the secular authority which preferred to use the badge as a means of exaction. Thus it was easy for individuals and even for whole communities to obtain exemption if the necessary funds could be provided. This lack of co-operation by the secular authority was a constant source of complaint at church councils which continued to re-issue the regulations with monotonous regularity. The badge was usually in the shape of a ring hence the name *rouelle* (wheel) and the colour was usually yellow, red or particoloured red and white. Its effect in different countries is discussed overleaf.

106 France: Fourteenth century. *The Jewish badge.* Miniature. Ms. français 820, f. 192. Bibliothèque Nationale. The bearded figure on the right is a Jew and wears a red and white badge, blue hood, pink cloak and green inner tunic.

Opposite page

107 Spain: Fifteenth century. *Jewish women wearing the badge.* Sculpture. North cloisters of Barcelona Cathedral. Part of a scene representing John the Baptist preaching. The badge worn on the forehead as prescribed by law.

108 Spain: Fourteenth century. *Descent from the Cross.* Fresco detail. Chapel of Santa Lucia, Tarragona, Spain. Jew and Jewess in the dress prescribed by law with the Jewish badge on the breast.

France. The badge in the shape of a ring originated in France where it is first mentioned in 1208. After the Council of Narbonne, 1227, it became the official distinguishing sign for Jews and it was confirmed for the Jews of Provence by a number of church councils during the thirteenth and fourteenth centuries. By the laws of Marseilles, 1255, they were given the choice of the badge or a yellow hat.

The age at which the badge had to be worn varied. At Marseilles it was seven. Elsewhere it was thirteen or fourteen for boys and twelve for girls.

Normally it had to be worn on the breast. Sometimes a second one had to be worn on the back. At Besançon it was worn on the hat or on the belt. In the fifteenth century at Grenoble a badge of mixed colours had to be worn by men on the middle of the chest (plate 106) and by women on the head. At Valence the women wore it on their clothes.

The colour prescribed was at first yellow. Under King John it became parti-coloured red and white.

Fines of varying sums were fixed for contravention and in some cases the informer was awarded the clothing of the offending Jew.

Exemption from wearing the badge was granted to individual Jews for a money consideration and travellers were frequently exempted.

It was also a source of revenue when Jews were required to buy the badge from an official source.

At Perpignan in 1314, the governor ordered all Jews to wear a cape with a badge of a different colour of cotton or silk worn on the middle of the chest. Offenders had their clothes forfeited and the informer received one third of their value.

Spain. In Spain the badge was usually yellow. It was imposed on the Jews of Castile by a bull of Pope Honorius III in 1219. James I, King of Aragon made a similar order in 1228. Pope Gregory IX in 1233 ordered the King of Navarre and the Archbishop of Santiago to enforce the badge. In 1313 a yellow or red badge was introduced at Barcelona. The penalty for not wearing it was a fine or twenty strokes of the whip.

In 1315 the Moorish King of Granada imposed a badge on Jews to distinguish them from Moslems. Many exemptions were granted and frequently the badge was not enforced but the former laws were renewed with great force in 1371 by Henry II King of Castile.

In 1396 a yellow badge was imposed on the Jews of Murviedro as well as special clothing (see below).

In 1415 Pope Benedict XIII issued a bull imposing a badge parti-coloured yellow and red to be worn on the breast by men and on the forehead by women (plate 107). The shape and size of the badge were reproduced. It is the only example of a parti-coloured badge in Spain and applied only to Aragon.

107

109 Portugal: *c.* 1465-7. *Detail from the Veneration of St Vincent.* Tempera and oil on oak by Nuno Goncalves. Museu Nacional de Arte Antiga, Lisbon. The picture, which is a polyptych, shows members of the Court and Portuguese society praying before St Vincent, the patron saint of Portugal. The rabbi, holding a Hebrew book, wears a cylindrical black hat and gown. On his breast is the Jewish badge, a six pointed star in red.

A municipal law of Barcelona in 1479 required all Jews entering the city and staying more than fourteen days to wear a red badge on the breast.

Portugal. The badge seems to have been first introduced in 1289. In 1391 John I substituted for the yellow hat a red badge with six points the same size as the royal seal (plate 109).

Italy. The badge was first enforced in Italy in 1222 when the Holy Roman Emperor, Frederick II, decreed that his Jewish subjects should wear a blue badge shaped like the Greek letter T (*tau*). He also ordered them not to shave their beards.

At about the same time the badge was introduced into Sicily, Naples and Pisa.

In 1257 it was enforced by Pope Alexander IV in the Papal States in the form of a yellow patch for men and two blue stripes for women.

The Council of Ravenna in 1311 and 1317 confirmed the badge for men and ordered women to wear it on their head-dress.

At Verona in 1433 the shape stipulated was a star.

At Palermo in Sicily in 1488 under Spanish-Aragonian rule the badge was a piece of red cloth the size of a ducat worn over the heart.

At Piedmont in the seventeenth century a strip of yellow material had to be worn on the right shoulder, in the Duchy of Modena a red band covering an eighth part of the hat, and at Mantua the badge had to be worn on the hat.[3]

Elsewhere the badge was usually yellow and took the form of the letter O by which it was called (plate 110). By the beginning of the seventeenth century it was being enforced in practically every Italian city inhabited by Jews and was not abolished until 1816. Exceptionally, it was unknown in the free city of Leghorn.

110   Italy: Mantua, early fifteenth century. *Daniel Norsa and his family.*
Detail of painting. Church of Sant' Andrea, Mantua. Both men are bearded
and wear the Jewish badge. The family group appears beneath a painting
of the Madonna which they had been compelled to present as an altarpiece
to the church to make amends for an alleged desecration of a fresco of the
Madonna in their house.

111 England: 1275. *English Jew.*
Drawing. British Museum.
Cottonian Ms. Nero D II.
He wears a *gardecorps* with Jewish
badge and hood.

England. On 30 March 1218 Henry III issued an order requiring all Jews to wear the *tabula* consisting of two broad strips of white linen or parchment (plate 111).

Exemption from wearing this badge was freely granted for a consideration which varied according to the wealth of the applicant and the poorer members of the community were covered by a general licence for which a lump sum was paid. After 1253 when the wearing of the *tabula* was required by statute, enforcement was probably much stricter.

The Statutum de Judaismo of 1275 provided that every Jew over the age of seven should wear on his outer garment a badge in the form of two tables made of yellow cloth six fingers long and three fingers wide.

Germany. Jews were sufficiently distinguished by their hats and beards and the badge is not heard of until 1434 when it was imposed by the Council of Augsburg. It was yellow and had to be worn on the breast. Similar orders were made at Cologne in 1442, Nuremberg and Bamberg in 1451, Frankfurt in 1452 and other cities (plates 112–4). When Skippon visited Frankfurt at the end of the seventeenth century the Jews were still wearing a yellow badge but according to Schudt it had disappeared shortly afterwards. A heart-shaped badge worn by a German Jew on an engraving published at the beginning of the eighteenth century is the only record of a badge of this shape (plate 115).

112–13 Germany: Worms sixteenth century. *'Tracht der Juden zu Worms'*.
Drawings. Stadtarchiv, Worms. Monumenta Judaica B.139. The man in a
cloak and *chaperon*, the woman in a cloak and veil. Both wear the Jewish
badge.

114　Germany: 1588. '*Jew of the Palatinate. Jew of Frankfurt a/m. Unmarried Jewess. Jewess dressed for synagogue*'. Engravings. From C. Rutz, *Sacri Romani Imperri Ornatus*, 1588. The Jew of the Palatinate wears a cloak with *chaperon* and *liripipe*. The Jew of Frankfurt has a Jewish badge on his cloak and wears a hat. Both women wear the *orales*, the Jewish veil, which had two blue stripes, and the married woman has the regulation topcoat for synagogue. She also wears the badge.

115　Germany: *c.* 1700. '*Ein Jud der nach der Synagog gehet*'. Engraving. Rubens (ii) 1598. Dressed for synagogue in a sleeveless cloak (*sarbal*) on which is fixed the Jewish badge in the shape of a heart. He has the round black hat (*barrette*) and pleated ruff typical of German Jewish costume.

87

The final infamy occurred under Nazi rule when the town commandant of Wloclawek in Poland ordered every Jew without distinction of age or sex to wear a distinctive sign on the back in the form of a yellow triangle (plate 116). By 1942 the badge in one form or another had been extended to Germany itself and to all occupied countries.[4]

Switzerland. A bull of Pope Benedict XIII of 31 August 1411 required the Jews of Geneva to wear a distinctive mark. At Schaffhausen in 1435 a Jew wore a badge shaped like a Jew's hat.

Austria and Hungary. In 1232 Andrew II, King of Hungary, undertook to impose the badge on the Jews. In 1279 the Council of Ofen decreed that the Jews should wear a red badge on their left breast subject to severe penalties.

By a decree dated 1551 the Emperor Ferdinand I of Austria referring to the fact that the Jews of his empire had abandoned their distinctive costume ordered them to wear a yellow badge over their left breast within one month of taking up residence in any town (plates 117–8).

Under Maria Theresa the Jews in the Austrian empire, which included Galicia, Bohemia and Hungary, suffered severe persecution. One of the first reforms introduced by Joseph II when he became emperor in 1765 was the abolition of the badge. Important Jewish merchants were permitted to wear fashionable dress and even to carry swords.

116 Germany: 1939. *Jewish badge.* Jewish Museum, London. The badge re-introduced in Poland by the Nazis in 1939.

117 Austria: Prague, Sixteenth century. *'Jobst Mellern'.* Woodcut. He is called *Der Gelb Geckl* (The yellow fop) because of his yellow badge. Fur hat; caftan buttoned at neck with armholes through which the long sleeves of the undergarment protrude. Jewish badge on left breast.

88

118 Austria: Vienna, 1551. *Decree of Emperor Ferdinand I.* Friedburg Stadtarchiv XIIᶜ· Monumenta Judaica B.359. All Jews are required to wear a yellow ring (as shown) on the left side of the chest or dress within one month of coming to reside in any town.

DISTINCTIVE DRESS IMPOSED ON MEN

In addition to the badge and the pointed Jewish hat (discussed below) Jews were also subjected to other requirements with regard to their dress. At Perpignan in 1295 they were ordered to wear a cape.

In 1396 John I of Aragon ordered the Jews of Murviedro to wear a *gramalla* (long outer gown) or other garment covering the toes (plate 119) in addition to a yellow badge on the breast. In Majorca the Jews were required to wear attached to their hood a cowl the length of a palm, shaped like a funnel, and sewn up to form a point. In addition they had to wear a *gramalla*,

At Valladolid in 1412 the laws were given more precisely:

All Jews and Moors are to wear long robes over their clothes as low as their feet, and are not to wear cloaks; and in all cities, towns and places, they are to wear their distinctive red badge. But it is my pleasure, that, to avoid the dangers they might otherwise incur in travelling, they may wear the clothes they now have, as well as in the places they may go to.

That all Jewesses and Moriscas of our kingdoms and dominions, shall, within ten days from this

89

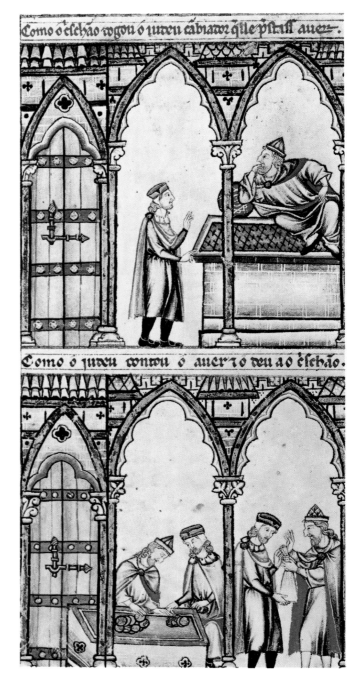

119 Spain: Fourteenth century. *Moses' blessing. Moses and Joshua.*
Miniatures: From the Sarajevo Hagadah. The monastic type of
dress prescribed for Spanish Jews. Full length gowns with capes.
The hoods are pointed. Labels, characteristic of academical dress
and consisting of two tongues of white fur or silk, appear to be
part of the hood.

120 Spain: Castile, thirteenth century. *Jews of Castile.* Miniature.
From *Las Cantigas* No. 25 f, 38. El Escorial, Madrid. Composed for
Alfonso X of Castile (1252–84), the *Cantigas*, of which there are 194,
describe the miracles performed by pictures or images of the Madonna.
Most of them are illustrated by miniatures, many of which show
attempts by Jews to desecrate a picture or image as the result of which
they are drowned, burned or converted. The Jews wear a curious
form of the Jewish hat with three-quarter length tunics and cloaks.

date, wear long mantles reaching to their feet, and cover their heads with the same. Those who act
contrary, for so doing, are to forfeit all the clothes they may have on to their under garment.

That no Jew or Moor, ten days after this date, shall wear cloth of which the entire suit costs
upwards of thirty maravedis; those who act contrary shall, for the first offence, forfeit the apparel
they have on to the shirt; for the second, lose all their clothes and receive a hundred lashes; and for
the third, all their property shall be confiscated to my treasury. But it is my pleasure that, if they
choose, they may make coats and cloaks of the clothes they now possess.

Henceforward Jews and Moors are not to shave their beards, or have them shaved with razors
or scissors; nor trim nor cut the hairs, but are to wear them long as they grow naturally, as they
were formerly accustomed. Any person who acts contrary hereto, shall receive a hundred lashes,
besides paying a fine of a hundred maravedis for each time he transgresses.[5]

A regulation of the city of Cologne dated 8 July 1404 required Jews and Jewesses of all ages to wear distinctive dress and in particular laid down the following rules:

Sleeves on coats and jackets may not exceed half an *elle* in width.
Collars on jackets and cloaks may not exceed one finger in width.
No fur may be shown at top or bottom of clothing.
Lace is permitted on sleeves only.
Cuffs on sleeves may not exceed the length of the hand.
Coats must be fringed and must reach the calves.
Cloaks may not be open on both sides and must reach to within a hand's width of the ground.
Hoods of males over the age of 13 must be one *elle* in length, the shoulder collar one and a half *elles* but not wider than one-eighth.
Silk shoes are forbidden both indoors and outdoors.
Unless close-cropped, the hair above the lobe of the ear may not be cut.
No child over the age of three may wear open clothing.
A girl may not wear a hair ribbon worth more than 6 gulden or wider than two fingers.
On ordinary days women may not wear more than one ring on each hand nor one worth more than 3 gulden.
On ordinary days women may not wear gold belts nor a belt wider than two fingers.
On festivals they may wear belts up to 2 silver marks in value and two rings up to 6 gulden in value.[6]

One result of the various dress regulations was that the Jews with their hoods and long cloaks were frequently mistaken for monks and to prevent this the Council of Albi in 1254 issued the following decree:

And since by reason of the round capes which Jews generally wear the respect due to the clergy is seriously impaired for they (the clergy) use round capes habitually we decree with the approbation of this Council that in the future Jews shall not dare to wear round capes. They may however wear capes with long sleeves the sleeves being as long as the capes but in these sleeves there must be no folds or creases.

DISTINCTIVE MARKS FOR WOMEN

Usually the badge applied to men, women and children but a special distinction for women was a veil with two blue stripes. This requirement is found in a Papal Bull of 1257 which remained in force at Avignon until the fifteenth century, was repeated by the Council of Ravenna, 1311, and by the Council of Cologne, 1442, by which time it applied all over Germany (plate 114). The veil, known at first by its simple medieval Latin name, *oralia* or *orales*, had by 1326 become a pointed veil called *cornalia* or *cornu*, which is presumably the same pointed veil as the Jewish women of Augsburg were ordered to wear in 1434. In German, where it was called *flieder*, *sendelbinde* or *riese*, it remained the typical head-dress for Jewish matrons until the seventeenth century or perhaps later (plates 158, 169).[7] In 1360 all Jews of Rome save physicians were required to wear a red *tabard* and the women a red petticoat. By a Papal decree of 1555 Jewish women were ordered to wear a head-dress made of yellow cloth but the *chapeau noir* was frequently permitted in the Papal States if it had a piece of yellow material or ribbon attached. When Thomas Platter visited Avignon in 1596 he made a sketch of the tall funnel-shaped head-dress worn by the Jewish women.[8]

THE JEWISH HAT

The outstanding characteristic of Jewish costume in medieval times was the pointed Jewish hat or *Judenhut*. In its simplest forms it was a plain cone similar to the Persian *kalansuwa* worn by non-believers in Moslem countries from which presumably it originated and it could have been introduced to Europe either through Spain or Byzantium.[9] It was probably accompanied by another Persian garment, the *caftan*, which with its girdle also became a feature of Jewish dress.

The first illustrations of the Jewish hat are found on miniatures in the Stavelot Bible which are not later than 1097 (plate 121), but the more characteristic form is found on the bronze doors of San Zeno at Verona in Northern Italy which are twelfth century or possibly earlier. Two different styles are seen on the same panel (plate 122), which make dating difficult, but

121   N. France: Eleventh century. *Joel.* Miniature. From the *Stavelot Bible*. British Museum, Add. Ms 28106–7. The earliest illustration of the Jewish hat. Medieval tunic with cloak fastened over shoulder.

122   N. Italy: Verona, twelfth century. *Moses with the Tablets of the Law.* Panel from bronze doors of San Zeno illustrating two different types of Jewish hat.

124 Germany: Fourteenth century. *The Jewish hat.* Miniature. From the Leipzig *Machsor*. Three Jews praying. The reader enveloped in a *tallith*: the others in full length tunics, cloaks and Jewish hat.

123 Germany: Thirteenth century. '*Süsskind der Jude von Trimberg*'. Miniature. University Library, Heidelberg. Süsskind of Trimberg, a Jewish troubador, stands before the bishop wearing a Jewish hat, beard and long hair.

the hat must have been a distinctive Jewish feature well before the twelfth century by which period it had become established as a universal symbol of Jewry equivalent to the *Magen David* of modern times. It was proudly displayed on Hebrew manuscripts, unlike the Jewish badge which was a mark of degradation and was always bitterly resented. It was commonly used as a design for a Jewish seal, as seen on the thirteenth–century seal of the Augsburg Jewish community[10] and other medieval seals (plate 125). The colour of the hat was usually yellow, like its counterpart in Moslem countries, but on manuscripts a variety of colours is found including red and white.

For heraldic purposes the Jewish hat was employed for 'canting' arms, i.e. coats of arms in which the armorial bearings contain an allusion to the name of the family. Thus the arms for *Jüdden*, *Juden* or *Judei* of Westphalia are given as *De gules à trois chapeaux d'argent* and those of *Judels* of Holland as *D'argent à trois chapeaux de juif de gules les cordons de sinople* while the crest was *Un chapeau de l'écu sans cordon* (plate 131). The arms for *Joeden* include a figure wearing the Jewish ruff.[11]

125 Germany: 1329. *Seal of S. Moses.* From *Revue des Etudes Juives* IV. 279. The Jewish hat was frequently used as the design on Jewish seals in medieval times. See *Monumenta Judaica* B. 160.

So long as the Jewish hat was generally worn it was a sufficient distinction and it was when the Jews began to abandon its use that the Church introduced the badge.

Drawings of the thirteenth century from England, France and Spain indicate that the Jewish hat survived in isolated cases only and it was for this reason that the badge was introduced into these countries first.

In Germany, apart from the cities of Mainz and Erfurth, the badge came much later because the Judenhut, a sufficient distinction, remained part of the Jew's prescribed costume by law.

The Schwabenspiegel, a code of law compiled about 1275, states specifically that all Jews must wear one and in the miniatures attached to the Sachsenspiegel, another code of laws prepared a century later the Jews can still be identified by their hats.

The Jewish hat was accompanied by a beard and usually a long coat. When Süsskind von Trimberg, a troubador, became a Jew, he announced that he intended to grow a beard and wear a Jewish hat and a long coat. He is thus portrayed in a miniature from the thirteenth-century *Manesse Codex* at Heidelberg, except that his cloak with its ermine collar is similar to that worn by the seated bishop (plate 123).

126 England: 1233. *Caricature of English Jews.* Drawing. Public Record Office. Ms. dated 1233. In medieval times under the Angevin kings the Jews and all their possessions belonged to the king who made himself responsible for their protection, and the chief Jewish centres had royal castles where they could seek shelter in times of danger. One of these centres was Norwich and the caricature shows various Jews on the ramparts of the castle there. Isaac of Norwich, the wealthiest Jew of his day, who is bearded, wears the royal crown of Henry III, possibly in order to indicate that he is the king's property. It has three fleur-de-lys on it like the crown on the first Great Seal of Henry III. The figure on the left, clean-shaven and holding a pair of scales, wears a pointed hood. Mosse-Mokke, also clean-shaven, wears a spiked hat shaped like a helmet, which is possibly the Norman-French version of the Jewish hat. Abigail wears a *barbette* and *fillet*, the contemporary head-dress. Her hair, in a long plait, hangs down her back.

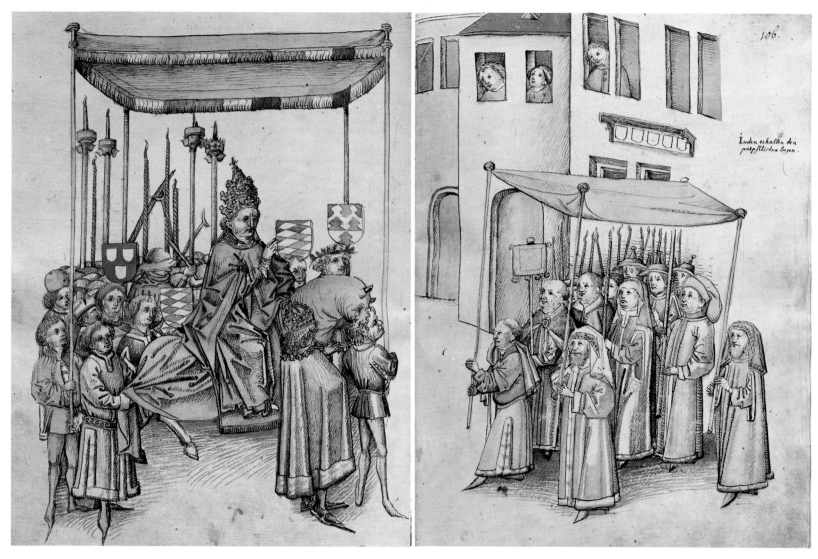

127   Germany: 1417. *Pope Martin V receives a Jewish deputation at Constance, 1417.*
Drawings. From the *Richenthal–Chronik*, Rosgarten Museum, Constance.
The most prominent Jewish figures (the rabbis?) have cloaks and chaperons;
others wear the Jewish hat.

In other countries, also, the Jewish hat was mandatory. At Gnesen in the
Kingdom of Poland, at Breslau, at Strasbourg and in Austria in 1267, the
Jews were ordered to retain the pointed hat (*pileus cornutus*).

In the fourteenth century, Alfonso IV of Portugal ordered all his Jews to
wear a yellow capuchon or hat.

In Nuremberg the Jews wore a red *Judenhut* until in the fifteenth century
the City Council decreed that those who were citizens or 'protected' should
adopt a *barrette* or flat hat while foreign Jews as a mark of distinction were
required to wear a *gugel*. Resident Jews were not permitted to wear a *kappe*
under penalty of a fine of a pound of hellers.[12]

The Jews were expelled from Nuremberg in 1490 and were not read-
mitted until the nineteenth century so that the engraving showing their
costume, although published in 1755, is presumably based on fifteenth-
century drawings (plate 158).

128 England: Thirteenth century. *A prophet*. After a fresco in the Holy Sepulchre Chapel of Winchester Cathedral. An example of the Jewish hat.

129 Germany: Fifteenth century. *The Seder*. Drawing. Hebrew Ms. *Hagadah*. Hebrew Union College, Cincinnati. The husband is bearded and wears the Jewish hat prescribed by the laws of Frankfurt a/M (see plate 130). The wife wears a contemporary bonnet called *gebende*.

JOSEPH DE BENI,

Par la grace de Dieu & du de cette Ville de Carpentras, le PAPE, &c.

S. Siége Apoſtolique, Évêque Aſſiſtant au Trône de N. S. P.

EN conformité des Articles XXXVII. & XXXVIII. de l'Edit du 5 Avril 1775, & de l'Article X. du Décret de la Sacrée Congrégation du Saint Office du 18 Juillet 1781, Nous permettons à   Juif de la Carrière de cette Ville, d'aller en voyage ſoit dans cette Province du Comté Venaiſſin, ſoit dans les différentes Villes du Royaume de France, à condition que ledit n'entreprendra point le ſuſdit voyage avec un Conducteur Chrétien un jour de Dimanche ou Fête chaumée par les Chrétiens ; qu'il ne pourra ſéjourner dans les Villes & Lieux du Diocèſe de cette Ville où il n'y a point de Juiverie leſdits jours des Dimanches & Fêtes ; & qu'en conformité de l'Art. XX. dudit Edit, s'il s'arrête plus d'un jour dans les Villes ou Villages du Comtat, il ſera tenu de porter le chapeau de couleur jaune. Les Préſentes valables pour le terme de   à compter de ce jour. DONNÉ à Carpentras au Palais Épiſcopal, ce

130 France: 1781. *Passport issued by Bishop of Carpentras, 1781*. Pursuant to Article 10 of the Decree of 18 July 1781 it grants a Jew liberty to travel provided he wears a yellow hat if he stays more than one day in any of the towns or villages of the province.

96

In Frankfurt a new form of hat was decreed in the fifteenth century (see plates 129–30).

Although the pointed Jewish hat went out of use in Europe during the Middle Ages, a hat of a specified colour remained a Jewish mark of distinction in the Papal States until the French Revolution. Clement VII on 13 June 1525 substituted a yellow hat for the badge and, although withdrawn after protests from the Jews, it was reintroduced later by Paul IV, in 1555. He ordered the Jews of the Papal States to wear a green *barrette* but allowed them to wear a black hat in towns and villages where they were accustomed to trade.[13]

In Venice the Jewish hat varied in colour from yellow to reddish brown; later it was encircled with red or striped material. In 1528 the Council of Ten granted permission to Jacob Mantino, the physician, to wear the *barrette noire*, only after the French and English ambassadors, the papal legate and other patients had pleaded for him.[14]

In Avignon and the Comtat Venaissin the law requiring Jews to wear a yellow hat (plate 132) and their women a yellow sign was confirmed as late as 1776 and it was not rescinded until 1791 when the Comtat was ceded to France. However, certain Jews refused to abandon the yellow hat until the Mayor of Carpentras, on 25 January 1791, published an order in accordance with 'the principles of the exalted French constitution' forbidding it to be worn under penalty of twelve livres (see Appendix 2).

In Germany also it seems that the pointed hat became so much part of Jewish tradition that it was retained for use in the home for Sabbaths and festivals long after it had ceased to be obligatory. Evidence of this is found in a German Machsor of 1717 (plate 167) and on a silver Hanukah lamp of 1720 from Altona in the Jewish Museum, London.

131 Germany: Fifteenth to sixteenth centuries. *The Jewish hat in German Heraldry*. From Sibmacher. Coat of arms of the German family of Jude. An example of 'canting' arms. Names like this probably originated as nicknames and are not necessarily evidence of Jewish ancestry.

132 Germany: Fifteenth century. *Jewish hat*. Engraving. From Schudt. Form of hat prescribed by the laws of Frankfurt a/M.

The Shulhan Aruch. The general principles with regard to Jewish dress are laid down in the *Shulhan Aruch.*[15] In compliance with Leviticus 18 : 3, 20 : 3 and Deuteronomy 12 : 30 one is forbidden to follow the customs of the gentiles or to be like them in the way they dress or cut their hair. The dress of a Jew should reflect modesty and humility and he should avoid wearing expensive clothes; he must observe the laws regarding *tsitsith* and *shaatnez*. In accordance with Leviticus 19 : 27 he is forbidden to shave the hair at the side of the ears or the corners of his beard with a razor and the sidelocks (*peoth*) should be allowed to grow below the ears to a point where the cheeks widen. He may not dye his hair and decency requires him to wear a girdle. Women must be modest in their dress and married women must always have their hair covered. Fine clothes should be worn on the Sabbath and even better ones for festivals.

Behind these principles is a long history of sumptuary laws and dress regulations of different Jewish communities to which their members were expected to conform.

JEWISH SUMPTUARY LAWS AND DRESS REGULATIONS

Jewish restrictions on dress in times of trouble go back at least to the time of the Mishnah. According to Sotah ix : 9. 'During the war of Vespasian the use of crowns by bridegrooms and the beating of the drums (at weddings) was forbidden. During the war of Titus the crowns of brides etc. were forbidden'. But the later dress regulations were designed mainly in order to resist Christian fashions and to avoid creating envy by extravagance and ostentation.[16]

There are frequent reminders of the Jewish attitude towards dress in the regulations and sumptuary laws issued by various communities. The *Takanoth* (laws) of the communities of Speyer, Worms and Mayence in Germany passed at rabbinical synods held during the thirteenth century contained the following provisions: 'No one shall cut his hair in non-Jewish fashion or shave his beard either with a razor or such a manner as approximates the effect of a razor nor shall one wear long hair'.

'No child of the Covenant shall dress after the manner of Gentiles nor wear sleeves'.

'No one shall go to the synagogue otherwise than with a cloak or topcoat but one should not wear a *suckenis*'[17] (*sargenes*).

A rabbinical synod held at Frankfurt-am-Main in 1603 having noted 'that many Jews wear clothing made after the manner of gentiles and that many dress themselves and their daughters in costly clothes' decreed that such practices should cease.

Probably most Jewish communities had their dress regulations. Extracts from the laws of Forli in Italy (1416); Valladolid in Spain (1432); Fürth; Metz (1690–4); Frankfurt-am-Main (1715); Hamburg (1715 and 1731) and Carpentras (1738) are given in the Appendix.

In Italy the restrictions became much more severe after the sixteenth century.[18] Most of them were aimed at women. All jewellery was severely restricted while *godrons* (a type of ruff) and the extravagant coiffures of the late seventeenth century (*en cheveux* and *fontanges*) were banned. At Metz veils of gold or silver were allowed on special occasions only and for some time *sivlonoth* belts were prohibited. Men's wigs were restricted to the size of clerical wigs. In Frankfurt women were obliged to wear hooded cloaks for synagogue[19] and their shoes had to be black or white while men were not allowed coloured or white wigs. At Carpentras wigs with ribbons and curls and bagwigs (*perrukes à bourse*) were prohibited. In Hamburg women were not allowed crinolines. At Mantua at the end of the seventeenth century women were forbidden to use gold or silver embroidery and they were allowed very little jewellery. Outdoors they had to wear a long cloak with a hood covering the whole head. Only brides were allowed to wear gold and silver headbands with flowers. Men were not allowed to wear *sarbals* or other outer garments made of bright materials and bagwigs were forbidden. At Rome in 1726 men were forbidden to spend more than three escudos on their wigs.[20]

From the laws of Ancona in 1766 we learn that it was normal for men to wear the *arba kanfoth* in the street, this practice being forbidden in future except for bridegrooms on their wedding day. By the same laws hats with brims were prohibited for men but they were allowed to have a gold or lace border of a finger's width with a little tassel on their *berretta* while bridegrooms were permitted to have it embroidered with silver or gold.[21]

At Modena in addition to the usual restrictions women were forbidden to wear trains to their dresses and they were not permitted to go into the town without a *cendale* (head-dress) nor were they allowed to carry clocks, repeater watches or jewel cases uncovered. Men were forbidden to wear plumes, cockades or other ornaments in their hats.[22]

The Dress Regulations for Fürth are printed in a historical treatise on the Jews of Fürth and Nuremberg by A. Wurfel published in 1755 (see p. 194). They are of particular interest because they are accompanied by the writer's comments. Garments forbidden for men included synagogue cloaks made of damask, silk cloaks, velvet jackets, embroidered stockings or *bonnets,* silver clasps or buckles. We learn that men usually had a special *tallith* for the Sabbath and a finer one for festivals and that the band was sometimes covered in gold and pearls. Wigs were permitted for synagogue provided they were not powdered. Large collars were a sign of distinction. When there was doubt about the propriety of a garment a picture of it was sent to Poland for a rabbinical opinion.

An ancient tradition still observed among Hasidic Jews is to drape or button the right side of a coat over the left. This is based on the theory that good springs from the right and evil from the left (sinister) side.

THE SARGENES OR KITTEL

The Jewish hat was not the only article of clothing which entered into Jewish tradition. The *sargenes* or *kittel*[23] which dates from Talmudic times is a shroud consisting of a white linen over-garment reaching the feet with voluminous sleeves, a collar laced in front, a girdle of the same material and a cap to match. It was worn on New Year (plate 184) and the Day of Atonement, by a bridegroom at his wedding and by the head of the house for the Seder meal during the feast of Passover (plate 166). Passover was originally a New Year festival and the wearing of a special costume for New Year was a common practice in ancient times. At the Greek spring festival of Anthesteria shrouds were worn in order to disguise the individual and feign death while the divine powers were fixing his fate during the coming year.[24]

A special belt was worn over the *sargenes* on the Day of Atonement (plate 135).

SIVLONOTH AND MARRIAGE CUSTOMS

Gifts between bride and bridegroom known as *sivlonoth* (*sablonoth*) go back to Talmudic times. An account of a fifteenth century wedding in the Rhineland describes how on the eve of the wedding the bride and bridegroom exchanged gifts through the rabbi. The bride received a gold-studded belt, a veil, a *kürse*[25] (plate 165) and a garland: the bridegroom, a sash, a ring and a pair of shoes. The bride's mother gave her a silver belt. On the wedding day the bridegroom appeared in his Sabbath clothes but he also wore the German *gugel, kappe* or *matran* (*chaperon*) and ashes on his head in mourning for Zion. The bride wore the *kürse* given to her by the bridegroom and a *turmkrone* (tower crown) consisting of a golden headband set with little towers but she was enveloped in a *sargenes*. During the ceremony the bridegroom wore a *tallith* which the rabbi also wrapped round the bride.

The *sivlonoth* marriage belts, which remained a feature of Jewish women's

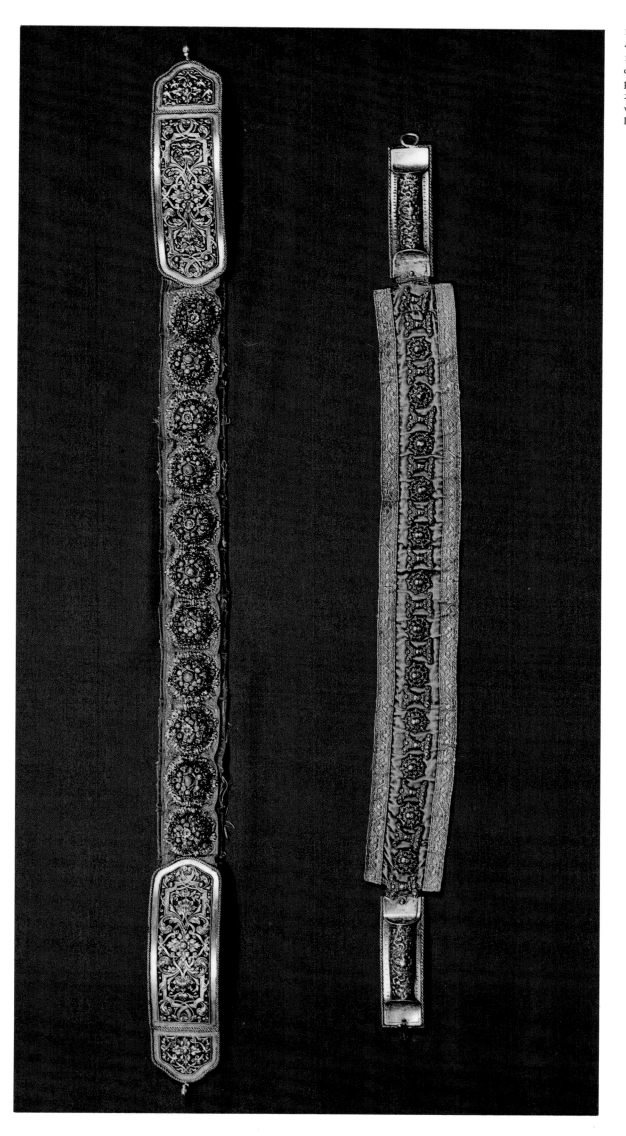

133 Germany: Seventeenth century.
Sivlonoth (marriage) belts.
1. Silver gilt; brocade on velvet and
eleven rosettes of silver set with
precious stones. Seventeenth century.
2. Silver; two strips of silver brocade;
violet velvet. Dated 1693.
Israel Museum.

134 Italy & Germany: Seventeenth century. *Jewish marriage rings.*
1. Gold filigree with blue and white enamel. Italian early seventeenth century.
2. Gold. South German late seventeenth century.
3. Gold. Italian early seventeenth century.
4. Gold. Italian early seventeenth century. Jewish Museum, London.

dress until modern times, were a survival from the medieval marriage belts originally worn in many parts of Europe. According to Buxtorf the bride sent the bridegroom one of silver and received from him one of gold. None of the gold ones seem to have survived but examples of silver belts are to be found in Jewish museums (plate 133). They are usually of massive weight with clasps like the one in the Oppenheim painting (plate 179); those seen in earlier pictures appear to be of thin chain hanging loosely from either hip (plate 170). Buxtorf (1661 edition) gives this account of the preparation for the ceremony:

When the day comes on which the wedding is to be solemnised, the bridegroom dons the clothes that he keeps for Sabbath wear; the bride puts on her wedding dress and in the manner in which Jews do things, is decked out as magnificently as possible. She is led by matrons of honour and bridesmaids, her head being unveiled and her hair loose, into a special room, where wedding songs are sung to her; they place her on a fair seat, comb her hair and arrange her tresses in curls and ringlets, then set thereon a magnificent fillet and spread a veil over her eyes—this for reasons of demureness and modesty, that she should not look at her bridegroom: following the example of Rebecca when her groom came to meet her. The women take a quite extraordinary delight in this ceremony of arranging the hair, evincing it in attractive songs, dancing and games of all kinds, designed to make the bride happy. That is why they have it in some spacious place and judge it to be something peculiarly gratifying to God. . .

In the 1728 edition Buxtorf continues:

At Venice the bride wears a sort of curls or favourites, which they call benetes, in imitation of those with which God himself, according to the rabbis, adorned Eve's head when he married her to Adam. The bride thus dressed and veiled is seated under a canopy supported by four young lads, or otherwise by four pillars. The nuptial throne is for the most part in some garden or open court and there the nuptial benediction is to be pronounced. The bridegroom is conducted thither by his friends and the bride too by her train.

The bride stood on the bridegroom's right. The wedding ring had to be of pure gold without stones and was placed on the first or index finger of the bride's right hand.[26] The ornate Jewish wedding rings, often in the shape of a house, are believed to have belonged to the community but there is no contemporary reference to their use nor, surprisingly, are they shown on any wedding pictures. Examples are to be seen in museums (plate 134).

Authorities: I. Abrahams; J. Aronius; K. von Amira; J. Bauer; A. Berliner; A. Boeckler; J. Charles-Roux; J. Buxtorf; C. W. & P. C. Cunnington; M. Davenport; *Encyc. Judaica*; J. Evans; L. Finkelstein; A. C. Fox-Davies; H. Gold; H. Graetz; S. Grayzel; M. Grunwald; D. de Haedo; J. N. Hahn; W. N. Hargreaves-Mawdsley; P. Hughes; *Jewish Encycl.*; *Jüdisches Lexikon*; B. Kisch; G. Kisch; S. Krauss; M. Letts; E. H. Lindo; J. G. Lovillo; J. R. Marcus; *Monumenta Judaica*; Müller & Schlosser; H. Norris; H. G. Richardson; U. Robert; E. v. Rünsberg; J. Sibmacher; R. Straus; E. W. Tristam; *Universal Jewish Encycl.* See Bibliography.

135   Germany: Eighteenth century. *Yom Kippur belt.* Brocade with silver clasp. Jewish Museum, London. Belt worn in synagogue on the Day of Atonement. The design follows a conventional form.

4 Poland and Russia

136 Poland: Fifteenth century.
Jewish Prosecutor. Painting.
St. Catherine's Church, Cracow.
From Schipper. He wears the
pointed Jewish hat.

An ecumenical council held at Breslau in 1266 decreed that the Jews living in the bishopric of Gnesen in Poland should wear a special hat, and the Council of Ofen in 1279 required the Jews to wear a red badge.

It was probably when the Jews began to abandon their medieval dress in favour of the Polish *caftan* and fur hat that the Piotrkov Diet of 1538 passed the following decree:

Whereas the Jews disregarding the ancient regulations have thrown off the marks by which they were distinguishable from the Christians and have arrogated to themselves a form of dress which closely resembles that of the Christians, so that it is impossible to recognise them, be it resolved for permanent observation that the Jews of our realm, all and sundry, in whatever place they happen to be found, shall wear special marks, to wit, a *barrette* or hat or some other headgear of yellow cloth. Exception is to be made in favour of travellers, who, while on the road, shall be permitted to discard or conceal marks of this kind.[1]

By paragraph twelve of the Lithuanian Statute of 1566 it was provided that 'the Jews shall not wear costly clothes nor gold chains nor shall their wives wear gold or silver ornaments. The Jews shall not have silver mountings on their sabres or daggers. They shall be distinguished by characteristic clothes; they shall wear yellow hats and their wives kerchiefs of yellow linen in order that all may distinguish Jews from Christians'.[2]

Thus is seems that the wearing of swords by Jews was accepted. The requirement that they should dress differently was reinforced by a rabbinical edict issued in 1607 prohibiting the adoption of Christian dress, and the Lithuanian Jewish Council between 1623 and 1762 also issued various sumptuary laws affecting dress.

Caftans with fur-trimmed hats were the basic features of Polish and Russian national dress in medieval times and were still being worn in 1576.[3] As the trend towards Western dress developed among the Polish upper classes, their original dress was gradually taken over by the Jews, and by the eighteenth century it had become their characteristic costume.

The features of this dress varied in different parts of Poland and included a skull-cap (*yarmulka, keppelche* or *kappel*); a cap with ear flaps (*lappenmütze* or *klapove hitl*); a high fur hat trimmed with plush called *spodic* (Polish＝

saucer) or one made of sable (*kolpak*). The *mosalka* was a silk skull-cap worn especially by Hasidim and a fur cap called *duchowny* was reserved for scholars. In Galicia the characteristic hat for the Sabbath was the *streimel* (Polish *stroj*= costume), a saucer shaped hat with a flat fur brim which in the case of rabbis was made from thirteen sables' tails. Gaily decorated yarmulkas were worn in the synagogue (plates 141, 144 and 151).[4]

From the eighteenth century onwards attempts were made by the authorities to persuade Polish and Russian Jews to abandon their Jewish costume and in 1804 Jewish council members in the provinces of Astrakan, the Caucasus, Little Russia and New Russia were required to wear either Polish, Russian or German dress. Nevertheless, in 1840 a Russian Council of State found that their dress was still one of the causes which prevented Jews from becoming assimilated and an imperial *ukase* issued 1 May 1850 prohibited *peoth* (side locks) and distinctive Jewish dress in any part of the empire, although aged Jews could wear out their old clothes on payment of a tax.[5]

In April 1851 a further order was made forbidding Jewish women to shave their heads on marriage. When Alexander II visited Poland in 1870 and saw Hasidic Jews still wearing *peoth* he gave instructions that the law should be rigorously enforced.

The following description of the dress of Polish Jews is given by Hollaenderski (1846):

a long coat or frock coat in black cloth edged in front with velvet and fastened from the neck to the waist; a wide belt, socks, shoes or slippers; a skull cap; a hat with a wide brim most of which is shaped like a sugar loaf or cut-off cone with a deep edge of sable or other fur. Finally a great coat as long as the under-coat. All this normally in black and in light material like silk. Rarely does a Jew, even if rich, possess more than two outfits, one for working day the other for Sabbath so that the colour gradually becomes unrecognisable and the whole costume gradually turns to rags. Eventually it is patched in many colours. The hair is normally shaved and hidden under the skull cap but there is a long side curl on each side; the beard is unkempt and reaches to the chest. The women dress like the Polish women. Their head is shaved and covered with a kerchief knotted in various ways. The rich ones wear little crowns decorated with pearls and diamonds and long earrings.[6]

Although the Hasidim retained their traditional dress the efforts of the Russian government began to take effect after the middle of the nineteenth century and Western dress was gradually adopted by most Jews with a peaked cap as its distinctive feature for men (see plate 154).

The Jewish women dressed like the Polish women but their wardrobe included certain distinctive types of head-dress: a crown of diamonds and pearls (see plate 152) or a lace cap adorned with flowers and birds (*kupkeh* or *binde*), and there were various types of forehead-band (*stirnbindel* or

137 Poland: Galicia, *c.* 1800. '*Des Juifs polonois avec un voiturier de Vienne*'. Aquatint. Rubens (ii) 1736. One Jew with prominent *peoth* wears a streimel, a fine embroidered caftan and high boots; the other has a large felt hat, a plain black *caftan*, white stockings and shoes.

138–39 Poland: 1812. *Polish Jews and French soldiers.* Lithographs. From *Blaetter aus meinem Portefeuille im Laufe des Feldzugs 1812 in Russland . . .* von C. W. Faber du Faur, Stuttgart 1831. The everyday dress of the Polish Jews; large felt hats worn over yarmulkas and prominent *peoth*.

sternstichl) some like diadems of pearls, others made of bands of satin, silk or velvet with tinsel or pearl embroidery and fastened by two ribbons. Another distinctly Jewish item of dress was the *brüsttüch* or plastron which also lent itself to elaborate and expensive decoration[7]. A favourite pose for Jewish women was with one or both hands concealed by the *brüsttüch* (plates 143, 147).

In Lithuania the feature of Jewish women's costume was the head-dress which consisted of a black velvet band studded with pearls and brilliants worn above the forehead and a smoothly fitting hood called *kupkeh* covering the back of the head. In the centre of this was fixed a bow of tulle and flowers. A lace frill with little earrings of brilliants was worn across the forehead. They also wore a special type of cloak usually made of satin with strips of gold embroidery called *güldenstick*.

The picture of Lithuanian Jewesses (plate 140) is accompanied by the following unflattering description of the Jewish women of Orcha, a town on the west bank of the river Dnieper:

(they) are clad in a most ridiculous and gaudy dress of silken rags; on their head is a large white napkin rolled round with three tails hanging over their shoulder; and under this head dress a kind of flapping cover of pearls with dangling steel ornaments hangs over the ear and forehead. The body is covered with   loose silk vest and a large petticoat of the same; the arms are hid in long loose shirt-sleeves terminated with a deep worked frill. The shoes are made without leather at the heels and everyone appears slipshod. Over their dress they wear a large silk gown (and in some instances even two) the sleeves of which hang down the back; a fur cloak is suspended from the neck . . . they take particular pride in their head-dress of pearls; the more valuable denotes the distinction of wealth.

The same writer has this to say of the men: 'The Lithuanian Jews are all dressed alike in long tunics of black silk with a broad silken sash round the waist; on the head they wear a small velvet cap and over it a huge one of fur'.[8]

Another traveller who stayed at a Jewish inn was struck by the curious cap decorated with pearls worn by the landlord's wife and learned that it was the mark of a married woman and was given as the bridal present by the husband.[9]

The Karaites of the Crimea were a Jewish sect with their own traditions and customs. They had their own village, Djufut-Kale, known as the fortress of the Jews because of its impregnable position, and they dressed like the

140   Poland: Lithuania 1815. 'Lithuanian Jewess'. Engraving. From R. Johnson, *Travels through Part of the Russian Empire*, 1815. Rubens (ii) 1651. The feature of the dress is the head scarf terminating in three tails.

141   Poland: 1817. 'Enfans Juifs'. From Norblin. Rubens (ii) 1740. The girl has her hair uncovered. Both boys wear *caftans* with girdles and both have their heads covered, the one on the left with a *yarmulka*, the other with a *streimel*.

other inhabitants of the region. All travellers who visited them are unanimous in praising their kindness, their civilised way of life and their high moral standards. An Englishman, who visited parts of Russia on behalf of the Bible Society, saw them in 1821 and attended the synagogue during Pentecost. He describes the Karaite *tallith* as consisting of two long belts of woollen material joined behind by a square piece of the same material ornamented in various ways and with *tsitsith* attached to its corners (see plate 14). The rabbi was dressed in a long robe of black silk over which a large white *tallith* was thrown covering his head. The ordinary people wore long blue top coats lined with lambskin and large lambskin caps.[10]

A Russian traveller, Prince Demidov, who visited the Karaite Jews of the Crimea in 1837, was impressed by the scrupulous care with which they dressed and their general air of distinction. A costume plate published by de Pauly some twenty years later conveys the same impression (plate 153).

A man and woman from the small Jewish community of Epifan in Central Russia are seen in regional dress (plates 155–6).

142   Poland: 1817. *'Juif revenant de la synagogue'*. Engraving. From Norblin. Rubens (ii) 1739. He wears a fur trimmed hat (*spodic*), coat with girdle, Sabbath cloak without sleeves, white stockings and buckled shoes.

143   Poland: 1817. *'Femme Juive'*. Engraving. From Norblin. She wears a scarf over a head-covering trimmed with lace, the typically Jewish plastron, the *brüsttüch*, and somewhat elegant shoes.

144   Poland: 1817. *'Polish Jew in his summer dress'*. Drawing. He wears a yellow *yarmulka* with red embroidery, white tunic with girdle, blue breeches, yellow stockings and mules.

145　Poland: Warsaw, 1846. *'Le Juif de Varsovie et sa Femme'*.
Engraving. Rubens (ii) 1751. He wears a tall fur-trimmed
hat, black *caftan* with a girdle, white stockings and shoes.
His wife has a crown of pearls.

146　Poland: Lithuania, 1846. *'Le Juif Lithuanien avec sa
femme et sa fille'*. Engraving. Rubens (ii) 1753. He wears a
fur-trimmed hat *(spodic)*, a black *caftan* with girdle, white
stockings and slippers. The daughter is allowed to show
her hair but the wife's head is completely covered.

147　Poland: 1846. *'Le chasside et sa femme'*. Engraving.
Rubens (ii) 1754. He wears a tall fur hat, white smock with
tsitsith on its corners, girdle, white stockings, black *caftan*.
His wife wears the typical Jewish plastron, the *brüsttüch*,
and an unusual head-dress.

148 Russia: 1843. *'Famille Juive dans son interieur'*. Lithograph. From *Scènes Populaires Russes*, 1843–4. The man holding the goat which is being milked is in a dark blue caftan and a *spodic*. The women wear a kind of turban. The boy on the right has long *peoth* and wears an *arba kanphoth*.

149 Russia: The Ukraine, *c.* 1845. *'Enfans Juifs'*. Lithograph. From *Costumes de la Petite Russie*. The boy has *peoth* and wears a black *caftan* and a fur-trimmed hat.

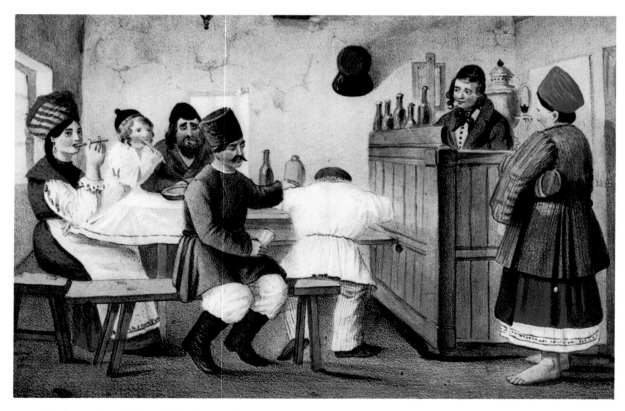

150 Russia: *c.* 1840. *'Cabaret Juif'*. Lithograph. Examples of Jewish and Russian costume. The Jewish innkeeper wears a *yarmulka* with Western dress.

151 Poland: 1878. *Day of Atonement in the Synagogue*. Painting by Maurycy Gottlieb (1856–79). Tel-Aviv Museum (Gift of Sidney Lamon, N.Y.). A self portrait of the artist in the foreground in *tallith* and *streimel* leaning on his right arm. Most of the women wear the characteristic head-dress the *sternstichl*.

152 Poland: *c.* 1878. *A Jewess*. Painting by Maurycy Gottlieb (1856–79).
Israel Museum. She wears the characteristic head-dress, the *sternstichl*.

153 Russia: Crimea, 1862. 'Karaimes'. Chromolithograph. From
T. de Pauly, *Description Ethnographique des Peuples de la Russie*,
St Petersburg, 1862. The Karaite Jews in this costume plate have
been sketched from life. There is an air of distinction about them
enhanced by the quality of their dress which to de Pauly displays
strong Turkish influence. The seated figure is Abraham Firkovich
(1786–1874), the Karaite leader.

154 Russia: 1862. '*Juifs* (*Talmudistes*)'. Chromolithograph. From
T. de Pauly, *Description Ethnographique des Peuples de la Russie*,
St Petersburg, 1862. This costume plate emphasises the difference
between the Talmudists and the Karaite Jews seen in No. 153. It
is also taken from life and shows the effect of Russian legislation
of the 1840's and 1850's. The older man now wears a frock coat
instead of a *caftan* but he still has a girdle and his coat buttons
right over left. The young man wears the peaked cap which was
to become a distinctive feature. The woman's cap completely
covers her hair.

155–56 Russia: Epifan, *c.* 1850. '*Juif D'Epiphan. Juive D'Epiphan*'. Engravings.
Rubens (ii) 1771–2. The man in turban and regional dress. The woman with
her child on her back wears her hair uncovered.

5 The Western world–The effects of emancipation and assimilation

The main features of Jewish costume in Western Europe in modern times are its continued conservatism in countries like Germany, Austria and Hungary contrasted with the rapid disappearance of any distinctive characteristics among the emancipated Jews of England, France and Holland.

The Venetian rabbi, Leon of Modena (1571–1648), in his *Historia dei Riti Ebraici* written for James I of England emphasises the conservatism of Jewish dress. He writes:

> They do not willingly imitate any other nation in the fashion of their apparell unless their own make them there seem very deformed. Neither may they shave their crown, nor wear locks of hair upon their head, nor any the like things. And in what country soever they are, they generally affect the long garment or gown. The women also apparell themselves in the habit of the countries where they inhabit. But when they are married, upon their wedding day they cover their own hair, wearing either a perruke, or dressing, or some other hair or something else that may counterfeit natural hair according to the custome of the women of that place, but they are never to appear in their own hair more. . . . They hold it also an unbeseeming thing for a man to make himself ready without putting on a girdle; or something that may divide the lower part of the body from the upper.[1]

A Dutch writer gives this description of Jewish dress at the beginning of the eighteenth century:

> As the men must not dress themselves like women, so the women are not allowed to disguise themselves in men's apparel. A Jew must avoid every thing that may make him appear effeminate; jewels, pomatums, paint, patches, Spanish white & c., must be banished from the toilet of the modest Jew, and left to the fops and the ladies; together with the glass, and all the childish and affected airs which are the consequences of consulting it. The faithful Jew must learn to be upon his guard, to shew a great soul and with patience suffer the fine black locks he had at twenty-five to turn grey at forty-five. He must despise the use of nippers, or of any such compositions as help to discolour the beard, smooth the wrinkles or fill up the holes in his face, or to fasten in false teeth. This is the duty incumbent on a devout Jew; but we will not say, that all of them inviolably observe it. As there are laws and rules relating to the beard, it must not wholly be omitted. The German Jews wear their beards from the extremity of one jaw to the other, like a cord, which is divided by a tuft into two equal parts, which falls very agreeably from the chin upon the breast.[2]

Germany, Austria, Hungary and Switzerland shared very much the same customs as regards Jewish dress. During the seventeenth century the Jewish cloak, the *sarbal*, remained the distinctive outer garment and Joseph Nördlingen Hahn (died 1637), in his *Sefer Yosef Ometz*, exhorts Jews to wear one when saying their prayers at home, instead of the short house-jacket. The Sabbath *sarbal* (*schülmantel*) was a cloak without an opening on the right-hand side to remind the wearer not to carry anything on the Sabbath day; Hahn recalls that in his youth, when times were better, most people had a *sarbal* exclusively for synagogue use and the wealthy gave one to their sons when they got married. He attacked the modern practice of wearing a *sarbal* with a vent at the back decorated with multi-coloured silk, which made it an ornamental garment instead of a practical one.

Hahn also deplored the disappearance of the *matran*, formerly worn especially at Frankfurt-am-Main and Worms. This was the *chaperon*, the most characteristic feature of Jewish dress in medieval times, the great virtue of which, according to Hahn, was that it served to cover the head and eyes so that a person was completely enveloped during prayer, a practice which went back to Talmudic times (plate 114).[3]

The *chaperon* had been replaced by the *barrette* (*beret*), a round hat made of felt or wool, which was originally a symbol of learning popular all over Europe during the fifteenth and sixteenth centuries. For a long time it was the normal daily head-dress of the Jew but gradually became reserved for synagogue use, hence the name, *schabbes deckel*, by which it was known to Jew and Christian alike. In its early form it had a loose floppy crown without

157 Germany: 1530. *Ceremony of Tashlik*. Woodcut. Rubens (ii) 1046. Men wearing *chaperons* with *liripipes*; the women wearing *chaperons* except for one whose head-dress is a *gebende*.

158 Germany: Nuremberg, fifteenth century. *Jewish costumes*. Engraving.
From A. Wurfel, *Historiche Nachrichten*, Nuremberg, 1755. From left to right:
1. The head of the congregation wears the medieval hood (*kappe*) and a deep
fringed collar. 2. Dress for synagogue. 3. Women's dress for synagogue
includes the *viereckiger schleier* (square veil). 4. Synagogue dress. The head-dress
seems to be the medieval *liripipe*. 5. Women's indoor dress. 6. Carrying the
Sabbath wine (see p. 95).

159 Germany: Eighteenth century.
Barrette. Bayerisches Nationalmuseum,
Munich. Round black felt hat worn
by German Jews during the eighteenth
century. *Monumenta Judaica* E 490.

any stiffening and the one example which has survived is a late version which was still being worn during the nineteenth century (plate 159).

An even more distinctive piece of costume for women as well as for men was the sixteenth-century ruff, the *Jüdenkragen,* which survived as a Jewish distinction either in its original form or as a pleated collar until well into the nineteenth century (plates 158, 160-2, 164). Another survival from medieval times was the *viereckiger schleier* (square veil) worn by Jewish women which was reserved for synagogue use and for the Sabbath. It was a cap with two stiffly starched pointed wings in front made of white linen. It closely covered the head and the bun of hair at the back and had two blue stripes as a Jewish distinction (see plates 114, 158). The normal everyday head-dress for German women in the seventeenth century was a bonnet with cone-shaped ears (plate 162).

For weddings the mothers of the bride and bridegroom wore the medieval *fret,* a head-dress made of gold or silver trellis-work (plate 170).

Maximilian Misson, who passed through Frankfurt in November 1687, remarked on the large number of Jews and was struck by their pointed beards and black coats with pleated ruffs.

Skippon, who also visited the Frankfurt ghetto towards the end of the seventeenth century, writes: 'Most of the men wear ruffs and the women are habited with a black mantle; their head-dress is of linen, which sticks out much on either side; several of the women also wear ruffs. All the Jews wear a little yellow mark upon the clothes for distinction.'[4]

Edmund Chishull, who travelled through Austria in 1698, visited one of the eight synagogues at Prague and found the Jews wearing a blue ruff as a mark of distinction.

160 Germany: Frankfurt a/M 1614. *Plunder of the Ghetto*. Engraving. Rubens
(ii) 1581. The Jews wear the Jewish *barrette*, the Jewish ruff and the Badge.
Their women wear the ruff, the Badge and bonnets with ears.

The Jewish Badge was no longer being worn at Frankfurt-am-Main in
1714 according to Schudt, who observes that the Jews everywhere were
discarding their distinctive clothing although this was not a sign of their
approaching conversion but more of their growing pride and insolence.
He says:

Now the Jews wear black coats, black hats and dark-coloured clothes with a turnover of linen
round the neck. The older and nobler ones often wear a round white pleated collar. . . . On the
Sabbath the married men wear this collar with a flat round beret of black cloth which has no iron
ring inside and hangs down from his head. Our people call it Schabbes Deckel. . . . The older men
go fully adorned to the synagogue wearing silk jackets and coats of costly material; some even
have fine wigs. They also wear slippers so as not to appear to be hurrying away from a holy place
but to be dressed for peace and quiet as if they were at home. . . . In Frankfurt the women wore up
to the last fire in 1711 pointed stiff veils with a blue stripe. These have now fallen into disuse like
the yellow rings of the men. When I visited three women's Schuls on the eve of Schabbes in

118

October 1713 I found among several hundred Jewish women only one wearing such a veil. All the others wore bonnets with a wide lace border. When I enquired the reason I was told that all the veils were burned in the great fire. . . . Round the neck they had large round collars like the men's but theirs were starched stiffly. Over their clothes they wore wide black cloaks. Widows cover their heads with a piece of white linen which hangs down the back. . . . The women are gradually discarding the coats and collars and wear instead large, often precious lace kerchiefs. Many wear gold tinsel, gold lace or other precious ornaments on their heads especially unmarried women. Usually they have a silver belt round their waist. On Schabbes and feast days one sees with surprise what precious materials silks and laces are worn by the women folk.[5]

The Sephardim of Hamburg, like their brethren in Amsterdam and London, wore wigs and the latest fashions in dress, much to the indignation of Schudt who notes that the unmarried women there wore such precious and fashionable clothes that they could not be distinguished from Christians. In plate 163 they are seen wearing *fontanges*. During the eighteenth century the Hamburg Senate forbade Jews to appear on the Bourse with walking sticks, swords and pistols 'thereby causing disturbances and envy'.

161 Germany: *c.* 1700. '*Die Jüdin nach der synagog gehend*'. Engraving. Rubens (ii) 1599. She is very simply dressed. The feature of her costume is the large ruff, while the cloak was obligatory for synagogue wear. Her bonnet completely cover her hair indicating that she is married.

162 Germany: Frankfurt a/M 1703. '*Franckfurther Jud und Jüdin*'. Engraving. Rubens (ii) 1584. For everyday use the man wears a broad-brimmed hat, knee-length coat and gown. His lace collar has become typically Jewish as has the woman's ruff and her bonnet with its curious ears.

163   Germany: Hamburg, 1690. *Ketubah*. Drawing. In possession of Mrs
Gomperts Teixeira de Mattos. Wedding of Samuel, son of Isaac Senior
Teixeira, and Rachel, daughter of Abraham Senior de Mattos, on 17 June
1690. The Sephardim of Hamburg, like those of Amsterdam and London,
wore contemporary dress; the men have full-bottomed wigs and the women
wear *fontanges*.

Ulrichs, a sympathetic and reliable observer, who in 1768 published a history of Swiss Jewry, could find little in the city archives at Zurich on the subject of Jewish dress apart from an order issued by Bishop Hugo in 1497 requiring Swiss Jews to wear a yellow badge and women to have two blue stripes on their veils (plate 114). Ulrichs writes:

Nowadays the Jews in Germany wear black cloaks, black hats and clothes commonly of dark colours. I do not remember ever to have seen a Jew in scarlet, green or sky blue or similar colours but I saw many dressed in black damask. The women however display much finery. They wear precious rings and beautiful dresses embroidered with gold and silver. The rabbis and Parnassim, the teachers and heads of the Jewish community, also the older and highly esteemed persons wear a round white linen collar with many pleats.[6]

The tendency noted by Schudt for Jews to drop their distinctive costume becomes increasingly noticeable in Germany and Austria as the eighteenth century progresses (plates 166–178). Physicians and Court Jews wore wigs and contemporary dress as did men of letters and the old dress regulations were no longer enforced.

There are no obvious characteristics about the dress of the Prague Jewish family seen in a sixteenth-century engraving (plate 181). For special occasions the Jews of Prague had a remarkable variety of costumes (plate 185) but it was not until 1781 that the Emperor Joseph II abolished all distinctions in Bohemia including the yellow cuffs of the Jews of Prague and the yellow stripes worn by unmarried Jewish women.

Closer social contacts between Jews and Christians also had their effect and Fanny von Arnstein (plate 190) was criticised by Rabbi Moses Schreiber for wearing her hair in curls. His chief objection probably was that her hair was uncovered, although she had been forestalled in this respect by Blumchen Friedlander (plate 173) at Berlin.

164 Germany: Fürth, 1705. *Costume of Jews and their wives*. Engraving. From Boener. The women in their distinctive Jewish ruffs with sleeves to match and cloaks. They seem to be wearing *frets* as head-dress. The man in the centre wears a ruff but the one on the right (the rabbi?) is in a plain collar, a Jewish *barrette*, a tunic buttoned down the front and a sleeveless cloak.

165 Germany: Fürth 1705. *Jewish bride*. Engraving. From Boener. The bride
wears a short jacket (probably the *kürse* presented by the bridegroom) and a
marriage belt. The other women are in their synagogue cloaks and have
enormous Jewish ruffs.

The traditional Jewish costume of the seventeenth and eighteenth
centuries was retained in Germany for the Sabbath and is seen in a striking
picture of the late eighteenth century (plate 177). This costume gradually
fell into disuse and a new tradition—a three-cornered hat, knee breeches and
buckled shoes—is seen in the Oppenheim pictures of the 1860's showing
Jewish life in Frankfurt-am-Main (plate 179). A somewhat similar costume
but with the customary Jewish barrette is found at Sulzbach in 1826 (plate
176), which again follows very closely the description of the communal
dress of the Jews of Mattersdorf in Hungary at the middle of the nineteenth
century. This, we are told, comprised shoes with silver buckles, white or
black silk socks, velvet knee breeches with silver buckles, a coloured waistcoat and a tail coat both with silver buttons, a Maria-Stuart collar called
krais and a green cloak fastened in front by a silver clasp called *schülmantel*.
This last was also worn in the house for prayers and seems to have been a
survival of the *sarbal*. A skull cap was worn under a barrette without which
no one could be called to the Law. The rabbi of Mattersdorf wore a *streimel*
on the Sabbath and a boat-shaped hat on other days. Learned men wore a
long coat trimmed with fur called a *power* but were clean-shaven, and the
custom of wearing a full beard came later after Simon Schreiber became
rabbi at Mattersdorf in 1842.[7]

166   Germany: 1716–17. *The seder*. Drawing. From an Hagadah dated
1716–17. Hebrew Union College. The master of the house wears the
prescribed dress for this occasion, the *sargenes*. The other men have contemporary three-cornered hats and white bands. The wife is elegantly dressed.

1

2

3

4

167 Germany: Westphalia (?), 1717. Miniatures from a Hebrew manuscript
prayer book (Amsterdam rite).
1. *Friday night service in the synagogue.* Men standing in front of the Ark of the
Law in traditional black synagogue dress: long cloaks, Jewish ruffs and berets.
Some are playing musical instruments, an unusual practice in synagogue but
presumably permitted by local custom.
2. *Friday night prayers.* The head of the house and his two sons in long tunics,
knee breeches, *sarbals* without sleeves and Jewish berets. The wife and daughter
wear the somewhat obsolete *fontanges* as head-dress.
3. *Singing Zemirot.* The head of the house in traditional Sabbath dress while
the three sons wear what appears to be the medieval Jewish hat: a surprising
survival perhaps retained only for the Sabbath. The two women again in *fontanges.*
4. *Prayers for the New Moon.* Men in black tunics, knee breeches, *sarbals*
without sleeves, Jewish ruffs and berets.

124

The Jewish woman seen on an etching published in Rome in 1602 (plate 193) wears a bonnet with a kerchief attached which may have been yellow in colour as a mark of distinction. The woodcuts in the early seventeenth-century *Minhagim* book (plates 195–6) and *Hagadah* published in Venice, show the men wearing *berets* and *sarbals* in synagogue while the women at home are in attractive contemporary costume. This is in keeping with the comments of the English traveller, Thomas Coyat, who visited the synagogue at Venice in June 1608 and saw in the gallery 'many Jewish women, whereof some were as beautiful as ever I saw, and so gorgeous in their apparel, jewels, chains of gold, and rings adorned with precious stones, that some of our English countesses do scarce exceede them, having marvailous long traines like Princesses that are borne up by waiting women serving for the same purpose'.

When Misson visited Venice in 1688 the men were wearing red hats lined and trimmed with black but the physician, Abraham Cohen, is seen in contemporary dress (plate 194).

Other distinctions existed in different parts of Italy from time to time (plate 197) except at the free port of Leghorn but they were not rigorously applied and at weddings contemporary dress is seen of a most luxurious kind (plate 192).

In the Papal States, which included the Comtat Venaissin, the Jews were required to wear a yellow hat up to the time of the French Revolution.

In Alsace and Lorraine the Jews probably followed the dress customs of German Jewry and a Jewish pedlar of Lorraine in 1841 wrote nostalgically of the days when 'we all wore the same Jewish dress and the beard was to all of us like a commandment' (plate 200).

168   Germany: *c. 1750. Prayer for the Succah.* Drawing. From the collection of Mr H. Eisemann. Jews wearing the traditional dress for sabbaths and festivals.

169 Germany: Frankfurt a/M 1714–8. *A wedding*. Engraving. From Schudt.
The men in the usual *barrettes* and ruffs; the women wear the *viereckiger schleier*
(square veil) which had become a distinctive feature of their dress and they are
in their synagogue capes and ruffs. The bride heavily veiled.

170 Germany: Fürth, 1734. *Wedding procession*. Engraving. Rubens (ii) 1170.
The mothers of the bride and bridegroom wear their marriage belts and each
is in a *fret* head-dress made of silver and gold trellis work. The other women
are in horned head-dresses, ruffs and synagogue cloaks. The men wear the
typical Jewish dress of the period.

171 Germany: Frankfurt a/M 1774. '*Beer Dann,
Schutz-Jude*'. Etching. Rubens (ii) 2044. The dress
of a protected Jew.

172 Germany. 1738. *Joseph Süss Oppenheimer*.
Mezzotint. Rubens (ii) 2166. The costume of a
Court Jew. He is fashionably dressed with a wig
and is clean-shaven.

173 Germany: 1785. *Blumchen Friedlander.* Engraving. Rubens (ii) 2063. Although married she wears her hair uncovered as a sign of emancipation.

174 Germany: 1789. *Isaac Daniel Itzig.* Engraving. Rubens (ii) 2095. As a reformer he breaks away from tradition, wears contemporary dress with a *toupee* and side curls and is clean-shaven.

In France, until the Revolution, the Ashkenazim followed the customs of German Jewry and the dress regulations at Metz which appeared at frequent intervals until the end of the eighteenth century were similar to those of German cities (see Appendix). When Jonathan Eybeschutz was rabbi at Metz in the 1740's he denounced Jews who shaved or wore wigs and he was shocked to find that the adoption of gentile dress had gone to such lengths that *tsitsith* were no longer being worn openly.

The French Sephardim did not wear beards or distinctive dress and when Joseph David Azulay visited Bordeaux and Paris in 1777–8 he commented on the fact that the Sephardim had adopted gentile customs including the wearing of swords (plate 202).[8]

No restrictions on Jewish dress existed in Holland and the Sephardim wore the latest fashions including wigs. Their women appeared in *fontanges* when this head-dress was introduced in the seventeenth century.[9]

Rembrandt's masterpiece, 'The Jewish Bride' (plate 207) has been known by its present title at least since 1825 before when it was in private hands. The Dutch archivist, Jac. Zwarts, wrote a monograph to prove that the couple represented the Spanish Jewish poet, Daniel Levy (Miguel) de Barrios (1635–1701) and his second wife Abigail de Pina whom he married at Amsterdam in 1662. His theory is based on the supposed similarity between the man's portrait and that of de Barrios in his engraved portrait.[10] There are numerous other theories and one must confess that the only Jewish feature about the picture is that the woman wears her wedding ring, *more Judaico*, on the first finger of her right hand.

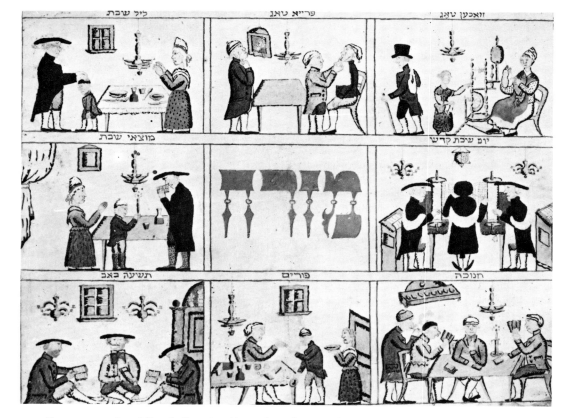

175 Germany: *c.* 1820. *Mizrach*. Drawing. From the collection of Mr H. Eisemann. The day by day life of a Jew showing the traditional costume worn at home for prayers and the everyday clothes for work.

176 Germany: Bavaria, 1826. *Feast of Tabernacles.* Engraving. Title page to a Machsor, Sulzbach, 1826. The men in traditional *barrette*. Jewish ruff, knee breeches, tail coat and buckled shoes.

The picture of the Dutch Suasso family painted by R. Jelgerhuis in 1793 (plate 210) complements the one of the English Montefiore family (plate 220) by the same artist painted four years later.

In general, it can be seen that the Dutch Sephardim wore fashionable dress while the Ashkenazim were distinguished by their beards and somewhat old-fashioned clothes (plates 204–211).

The first Jews to return to England in the seventeenth century were Sephardim. They were indistinguishable from Englishmen in their dress; they had neat pointed Spanish beards and wigs. John Greenhalgh described them after a visit to their synagogue in 1662 as 'all gentlemen and most of them rich in apparel, divers with jewels glittering . . . several of them are comely, gallant, proper gentlemen'.[11] The Ashkenazim could usually be recognized by their ragged beards and foreign dress but by the middle of the eighteenth century Naphtali Franks, a warden of the Great Synagogue, was wearing fashionable dress with wig and sword (plate 215). Born in New York, he characterised the members of this influential Anglo-American family.[12] Both in England and America important Ashkenazim like Abraham Goldsmid (plate 223) and Michael Prager (plate 225) invariably followed contemporary fashion and even an orthodox Jew like David Levi (plate 218) wore a wig and was clean-shaven.

New immigrants tended to retain their native mode of dress and the beard remained a Jewish mark of distinction until it came into general fashion towards the middle of the nineteenth century. The 'ol-clo' man wearing a tier of hats as a sign of his calling was always a Jew (plate 224). Sephardi and Ashkenazi women dressed according to the fashions of the day but it was usual for married women to keep their heads covered (plate 222).

The romantic notion of Jewish women's dress is sometimes reflected in English literature and engraving. Rebecca in Scott's *Ivanhoe* wears an Eastern dress and a turban of yellow silk while the *Ladies' Cabinet* for November 1835 forecasts greater popularity for the Jewish style of coiffure following the recent turbans *à l'Israélite*.

177 Germany: *c.* 1800. '*Der Samstag*'. Engraving. Jewish Museum, London. The women are in Directoire dresses. The men have retained their traditional costume for synagogue: they have flat round hats (*barrettes*), sleeveless gowns (*sarbals*) and frilled collars and wear beards.

178   Germany: *c.* 1820. '*A Hamburg Jewess on her sabbath*'. Drawing. Rubens (ii) 1636.
She holds a pompadour parasol and wears very décolleté clothes under her synagogue cloak.

179   Germany: Frankfurt a/M 1866–9. *Wedding*. Painting by M. D. Oppenheim. Israel Museum.
In the text accompanying the engraving of the picture the writer explains that many of the men
are wearing dress belonging to former times. The rabbi in a *tallith* wears the Polish *streimel*. The other
men have three-cornered hats, knee-breeches and buckled shoes—the dress for synagogue and special
occasions. The bridal couple wear gold *sivlonoth* belts (see p. 102). The bride, in accordance with Jewish
custom, receives the wedding ring on the first finger of her right hand (see p. 103).

180 Switzerland: 1768. *Funeral*. Engraving. From Ulrichs. The men are dressed like the German Jews in cloaks and round hats (*barrettes*).

181 Austria: Prague, 1514. *Kiddush*. Woodcut. From *Seder Zemirot Ubirchat Hamazon*, Prague, 1514. Statni Zidovske Museum, Prague. The woman's coiffure is the *gebende* which covers the chin and holds the head-covering in place. The men on each side of her wear a *barrette* and a coat with a deep collar called *schaube*. All are in contemporary costume.

182 Austria: Prague, c. 1650. *Ber Teller*. Etching. From his *Be'er Majjim Hajjim*, Prague, c. 1650. Statni Zidovske Museum, Prague. As a physician he is permitted by the communal regulations to wear the contemporary dress of his profession.

183   Austria: 1710. *Jacob Ries.* Engraving. Rubens (ii) 2189. Court jester at Vienna.
As a Court Jew he wears contemporary dress and full-bottomed wig.

184   Austria: Prague, 1734. *Prague. Synagogue service for New Year.* Engraving.
Rubens (ii) 1157. Most of the men wear the prescribed dress for this occasion,
the *sargenes* or *kittel*, accompanied by the Jewish ruff.

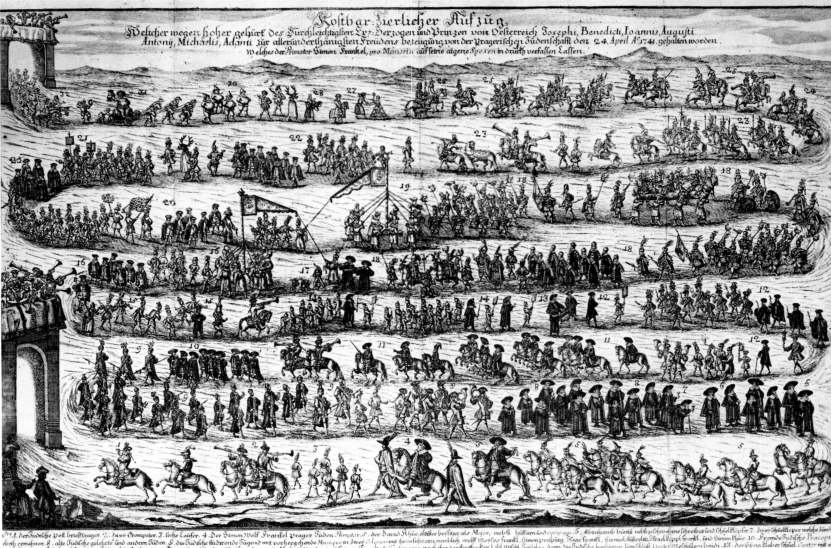

185   Austria: Prague, 1741. *Procession of Jews of Prague on the birth of the Archduke Joseph 24 April 1741.* Engraving. Israel Museum. A record of the remarkable variety of costumes worn by the Jews of Prague.

1. The Jewish postman. 2. Two trumpeters. 3. Six runners. 4. Simon Wolf Frankel, Prague, Jewish 'Primator'. 5. David Khuf, senior councillor, as major with hussars and equipage. 6. Abraham Guntzel and sworn scribe and 'schulklopfer'. 7. Two 'schulklopfers' who call for the early service. 8. Old Jewish sage and other Jews. 9. Young Jewish students preceded by musicians and two columns with their leaders: Wolf Moses Frankl, Simon Presburg, Isaak Frankl, Samuel Austerlitz, Israel Koppl Frankl and Simon Lhue. 10. Foreign Jewish 'praeceptores'. 11. Simon Neustaettl and other Jews on horses preceded by a trumpeter. 12. Moses Gumpertz, doctor of medicine with his faculty 'testemonia'; behind him, the pharmacist, Loebl Mischl Jaiteles, the Jewish barber and last, Doktor Meshulem Boudi. 13. The 'Synaklaber Schuel' cantor with a positiv (portable organ). 14. The poor orphans from the cheder. 15. Players with their gilt tankard. 16. The butchers with their privileged standard and key. 17. Two curious tumblers. 18. Furriers clad with Persian furs with 2 standards and portable stuffed animals preceded by trumpeters. 19. The butchers' other privileged standard, the boy Juda Iserles sitting on the pinnacle. 20. The Taylor's Guild with a small flag embroidered by Kestler. 21. The makers of gold and silver lace and button makers' Guild with their workstools. 22. The shoemaker with the Guild tankard preceded by musicians. 23. Company of hussars. 24. Bride and bridegroom. 25. Company of hussars, unmarried, with trumpeter. 26. A wedding jester. 27. A buffoon. 28. Various jesters, with the woman carrying her husband in a basket. 29. A horned man. 30. Two pairs of gluttons. 31. Bacchus. 32. A peasant wedding.

186–7 Austria: Prague, *c.* 1760. '*Reicher Jud in Prag. Reiche Jüdin in Prag*'. Etchings. From the collection of Dr Arthur Polak. The costumes are marked by their simplicity and subdued colours. The woman has her hair partially covered and carries a bonnet for outdoor wear.

188 Bohemia: *c.* 1750. *Jewish wedding.* Detail from painting. Israel Museum.
The bride's procession. She wears a ruff as part of her traditional dress.

189   Austria: *c.* 1690. *Samuel Oppenheimer*. Engraving. Rubens (ii) 2179.
As a Court Jew he is permitted to wear contemporary dress and a wig
but he retains a beard and his dress is very simple.

191   Italy: Padua, 1594. '*Judaeus Mercator
Patavinus*'. Engraving. Rubens (ii) 1728.
Although described as a Paduan, he speaks
Yiddish. He wears the Jewish *barrette*.

190   Austria: 1804. *Fanny von Arnstein*. Mezzotint. Rubens (ii) 2011.
She wears the dress of fashionable Viennese Society in which she figured
prominently, and although married she has her hair uncovered and in
curls, for which she is said to have incurred rabbinic censure.

192 Italy: Parma, 1452. *Wedding*. Miniature. From a Wedding Service, Parma, 1452. Montefiore Ms. 249. Jew's College, London. The wedding at Parma of Judah Ben Elhanan of Ascoli and Stella, daughter of Solomon Ben Abraham of Mantua. Reproduced by kind permission of the Montefiore Endowment Committee.

193

194

195 Italy: Venice, 1601. *Wedding*. Woodcut. From *Minhagim*, Venice, 1601. Bodleian Library. The men wear berets (the Jewish *barrettes*) and cloaks: the women have kerchiefs attached to their bonnets.

196 Italy: Venice, 1601. *Lighting the lights. Eve of Yom Kippur*. Woodcut. From *Minhagim*, Venice, 1601. Bodleian Library. The mother of the family has her head covered and wears a high collar.

193   Italy: Rome, 1602. *'Hebrea'*. Etching.
British Museum. She wears a long robe and
cloak and has a kerchief attached to her bonnet.

194   Italy: Venice, 1719. *Abraham Cohen of Zante*.
Engraving. Rubens (ii) 2006. A physician, he wears
full-bottomed wig and is clean shaven.

197   Italy: *c.* 1750. *Jewish funeral*. Painting. Israel Museum. The men have red
or yellow kerchiefs attached to their hats as a distinctive mark.

139

198   Italy: *c. 1750. Jewish wedding.* Painting by Longhi. Israel Museum. The rabbi in a
red hat and *tallith* the remainder in contemporary dress.

199　Italy: Florence, 1806. *S. Fiorentino*. Engraving.
From his *Poesie*, Florence, 1806. He is clean-shaven
and wears a short wig with contemporary dress.

200　France: 1664. *Jew of Lorraine*. Etching. From S. Le Clerc,
Divers estats et conditions de la vie humaine, Paris, 1664. In a *barrette*
and ruff as worn by the German Jews.

201　Italy: *c.* 1780. '*Dalla tribu di Ruben io discendo e trine e tele a chi
ne vuol le vendo*'. Drawing. Jewish pedlar in contemporary dress.

202   France: 1806. *Furtado de la Gironde*. Engraving.
Rubens (i) 101. A member of the Sephardi community of
Bordeaux in a tye-wig (*à noeud*) and contemporary dress.

203   France: Nancy, *c.* 1810. *Interior of Synagogue at Nancy*.
Lithograph. Rubens (ii) 1576. The rabbi, who is bearded,
wears the traditional fur hat and there are a few Levantine
Jews in turbans; otherwise the dress is contemporary and
some of the men are in military uniform.

204   Holland: 1709. *Daughters of Francisco Lopes Suasso*. Painting by C. Netscher.
Stedelijk Museum, Amsterdam. Sephardi children in contemporary dress.

205   Holland: 1642. *Zacutus Lusitanus*. Engraving.
Rubens (ii) 2241. The famous physician is bearded and
wears a deep collar edged with lace and a cuff to match.

206   Holland: 1668. *Circumcision*. Drawing by
Romeyn de Hooghe. Rijksmuseum, Amsterdam. The
two rabbis are bearded and wear skull caps, knee breeches
and coats buttoned to neck. The other men with one
exception are clean shaven and wear wigs.

207 Holland: 1662 (?). *The Jewish Bride*. Painting by Rembrandt. Rijksmuseum, Amsterdam. The couple are doubtfully identified as Miguel de Barrios and Abigail de Pina who were married in 1662. The only Jewish feature is that the woman wears her wedding ring on the index finger of the right hand (p. 103).

208 Holland: 1681. *A Sephardi merchant.*
Detail from a *vanitas* painting. Rubens (ii) 1694.
Jewish Museum, London. He is standing in
the Jewish cemetery at Oudekerk dressed in the
height of fashion with full-bottomed wig
and sword.

Below:
209 Holland: 1723. '*Nuptial ceremony of the
German Jews*'. Engraving. From Picart. Rubens
(ii) 1240. The bridegroom wears a wedding belt,
and according to Picart he sends the bride a
marriage belt of gold the day before the wedding
while she sends him one of silver. On the wedding
day the bride has her head uncovered and her
hair in tresses which in Venice are curled and
called *banetes*.

210 Holland: 1793. *The Suasso family*. Pastel by R. Jelgerhuis (1729–1806).
Stedelijk Museum, Amsterdam. A Sephardi family. The men in contemporary
dress and wigs, the women with their hair covered. Cf. No. 220.

211 Holland: 1825. '*Habitant du quartier juif a Amsterdam*'.
Lithograph. From *Costumes du Peuple de Toutes les Provinces
du Royaume du Pays-Bas*, Brussels 1825–8. The ancient style
of dress as well as its dilapidated condition seem to make it
distinctively Jewish.

212 England: *c.* 1788. *Lord George Gordon*. Mezzotint. Rubens (i) 139.
In the dress he adopted after his conversion to Judaism; long beard and the
large felt hat worn by Polish Jews.

213 England: 1749. '*The Jerusalem Infirmary*'. Engraving. Rubens (i) 295. The chief figures in this
caricature represent prominent members of the English Sephardi community and the medical staff
of the Infirmary. All are clean-shaven and wear contemporary dress but various types of wig are
shown. The caricaturist evidently regards as affectations the bag-wig of the man at the table and the
divided or campaign wig of the physician, Jacob de Castro Sarmento (standing behind the monkey),
as well as the sword which he alone carries.

214   England: 1788. *The Royal Exchange* (London). Engraving (detail).
A figure in a long cloak is seen on the right. His beard and outlandish dress
identify him as a foreign–born Ashkenazi Jew.

215–16　England: *c.* 1760. *Naphtali and Phila Franks*. Paintings by Thos. Hudson.
Jewish Museum, London. A warden of the Great Synagogue dressed in the height of fashion
with wig and sword. She is also fashionably dressed and wears her hair uncovered.

217

218

217   England: *c.* 1780. *David Alves Rebello.*
Engraving. Sephardi notability in short powdered
wig, frilled shirt and silk waistcoat.

218   England: 1799. *'David Levi'.* Engraving.
Rubens (i) 162. Although an orthodox Ashkenazi he
wears a short bob powdered wig, is clean-shaven
and his dress conforms to current fashions.

219   England: 1721. *Dr Fernando Mendez.* Miniature
by Catherine da Costa. Spanish and Portuguese
Synagogue, Bevis Marks, London. In full-bottomed
wig, contemporary dress and doctor's gown.

220   England: 1797. *The Montefiore family.* Pastel by R. Jelgerhuis. By kind permission of Mr Michael R. Q. Henriques. Joseph Elias Montefiore in a short wig, tail coat and knee breeches; his wife, Rachel, also apparently in a wig and a remarkable hat. Cf. No. 210

221 England: *c.* 1820. *Rachel de Crasto*. Oil painting. National Trust.
Member of a leading Sephardi family in dress of the period.

222   England: *c.* 1880. *Mrs Nathan Marcus Adler.* Painting. Jewish Museum, London.
The chief feature of the dress of the Chief Rabbi's wife is the covering of the hair.

223   England: 1806. '*Abrm Goldsmid Esq.*' Etching. Rubens (i) 118.
Powdered tye-wig, frock, frilled shirt, high boots and knee breeches.

224   England: *c.* 1820. '*Old clothes to sell*'. Etching. Rubens (ii) 1516. Jewish old-clothes-
man in typical costume with a tier of hats on his head as the sign of his trade.

225　America: Philadelphia, *c.* 1775. *Michael Prager*. Oil painting by Jas. Peale.
The Insurance Company of North America. He wears a wig with a pigtail queue,
frock, waistcoat and frilled shirt.

226 Sephardi rabbinical dress. Holland: 1671. *Jacob Sasportas.*
Painting by I. Luttichuys. Israel Museum. The rabbi has a bush beard
and wears a clerical robe, deep white collar and skull cap.

6 Rabbinical dress

In Talmudic times only rabbis wore the *tallith* and probably only they were privileged to keep their heads covered at all times (see p. 11). In later times there were no permanent traditional features about their dress but there was usually some distinction and in the fourteenth century Holkham Bible Zachariah wears a rather unusual collar.[1]

The Sephardim were the first to accept conventional Western clerical dress derived from the black Geneva gown and white bands of the Calvinist or Reformed Church, while the round black hat adopted by the Ashkenazim in Austria and Germany during the nineteenth century must have been borrowed originally from the Greek Orthodox clergy.

The fifteenth-century Portuguese rabbi painted by Nuno Goncalves is clean-shaven and wears a tall cylindrical hat with a black gown (plate 109) which appears to be contemporary academical dress. In the seventeenth century the Dutch Sephardi rabbis wore a black coat buttoned to the neck with a white collar, knee breeches, a sombrero outdoors and a skull cap indoors (plate 206). All this was in keeping with current fashion like their stiletto or Vandyke beards and there was no fetish about keeping the head continuously covered as there was with the Ashkenazim. In England, already in 1705, Haham David Nieto (plate 228) was wearing a full-bottomed wig without a hat and a clerical robe with bands. Moses Cohen d'Azevedo, appointed Haham in 1761, was clean-shaven and wore a powdered physical wig without a hat,[2] like his Hazan, David de Crasto (plate 232). This remained the recognised Sephardi rabbinical dress in England and Holland until the middle of the nineteenth century.

The Ashkenazi rabbis were much more conservative. In Germany persons holding the rabbinical diploma (*morenubrief*) wore a very deep collar. The fifteenth-century illustration of the rabbi at Nuremburg shows such a collar accompanied by a distinctive kind of *gugel* or *chaperon* (plate 158). The Prague rabbi seen in a woodcut dating from 1617 has a distinctive gown (plate 229) and the rabbi at Fürth wears a deep white collar instead of the usual Jewish ruff of the early eighteenth century (plate 164).

In Amsterdam during the seventeenth century the rabbis were known as 'the bearded ones'.

227 Sephardi rabbinical dress. Holland: 1686. 'Yshack Aboab'. Mezzotint. Rubens (ii) 2004. With full beard and wearing a skull cap, plain white collar and clerical gown.

228 Sephardi rabbinical dress. England: 1705. *David Nieto*. Mezzotint. Rubens (i) 219. The English Haham is bareheaded and has a stiletto beard. He wears a full-bottomed wig and clerical robes with white bands. His dress is an expression of his independent and liberal outlook.

By the middle of the eighteenth century, probably because of the large number of Polish rabbis, the typical European Ashkenazi rabbi was heavily bearded and wore the Polish fur trimmed gown with a fur trimmed hat (*spodic*) perhaps exchanged for a *streimel* on the Sabbath and festivals (plates 237–9 etc.). The rabbinical *streimel* was made of thirteen sables' tails. At Mattersdorf in Hungary in the middle of the nineteenth century the rabbi wore a *streimel* for Sabbath and festivals and a boat-shaped hat on weekdays.

In England and America Christian dress was adopted much earlier and already in the eighteenth century, Isaac Polack, Hazan of London's Great Synagogue, was clean-shaven and wore a three-cornered hat, clerical robes with white bands and a wig (plate 243). The latter was unusual for an Ashkenazi minister. The three-cornered hat survived for rabbinical use in England until the latter part of the nineteenth century. For Solomon Hirschel, the Chief Rabbi, it was his week-day hat exchanged for a *spodic* on Sabbaths and festivals (plates 245–6).

Ashkenazi rabbis attached great importance to the covering of the head.

The surprising absence of a hat in the case of Samson Raphael Hirsch, the pillar of orthodoxy (plate 252), is said to be due to the fact that he deliberately wore a wig.

A new style of Ashkenazi rabbinical dress was introduced into England from Hanover by Nathan Marcus Adler when he was appointed Chief Rabbi in 1845 (plate 253). His son, who succeeded him, is said to have worn bishop's gaiters and his dress as seen in plate 254 betrays more than a suspicion of Anglican influence.

In France the rabbis originally followed the customs of the Ashkenazim of Germany and Holland but at a rabbinical conference held in 1856 the dress of French Catholic priests was officially adopted with slight modifications (plate 255).

Italian rabbis were usually clean-shaven and wore clerical robes with white bands (plate 249). They had no objection to wigs.

In eastern countries a few instances of distinctive dress can be cited. In Morocco in 1781, the rabbi wore very large sleeves and usually a blue handkerchief around his cap (see p. 70). The Palestinian rabbi, Hezekiah da Silva, wore a distinctive red turban (plate 257); otherwise, as in Turkey, regional costume was the customary practice. At Constantinople in the 1860's the rabbis wore a dark blue felt cap around the base of which was bound a white kerchief or turban with fine blue stripes. At Smyrna in 1873 the rabbi wore a *bonneto*, a type of turban reserved for doctors and priests (plate 48).

The Karaite rabbi from Cairo, Moses ben Abraham, sat for his portrait expressly in order that future generations might know what he wore (plate 263).

The rabbi of the Reform congregation at Hamburg wore a round cap with a pompon, black gown and bands (plate 264).

At the present time it would be difficult to find any distinctive features in rabbinical dress either in Eastern countries or in the West.

229 Ashkenazi rabbinical dress. Austria: Prague, 1617. *Synagogue Interior.* Woodcut. From *Shoshanat Haamakim*, Prague, 1617. The rabbi on the left wears a beret (*barrette*) with short-sleeved gown. The preacher on the right wears a hood and the congregation are in berets and cloaks.

230 Sephardi rabbinical dress. Holland: *c.* 1650.
Jacob Yehudah Leon Templo. Engraving. Rubens (i) 158. His
collar has a lace border; otherwise the skull cap and gown
form the usual dress of a Sephardi rabbi His moustache and
stiletto beard are in keeping with current fashion.

231 Sephardi rabbinical dress. Holland: 1728. *'Salomon
Aelyon'*. Engraving. Rubens (i) 13. Without a hat, in a
full-bottomed wig, square-cut beard and gown with
white border and clerical bands.

232 Sephardi rabbinical dress. England: 1790. *'David de
Crasto'*. Engraving. Rubens (i) 72. He is clean-shaven and
wears clerical robes with white bands and a physical wig.

233 Sephardi rabbinical dress. England: 1751. 'Moses Gomes de Mesquita'. Mezzotint. Rubens (i) 210. The English Haham has a bush beard and wears a three-cornered hat, full-bottomed wig and clerical robes with white bands.

234 Sephardi rabbinical dress. Holland: 1824. David Leon. Engraving. Rubens (ii) 211. Clean-shaven and wearing a three-cornered hat, bob wig and clerical bands.

235 Sephardi rabbinical dress. England: 1806. 'Raphael Meldola'. Engraving. Rubens (i) 180. The English Haham is clean-shaven and wears a three-cornered hat, long bob powdered wig, clerical robes and bands.

236 Ashkenazi rabbinical dress. Holland: Amsterdam 1709. *Aryeh Judah Kalisch*. Engraving. Rubens (ii) 2101. In a fur-trimmed hat, frilled collar and ornamental cuffs.

238 Ashkenazi rabbinical dress. Holland: *c.* 1805. *Moses Nasj.* Engraving. Rubens (ii) 2156. He has a long trimmed beard and wears a three-cornered hat.

237 Ashkenazi rabbinical dress. Holland: 1700. *Jehiel Michael.* Engraving. Rubens (ii) 2148. Rounded unkempt beard, broad-brimmed hat and full length clerical robes with white bands.

239   Ashkenazi rabbinical dress. Holland: *c.* 1715. *Zevi Ashkenazi.*
Painting. Jewish Museum, London. The Dutch Chief Rabbi wears
a *spodic* and fur–trimmed robes.

240   Ashkenazi rabbinical dress. Holland: *c.* 1770.
Emanuel Cohen. Drawing. Rubens (ii) 2040. With unkempt
beard, traditional fur hat (*spodic*) and voluminous gown.

241   Ashkenazi rabbinical dress. Austria: Prague,
c. 1790. *Ezekiel Landau.* Engraving. Rubens (ii) 2103.
Wearing the traditional rabbinical hat, the *spodic*.

242   Ashkenazi rabbinical dress. France: *c.* 1820.
Jacob Meyer. Lithograph. Rubens (ii) 2143. In a full
beard and wearing a three-cornered hat with clerical
robes and white bands.

243　Ashkenazi rabbinical dress. England: 1779. '*Rev. Isaac Polack*'. Mezzotint. Rubens (i) 224. He is clean-shaven and wears a three-cornered hat, clerical robes with white bands and a short bob powdered wig.

244　Ashkenazi rabbinical dress. Germany: 1808. '*Aron Beer*'. Mezzotint. Rubens (ii) 2014. He has only a very slight beard and wears a gown with clerical bands and a three-cornered hat.

245   Ashkenazi rabbinical dress. England: *c.* 1805. *Solomon Hirschel.*
Engraving. Rubens (i) 149. The English Chief Rabbi in traditional fur hat and
a robe with clerical bands. Probably his Sabbath dress.

246   Ashkenazi rabbinical dress. England: 1808. *Solomon Hirschel.* Painting.
Jewish Museum, London. Rubens (i) 148. In three-cornered hat with clerical
robes and white bands. Probably his everyday dress.

247 Ashkenazi rabbinical dress. France: 1807. *Grand Sanhedrin des Israélites de L'Empire Français et du Royaume d'Italie*. Aquatint. Rubens (i) 102. The engraving shows the forty-five ecclesiastical members of Napoleon's Sanhedrin. The French rabbis wear their characteristic long white bands; some are clean shaven and bare-headed. The president, David Sintzheim, has a peculiar fur-trimmed hat with two horns.

248 Ashkenazi rabbinical dress. Holland: 1813.
Samuel Berenstein. Engraving. Rubens (ii) 2022.
The Amsterdam Chief Rabbi wears a three-
cornered hat, beard, clerical gown, broad silk
girdle and white bands.

249 Italian rabbinical dress. Italy: Turin, *c.* 1806.
'Abraham de Cologna'. Engraving. Rubens (ii) 2007.
Bare-headed, clean-shaven and wearing
clerical bands.

250 Ashkenazi rabbinical dress. Hungary: Presburg, *c.* 1830. *Moses Schreiber.* Lithograph. Rubens (ii) 2200. Heavily bearded, in a fur-trimmed hat (*spodic*) and fur-trimmed robe.

251 Ashkenazi rabbinical dress. England: 1827. *Myer Levy.* Lithograph: Rubens (i) 166. He is clean-shaven and wears a three-cornered hat which by this time was completely out of fashion.

252 Ashkenazi rabbinical dress. Germany: Oldenburg, *c.* 1835. *Samson Raphael Hirsch.* Lithograph. Formerly in the possession of Mr H. Eisemann. The leader of German orthodox Jewry has a short trimmed beard and wears clerical robes with white bands. No hat is visible (see p. 161).

253 Ashkenazi rabbinical dress. England: *c.* 1850. *Nathan Marcus Adler.*
Painting by Kempf. Jewish Museum, London. The English Chief Rabbi
wears clerical robes, white bands and a black velvet cap the future
pattern for orthodox rabbinical dress in England.

254   Ashkenazi rabbinical dress. England: 1904. 'The Chief Rabbi'. From *Vanity Fair*, 31 March 1904. Rubens (i) 391. Herman Adler in clerical robes, white bands and round hat, the dress introduced from Hanover by his father and as worn at the present time by the English Chief Rabbi.

255   Ashkenazi rabbinical dress. France: 1850. 'Le Rabbin'. Engraving. Rubens (ii) 1578. Full beard; three-cornered hat, clerical robes and long white bands.

256　Italian rabbinical dress. Italy: 1735. *Menachem Vivante of Corfu aged 85.* Painting.
Jewish Museum, London. In skull cap, full beard, clerical robes and girdle.

257   Oriental rabbinical dress. Palestine: *c.* 1690. *Hezekiah da Silva*. Painting. Israel Museum. He wears a *kaveže*, the traditional head-dress of Turkish Jews, coloured red and a fur-trimmed pelisse.

258 Oriental rabbinical dress. Turkey:
Adrianople, *c.* 1760. *'Selomoh Salem'*.
Engraving. Rubens (ii) 2196. The rabbi
still wears the *kaveze*, the traditional
Jewish turban of his native city, after
settling at Amsterdam.

259 Oriental rabbinical dress. Morocco: 1836.
'Rev Dr M. Edrehi. A native of Morocco'. Engraving. Rubens
(ii) 88. The rabbi, who settled in London, wears a turban
and Eastern costume. A seal is suspended from his neck.

260 Oriental rabbinical dress. Tunis: 1850.
'Rabbi Abraham Belais'. Lithograph. Rubens (i) 316.
The rabbi, who was born in Tunis, retained his
native costume after settling in London.

262　Oriental rabbinical dress: 1839. '*Moses Doweck Cohen Chief Priest of the Israelites, Calcutta*'. Etching. Rubens (i) 71. Although a native of Aleppo, he ranks as a Baghdadi and wears their traditional costume.

261　Oriental rabbinical dress. Turkey: *c.* 1880. '*Moise Halevy, Grand-rabbin de Constantinople*'. Engraving. His dress seems to be similar to that worn by Turkish dignitaries.

263　Karaite rabbinical dress. Palestine: 1901. '*Moses Ben Abraham the Rabbi of the Karaite Jews*'. Drawing. From M. Thomas, *Two Years in Palestine and Syria*, London, 1901. He wears Turkish dress, a striped *entari* under a dark purple *djubba* with a turban of the same colour surmounted by a red kerchief. The rabbi who originated from Cairo consented to sit for his portrait 'in order that future generations might know what he wore'.

177

264   Reform rabbinical dress. Germany: Hamburg, 1843–7. *Naphtali Frankfurter*.
Lithograph. Rubens (ii) 1637. The reform rabbi is clean-shaven and wears a skull cap
with a pompon, clerical bands, full length gown and *tallith*.

Appendices

Exodus 28, 29

(28) You yourself are to summon to your presence your brother Aaron and his sons out of all the Israelites to serve as my priests: Aaron and his sons Nadab and Abihu, Eleazar and Ithamar. For your brother Aaron make sacred vestments, to give him dignity and grandeur. Tell all the craftsmen whom I have endowed with skill to make the vestments for the consecration of Aaron as my priest. These are the vestments they shall make: a breast-piece, an ephod, a mantle, a chequered tunic, a turban, and a sash. They shall make sacred vestments for Aaron your brother and his sons to wear when they serve as my priests, using gold; violet, purple, and scarlet yarn; and fine linen.

The ephod shall be made of gold, and with violet, purple, and scarlet yarn, and with finely woven linen worked by a seamster. It shall have two shoulder-pieces joined back and front. The waist-band on it shall be of the same workmanship and material as the fabric of the ephod, and shall be of gold, with violet, purple, and scarlet yarn, and finely woven linen. You shall take two cornelians and engrave on them the names of the sons of Israel: six of their names on the one stone, and the six other names on the second, all in order of seniority. With the skill of a craftsman, a seal-cutter, you shall engrave the two stones with the names of the sons of Israel; you shall set them in gold rosettes, and fasten them on the shoulders of the ephod, as reminders of the sons of Israel. Aaron shall bear their names on his two shoulders as a reminder before the LORD.

Make gold rosettes and two chains of pure gold worked into the form of ropes, and fix them on the rosettes. Make the breast-piece of judgement; it shall be made, like the ephod, by a seamster in gold, with violet, purple, and scarlet yarn, and finely woven linen. It shall be a square folded, a span long and a span wide. Set in it four rows of precious stones: the first row, sardin, chrysolite and green felspar; the second row, purple garnet, lapis lazuli and jade; the third row, turquoise, agate and jasper; the fourth row, topaz, cornelian and green jasper, all set in gold rosettes. The stones shall correspond to the twelve sons of Israel name by name; each stone shall bear the name of one of the twelve tribes engraved as on a seal.

Make for the breast-piece chains of pure gold worked into a rope. Make two gold rings, and fix them on the two upper corners of the breast-piece. Fasten the two gold ropes to the two rings at those corners of the breast-piece, and the other ends of the ropes to the two rosettes, thus binding the breast-piece to the shoulder-pieces on the front of the ephod. Make two gold rings and put them at the two lower corners of the breast-piece on the inner side next to the ephod. Make two gold rings and fix them on the two shoulder-pieces of the ephod, low down in front, along its seam above the waist-band of the ephod. Then the breast-piece shall be bound by its rings to the rings of the ephod with violet braid, just above the waist-band of the ephod, so that the breast-piece will not be detached from the ephod. Thus, when Aaron enters the Holy Place, he shall carry over his heart in the breast-piece of judgement the names of the sons of Israel, as a constant reminder before the LORD.

Finally, put the Urim and the Thummim into the breast-piece of judgement, and they will be over Aaron's heart when he enters the presence of the LORD. So shall Aaron bear these symbols of judgement upon the sons of Israel over his heart constantly before the LORD.

Make the mantle of the ephod a single piece of violet stuff. There shall be a hole for the head in the middle of it. All round the hole there shall be a hem of woven work, with an oversewn edge, so that it cannot be torn. All round its skirts make pomegranates of violet, purple, and scarlet stuff, with golden bells between them, a golden bell and a pomegranate alternately the whole way round the skirts of the mantle. Aaron shall wear it when he ministers, and the sound of it shall be heard when he enters the Holy Place before the LORD and when he comes out; and so he shall not die.

Make a rosette of pure gold and engrave on it as on a seal, 'Holy to the LORD'. Fasten it on a violet braid and set it on the very front of the turban. It shall be on Aaron's forehead; he has to bear the blame for shortcomings in the rites with which the Israelites offer their sacred gifts, and the rosette shall be always on his forehead so that they may be acceptable to the LORD.

Make the chequered tunic and the turban of fine linen, but the sash of embroidered work. For Aaron's sons make tunics and sashes; and make tall head-dresses to give them dignity and grandeur. With these invest your brother Aaron and his sons, anoint them, install them and consecrate them; so shall they serve me as priests. Make for them linen drawers reaching to the thighs to cover their private parts; and Aaron and his sons shall wear them when they enter the Tent of the Presence or approach the altar to minister in the Holy Place. Thus they will not incur guilt and die. This is a rule binding on him and his descendants for all time.

(29) In consecrating them to be my priests this is the rite to be observed. Take a young bull and two rams without blemish. Take unleavened loaves, unleavened cakes mixed with oil, and un-leavened wafers smeared with oil, all made of wheaten flour; put them in a single basket and bring them in it. Bring also the bull and the two rams. Bring Aaron and his sons to the entrance of the Tent of the Presence, and wash them with water. Take the vestments and invest Aaron with the tunic, the mantle of the ephod, the ephod itself and the breast-piece, and fasten the ephod to him with its waist-band. Set the turban on his head, and the symbol of holy dedication on the turban. Take the anointing oil, pour it on his head and anoint him. Then bring his sons forward, invest them with tunics, gird them with the sashes and tie their tall head-dresses on them. They shall hold the priest-hood by a rule binding for all time.

Josephus, Jewish Antiquities, III, 150–174

(vii. 1) Moreover, vestments were made for the priests, both for the general body, whom they call *chaanaeae*, and in particular for the high-priest, whom they entitle *anarabaches*, signifying 'high-priest.' Now the vestments of the priests in general were as follows. When the priest is proceeding to perform his sacred ministrations, after undergoing the purification which the law prescribes, first of all he puts on what is called the *machanases*. The word denotes a 'binder,' in other words drawers covering the loins, stitched of fine spun linen, into which the legs are inserted as into breeches; this garment is cut short above the waist and terminates at the thighs, around which it is drawn tight.

(2) Over this he wears a linen robe, of a double texture of fine *byssus*; it is called *chethomenê*, that is to say 'of linen,' *chethon* being our name for linen. This robe is a tunic descending to the ankles, enveloping the body and with long sleeves tightly laced round the arms; they gird it at the breast; winding to a little above the armpits the sash, which is of a breadth of about four fingers and has an open texture giving it the appearance of a serpent's skin. Therein are interwoven flowers of divers hues, of crimson and purple, blue and fine linen, but the warp is purely of fine linen. Wound a first time at the breast, after passing round it once again, it is tied and then hangs at

length, sweeping to the ankles, that is so long as the priest has no task in hand, for so its beauty is displayed to the beholders' advantage; but when it behoves him to attend to the sacrifices and perform his ministry, in order that the movements of the sash may not impede his actions, he throws it back over his left shoulder. Moses gave it the name of *abanêth*, but we have learnt from the Babylonians to call it *hemian*, for so is it designated among them. This tunic is nowhere folded, but has a loose opening at the neck, and by means of strings fastened to the border at the breast and at the back is supported on each shoulder. It is called *massabazanes*.

(3) Upon his head he wears a cap without a peak, not covering the whole head but extending slightly beyond the middle of it. It is called *masnaephthes*, and is so fashioned as to resemble a coronet, consisting of a band of woven linen thickly compressed; for it is wound round and round and stitched repeatedly. This is then enveloped by a muslin veil descending from above to the forehead, thus concealing the stitches of the head-band with their unsightly appearance and presenting to the skull a completely even surface. This head-gear is adjusted with care so as not to slip off while the priest is busy with his sacred ministry. We have now described the nature of the vestments of the ordinary priests.

(4) The high-priest is arrayed in like manner, omitting none of the things already mentioned, but over and above these he puts on a tunic of blue material. This too reaches to the feet, and is called in our tongue *meeir*; it is girt about him with a sash decked with the same gay hues as adorned the first, with gold interwoven into its texture. To its lower edge were stitched depending tassels, coloured to represent pomegranates, along with bells of gold, disposed with a keen regard for beauty, so that between each pair of bells there hung a pomegranate and between the pomegranates a little bell. But this tunic is not composed of two pieces, to be stitched at the shoulders and at the sides: it is one long woven cloth, with a slit for the neck, parted not crosswise but lengthwise from the breast to a point in the middle of the back. A border is stitched thereto to hide from the eye the unsightliness of the cut. There are similar slits through which the hands are passed.

(5) Above these vestments he puts on yet a third, which is called an *ephod* and resembles the Grecian *epômis*, being made in the following fashion. A woven fabric of the length of a cubit, of all manner of colours along with gold embroidery, it leaves the middle of the breast uncovered, is provided with sleeves, and in general presents the appearance of a tunic. But into the gap in this vestment is inserted a piece of the dimensions of a span, variegated with gold and with the same colours as the ephod; it is called *essên*, a word signifying in Greek speech *logion* ('oracle'). This exactly fills the space in the fabric which was left vacant at the breast, and is united by gold rings at each of its angles to corresponding rings attached to the ephod, a blue thread being passed through the rings to bind them together. Furthermore, to prevent any sagging of the middle portion between the rings, they devised the plan of stitching it with blue thread. The *epômis* is buckled on to the shoulders by two sardonyxes, fitted on this side and that with golden extremities extending over the shoulders and serving to hold the pins. On these stones are graven the names of the sons of Jacob in our tongue and in the native characters, six on each stone, those of the elder sons being on the right shoulder. On the *essên* also there are stones, twelve in number, of extraordinary size and beauty—ornament not procurable by man by reason of its surpassing value. Now these stones are ranged three in a row, in four lines, and worked into the fabric, being enclasped in gold wire whose coils are so inserted into the fabric as to prevent them from slipping out. The first triad comprises sardonyx, topaz, emerald; the second exhibits carbuncle, jasper, sapphire; the third begins with jacinth, then comes amethyst, and in the third place stands agate, ninth in the whole series; the fourth row is headed by chrysolite, next onyx, and then beryl, last of the series. All the stones have letters graven upon them, forming the names of the sons of Jacob, whom we esteem withal as our tribal chiefs, each stone being honoured with one name, according

to the order in which each of them was born. And since the rings were too feeble by themselves to support the weight of the gems, they made two other larger rings and inserted them into the fabric at the border of the *essên* nearest to the neck; these were designed to receive wrought chains, which on the top of the shoulders joined and were linked to cords of golden twine, whose extremity in the reverse direction passed through a ring projecting from the border at the back of the ephod. This secured the *essên* against any slip. The *essên* moreover had stitched to it a band, of the like hues of which I have spoken, along with gold; this after passing round the body was then tied at the seam and hung down. The tassels at either extremity of this band were caught into golden sheaths which embraced them all.

(6) For head-dress the high-priest had first a cap made in the same fashion as that of all the priests; but over this was stitched a second of blue embroidery, which was encircled by a crown of gold wrought in three tiers, and sprouting above this was a golden calyx recalling the plant which with us is called *saccharon*, but which Greeks expert in the cutting of simples term henbane. In case there are any who, having seen the plant, never learnt its name and are ignorant of its nature, or, though knowing the name, would not recognize it if they saw it, for the benefit of such I proceed to describe it. It is a plant which often grows to a height of above three spans, with a root resembling a turnip—one may not incorrectly draw this comparison—and leaves like those of the rocket. Now out of its branches it puts forth a calyx closely adhering to the twig, and enveloped in a husk which detaches itself automatically when it begins to turn into fruit; this calyx is as big as a joint of the little finger and resembles a bowl in contour. This too I will describe for those unfamiliar with it. Imagine a ball cut in two: the calyx at the stem presents the lower half of this, emerging from its base in rounded form; then gradually converging with a graceful re-entrant curve, it broadens out again gently near the rim, where it is indented like the navel of a pomegranate. Its hemispherical lid adheres closely to it, turned (as one might say) to a nicety, and is surmounted by those jagged spikes whose growth I compared to that on the pomegranate, prickly and terminating in quite a sharp point. Beneath this lid the plant preserves its fruit which fills the whole of the calyx and resembles the seed of the herb *sideritis*; while the flower which it produces may be thought comparable to the broad petals of a poppy. It was, then, on the model of this plant that was wrought the crown extending from the nape of the neck to the two temples; the forehead, however, was not covered by the *ephielis* (for so we may call the calyx), but had a plate of gold, bearing graven in sacred characters the name of God. Such is the apparel of the high priest.

Josephus, Jewish War, V. 227–236

(7) All who were of priestly lineage but were prevented from officiating by some physical defect, were admitted within the parapet, along with those free from any imperfection, and received the portions which were their birthright, but wore ordinary dress; none but the officiating priest was clad in the holy vestments. The priests who were without blemish went up to the altar and the sanctuary clothed in fine linen, scrupulously abstaining from strong drink through reverence for the ritual, lest they should be guilty of any transgression in their ministrations.

The high priest accompanied them, not on all occasions, but on the seventh days and new moons, and on any national festival or annual assemblage of all the people. When ministering, he wore breeches which covered his thighs up to the groin, an under vest of linen, and over that a blue robe reaching to the feet, full and tasselled; and from the tassels hung golden bells and pomegranates alternately, the bells symbolizing thunder and the pomegranates lightning. The embroidered sash which attached this robe to the breast consisted of five bands of variegated colours, gold, purple, scarlet, fine linen and blue, with which, as we have said, the veils in the sanctuary were also interwoven. Of the same mixture of materials, with gold preponderating, was the high-priest's ephod. In form like an ordinary cuirass, it was fastened by two golden brooches, set with very large and beautiful sardonyxes, on which were engraved the names of those after whom the tribes of the nation were called. Attached to the other side were twelve more stones, in four rows of three each: sardius, topaz, emerald; carbuncle, jasper, sapphire; agate, amethyst, jacinth; onyx, beryl, chrysolite; on each of which, again, was engraved the name of one of the heads of the tribes. His head was covered by a tiara of fine linen, wreathed with blue, encircling which was another crown, of gold, whereon were embossed the sacred letters, to wit, four vowels. These robes were not worn by the high priest in general, when he assumed plainer attire, but only when he penetrated to the innermost sanctuary; this he entered alone once in the year, on the day on which it was the universal custom to keep fast to God. Of the city and the temple and of the customs and laws relating to the latter we shall speak more minutely hereafter; for on these topics much yet remains to be told.

APPENDIX 2 EXTRACTS FROM JEWISH SUMPTUARY LAWS AND DRESS REGULATIONS

Extracts from Laws made by a Commission held in 1416 at Forli in Italy[1]

In order that we may carry ourselves modestly and humbly before the Lord, our God, and to avoid arousing the envy of the Gentiles, we decree that until the end of the above-mentioned term (ten years, 1416–26) no Jew or Jewess shall be permitted to make a *foderato-cinto*, unless it be black, and that the sleeves shall be open and that the sleeves shall have no silk lining whatever on them. Those who already possess such cloaks *(foderato-cinto)* of any colour other than black, may continue to wear them, provided the sleeves are not open, and the cloaks are closed both in the front and back.

Neither shall any man or woman wear any cloak of sable or ermine or mixed fur or of red material of mixed colour or of muslin or of violet colour. However, a cloak lined with fur may be worn, if none of the fur is placed on the outer covering of the cloak.

Women's cloaks which have already been made with open sleeves and are lined with fur, may be worn within the house but not in public, unless the sleeves are sewn or the cloaks are worn under an overcoat, so that the cloak cannot be seen at all. Also the coats of women which are lined with fur, must as far as possible be so made so as not to show the fur.

No man shall be permitted to wear a silk or velvet *giubetta* (cloak) except in such manner that it is completely concealed. Neither shall women wear any silk or velvet dress except in such manner that it is completely concealed. Neither shall they wear any dress having fringes attached to it other than at the opening of the neck or the sleeves.

No woman shall wear any necklace on her neck or a gold hair-net on her head unless it be concealed except that newly-married brides may wear golden hair-nets unconcealed for thirty days after the wedding; after that time they must wear the veil over the net. No girdle which has a silver buckle more than six ounces in weight, or which is covered with velvet in any form, shall be worn by men in public.

No more than one gold ring may be worn by a man, but the ring may be placed on any finger. Women shall under no circumstances wear more than two or three rings.

Neither shall women wear a girdle or belt the silver of which weighs more than ten ounces.

The fine for the transgression of any of these provisions regarding the use of clothes and ornaments shall be ten Bolognini of silver or their value for the treasury of the city for each offence. Men shall be held responsible for the infractions of these rules by their wives. If anyone refuses to obey the ordinances, the community shall refuse to admit him to *minyan* or to read the Torah or to perform the *Gelilah*.

We have also decreed that it shall be prohibited for more than three ladies and two maids to walk together in the streets except in the performance of some religious duty. Nor shall it be permitted for women to promenade through the streets and avenues except on festival days, when they shall be limited in the said manner. Men shall be held responsible for the observance of this section by their wives as in the case of the dresses.

Extracts from Laws made by a Synod of Castilian Jews convened at Valladolid in 1432[2]

No woman unless unmarried or a bride in the first year of her marriage, shall wear costly dresses of gold-cloth, or olive coloured material or fine linen or silk, or of fine wool. Neither shall they wear on their dresses trimmings of velvet or brocade or olive-coloured cloth. Nor shall they wear a golden brooch nor one of pearls, nor a string of pearls on the forehead, nor dresses with trails

[1] Finkelstein, 292–3.　　　　[2] Finkelstein, 373–4

on the ground more than one third of a *vara* in measure, nor fringed Moorish garments, nor coats with high collars, nor cloth of a high reddish colour, nor a skirt of *bermeia* thread, except as for the skirt and stockings, nor shall they make wide sleeves on the Moorish garments of more than two palms in width, but they may wear jewellery like silver brooches and silver belts provided that there is not more than four ounces of silver on any of them.

No son of Israel of the age of fifteen or more shall wear any cloak of gold-thread, olive-coloured material or silk, or any cloak trimmed with gold or olive-coloured material or silk, nor a cloak with rich trimmings nor with trimmings of olive-coloured or gold cloth.

This prohibition does not include the clothes worn at a time of festivity or at the reception of a lord or a lady, nor at balls or similar social occasions.

Because of the diversity of custom among the Communities in regard to the wearing apparel, we find it impracticable to make a general ordinance which shall provide for all the details that ought to be included, and we therefore ordain that each Community shall make such ordinances on the subject so long as this Ordinance endures, as will keep before their minds that we are in Dispersion because of our sins, and if they desire to establish more rigorous rules than this they have the power to do so.

Extracts from Sumptuary Laws of the Jewish Community of Metz
published the 1st day of Ellul 5450 (1690)[3]

GENTLEMEN:

I have been instructed by the 9 honourable members of the Executive Commission to publish the articles of the following law which the Special Committee of 12 members has discussed and adopted.[4]

The public is warned that no one will be allowed to plead ignorance of the law as an excuse; for that reason it is published afresh drawing attention to the fact that no excuse will be accepted and that the penalties will not be waived for anyone.

Also remember gentlemen and let it be emphasized that the publication of this law is ordered in order to remove the slightest possible excuse.

No women may wear on Saturdays or festive occasions more than 4 rings. Godmothers, midwives, those who conduct the bride under the *chupah*, those who conduct her to the synagogue for the morning prayers and the young bride herself on the Saturday following her marriage are allowed to wear more than 4 rings. Likewise the godmother, the mother on the wedding anniversary, the woman who accompanies the bride to synagogue on the morning of the wedding and she herself on the first Saturday following the wedding until leaving the synagogue; also the woman who accompanies the bride under the *chupah* from the time her *flechten* (head-dress) is put on until after the wedding ceremony.

Large or small diamonds, even imitation ones, whether solitaire or set with other stones are forbidden to everyone, men, women and young people whatever their position, even during religious ceremonies.

Gold belts, gold chains, large or small, gold coins, precious stones or pearls worn round the neck or on the arms or ears are completely forbidden. But a betrothed woman may wear any of these jewels received as a present on the first Saturday only.

Gold and silver bracelets and gold belts are expressly forbidden except to godmothers, the women who accompany the bride to the synagogue, those who accompany her there on the

---

[3] Original in Yiddish. Translated from the French version in *Annuaire de la Société des Etudes Juives*, Paris, 1880, i: 77 ff.
[4] The Committee of Twelve *(Commission des Douze)* was responsible for framing the laws and the Committee of Nine *(Commission des Neuf)* for enforcing them.

morning of the wedding and to midwives who are allowed to wear them up to the time they leave the synagogue. The women who accompany the bride under the *chupah* may wear them from the time she puts on her head-dress until returning from the ceremony. The young bride is allowed to wear them on the first Saturday following the wedding for the whole day.

On Saturdays and festive occasions women are allowed to wear only ordinary veils. Godmothers are allowed to wear others only on the evening before a circumcision or the Saturday following the birth of a boy. Veils of gold or silver are expressly forbidden, except on the Saturday preceding a wedding, to the mother of the bride, her mother-in-law, sisters, sisters-in-law, grandmothers and aunts. This privilege lasts for the two days before the wedding and extends to women who conduct the bride to the synagogue on the morning of the wedding and those who accompany her under the *chupah*.

But veils spangled with gold or pearls are permitted only to godmothers or women who accompany the bride to the synagogue on the morning of her wedding or to the bride herself on the Saturday following the wedding up to the time she leaves the synagogue. The women who accompany the bride under the *chupah* are also allowed to wear them from the moment they begin to put on the bride's head-dress until returning from the synagogue.

Midwives are allowed to wear gold or silver veils, gold belts or gold bracelets only up to the time they leave the synagogue. The same applies to the mother of a *Bar Mitzvah*.

No unmarried woman may wear a head-dress spangled with gold or with pearls except a betrothed girl on the first Saturday following the ceremony when the betrothal becomes definite and subject to a pledge. She may also do so on the two Saturdays following but only until just after the dance. On returning from the dance she must immediately take off her coiffure spangled with gold or pearls and in any case she is forbidden to go out in this attire on the Rhinport (the quay of the Moselle).

Expectant mothers and the young bride during the wedding week (who are allowed to wear all the ornaments and clothing otherwise forbidden) may not sit in front of the entrances to their houses or in the streets nor stand up or sit in front of the windows so dressed if they can be seen outside.

All coiffures made to imitate non-Jewish fashions like *godrons, en cheveux, fontanges,* are strictly forbidden but young girls under 12 years of age are allowed to wear *en cheveux* coiffures.

All ribbons of silk or taffeta of any colour except black are expressly forbidden; ribbons of silk or taffeta which women and young girls tie round their waist even black are completely forbidden but crowns and bows on these crowns are allowed whatever the material; also black ribbons worn round the neck or on the cornettes (head-dress).

Bows which women and young girls put on *juste-au-corps* or on *jaquettes* are completely forbidden whether made of ribbons of silk or taffeta and regardless of colour even black.

Manteaux plissés (pleated coats) are completely forbidden for women and young girls.

Pingwoi are forbidden for women and young girls except those under 12 years of age.

Brocades of all kinds and colours or silk material embroidered with flowers regardless of the shade are forbidden except for religious ceremonies. Nevertheless for corsages and sleeves these materials are allowed.

But the gold or silver brocades or other materials with flower patterns in gold or silver are completely forbidden to everyone even for corsages and sleeves and religious ceremonies.

All kinds of lace, braid, fringes of gold or silver or in gold or silver thread are forbidden to everyone, men, women and children, whether for clothes or for shoes or other articles of attire but this does not apply to the caps of small boys or the bonnets of women and young girls. Unmarried servant girls are not allowed to wear lace of gold or silver even imitation but they may wear on their bonnets any other kind of lace.

Shoes of red or blue leather or any other colour except black and white are forbidden to everybody. The same applies to shoes of velvet or any other material *bordées* or *piquées*.

Aprons and *moscous* may not be decorated with lace higher than a quarter of a Metz ell, including the *biais*. This applies to women married or otherwise even during fêtes and religious ceremonies.

All married women must wear top coats in the synagogue on all occasions under a penalty of one *reichsthaler*. A newly married woman is allowed in the synagogue without a top coat for the first month following her wedding.

No woman whether married or otherwise is allowed to wear two or more skirts one over the other the colours of which are different under a penalty of one *ducat*.

All wigs are forbidden to young and old alike if they are longer than those worn by priests under a penalty of one *ducat*.[5]

Buttons made of silver thread are forbidden under a penalty of one *ducat*. Those in use at the time when this law is published are permitted until the clothes are worn out.

The borders of women's coats may not exceed one quarter of a Metz ell or a little more including the lace. Moreover this type of coat is not allowed on Saturdays or festive occasions. Coats already in use which have deeper borders may be worn on ceremonial occasions and fetes.

In any case nothing spangled with gold is allowed except on ceremonial occasions under a penalty of one *ducat*.

The present law applies to everyone, men, women and children with the exception of the honourable syndics[6] and administrators, their wives, sons and unmarried daughters to whom the Articles 1, 5, 9, 10–14, 17, 24, 25, 27 and those following do not apply. But the prohibition of diamonds, gold chains, veils and borders spangled with gold or with pearls, the coiffures called *godrons* and *fontanges*, gold lace, lace wider than a quarter of a Metz ell applies to the syndics and their family as to everyone else. They are also forbidden to wear brocades, gold belts, coins, precious stones and pearls on the neck or arms.

This law also applies to all who intend to settle at Metz even for three months. They are obliged to conform from the time they arrive in the town.

It is further ordered that during week-days clothes made of velvet, silk or taffeta are forbidden regardless of colour and no matter who the person is and whether man, woman or child excepting only little velvet caps for boys and bonnets of velvet or silk for little girls which are allowed.

Any infringement of this article will be punished by a fine of one *ducat*. False sleeves and cuffs in the materials above mentioned are allowed.

No woman may walk in the streets with her collar open under a penalty of one *schilling*. Still more is it forbidden to enter the synagogue dressed in this way.

Signed: MOISE, Chamass

Additional Sumptuary Laws of the Jewish Community of Metz
published the 12th day of Nissan 5451 (1691)

GENTLEMEN:

I am instructed to publish the following in the name of the *Commission des Douze*:

Whereas a law has been made on the subject of dress and whereas new fashions are continually being introduced for women so that they are now wearing very wide trimmings with pendants and fringes and lace or braid between the trimmings and that sometimes there are even two rows of lace: therefore it is publicly announced that all these new fashions are forbidden and that the law made on the 1st Elloul 5450 must be obeyed under a penalty of one *ducat* for each offence; the

---

[5] During the seventeenth century Catholic priests were permitted to wear only very short wigs.

[6] The *Syndics*, seven in number, formed the supreme council of the community.

same penalties still apply to veils which are too large or do not comply with the law or are decorated with lace exceeding the amount then allowed.

Marten and any other kind of fur which married women and young girls wear round their neck is equally forbidden under a penalty of one *ducat* but children may still wear it.

It has also come to the knowledge of the Council that slanderous statements are being made about the honourable members of the *Commission des Neuf* on the subject of the enforcement of these laws. The community is therefore notified that such conduct must not be repeated and that if any person continues to spread these stories he will have to pay immediately a fine of one *ducat* in addition to any other penalties ordered by the *Commission des Neuf*.

The *Commission des Neuf* wishes to draw particular attention to this regulation and will not remit any part of the penalties.

Therefore let everyone be warned and take care.

Published the 12th day of Nissan 5451 (1691) by order of the *Commission des Douze*.

Signed: MOISE, Chamass

Additional Sumptuary Laws of the Jewish Community of Metz published 4th Tammouz 5452 (1692)

GENTLEMEN:

I am ordered to publish the following in the names of the syndics and council of the community with whom are joined certain private members.

Whereas it has come to our knowledge that many women have their veils embroidered by non-Jews which may arouse great jealousy and animosity because formerly non-Jews were under the impression that the gold which Jewish women wore on their dress was imitation and now they know that it is real. Therefore it is announced that as from today no one, man, woman or child may directly or indirectly have veils, bonnets, coat borders or any other part of their dress embroidered by non-Jews. Any work sent out to be done by non-Jews must immediately be returned under a penalty of 20 *reichsthaler*.

I am also instructed by the *Commission des Douze* that they had considered not applying the preceding requirements to midwives, godmothers, women who conduct the bride under the *chupah*, to brides during the celebration of their marriage or the following Saturday and to mothers of a *Bar Mitzvah*. But at this moment the *Commission des Douze* has become aware of the pride, luxury and extravagance resulting from too much latitude to the extent that a large number of honourable merchants of this City are astonished at the display of luxury and wealth and their jealousy is greatly aroused against the Jews wherefore the 12 honourable members of the Commission have decided to make the following regulations:

From today and for a whole year neither midwives nor godmothers nor the others previously mentioned, may wear veils of gold or spangled with gold still less those with pearls but only plain veils with ribbons and without braid. They may not wear more than 9 rings and no diamonds. For family celebrations they may wear their Sabbath coats only and not those reserved for festivals. No belts embroidered or set with precious stones or of gold nor *sibloness* belts. No gold, no bracelets, no chains round the neck. No clothing made of brocade whether corsage, plastron with sleeves, sleeves alone or still less any dress made entirely of this material.

No women, married or single, large or small, may wear short aprons imitating non-Jews nor scarlet coats (*manteaux ecarlates*) nor *juste-au-corps* decorated with taffeta inside or out; the same applies to dresses and coats.

In short what is forbidden to everyone in the former law made by the *Commission des Douze* is also forbidden for the period of one year to the people mentioned above for whom formerly an exception was made.

It will undoubtedly be necessary to make many further restrictions under the present circumstances but it has not been considered advisable to prohibit everything at one time.

All the offences mentioned above are subject to a penalty of one *ducat* for each offence exclusive of any other disciplinary measures which may be taken.

The Executive Commission is required to exercise an active surveillance in this matter and in no case will a fine be remitted.

This entire regulation will be inscribed in the communal register held by the *Commission des Neuf* in which the honourable members will enter the names of any offenders so that they are punished with the greatest possible severity.

Published in the synagogue by order of the council the 4th day of Tammouz 5452 (1692).

Signed: MOISE, Chamass

In 1694 the laws were revised. It was again emphasized that no fashionable coiffures were allowed. Even children were forbidden to wear ostrich feathers or fur in their hats but the council, the syndics and the physician were permitted to wear wigs of the largest size.

New regulations made in 1697 commence with a statement that the laws made in 1691 had been well received and considered fair and just. Nevertheless there was a growing tendency to neglect them and a greater trend than ever towards extravagant dress which offended Jews and non-Jews alike. Equally objectionable was the adoption of the new fashions introduced among non-Jews despite the requirement of Leviticus 18.3: 'You shall not walk in their ways'. The council therefore laid down new rules which were even stricter than those of 1691. All women except girls of fourteen or under were required to wear plain veils for synagogue and again any kind of tall coiffure worn by non-Jews was forbidden. Moreover anyone attending a ball in the town still had to conform to the dress regulations. Wigs were forbidden to young unmarried men except to hide a blemish on the head and men were not allowed to dance with their hats on.

The New Frankfurt Clothes Regulations[7]

By order of our holy community, on the instructions of the head of the community and other officials and with the consent of our excellent rabbi, whom God may keep, the following regulations were announced publicly on Thursday, 18 July 1715 in the old and new synagogues. These regulations are to be strictly observed from today for the next twenty full years.

The following regulations concerning the clothes of married and unmarried women are to be strictly observed under penalty of excommunication:

All clothes made of velvet or with gold or silver thread whether old or new, are forbidden. The same applies to *par terre* (down to the ground) clothes, with one exception. The mothers of the bride and bridegroom are allowed to wear old *par terre* clothes under the *chupah*.

From today women's clothes for Schabbes and feastdays must not be made of more than one colour. The material of which the clothes are made must not cost more than $2\frac{1}{2}$ thalers the stab. The clothes already made may be used by married and unmarried women in the following way. Clothing made of a material costing up to $3\frac{1}{2}$ florins per stab may be worn on Sabbath, even if it has more than one or two colours. Material costing from $3\frac{1}{2}$ florins up to 3 thalers per stab, may be worn only on feast-days. But clothing made of a material costing 3 thalers per stab and more is altogether forbidden in the same way as *par terre* garments.

On workdays no married or unmarried woman is allowed to wear silk clothes. Little silk caps of a single colour are allowed. Dressing gowns of silk, pleated skirts and skirts with frills are forbidden.

Married and unmarried women are forbidden to wear corselets or bodices without sleeves in the street under penalty of excommunication.

[7] Translated from the German version in Schudt iv, Part 3, 95 ff.

Night coats (night gowns), housecoats of silk or cotton and Leipzig caps (fur caps of marten or sable) may be worn at home, but not outside the house. Unmarried women are forbidden to wear any of these coats even in the house.

Short aprons are completely forbidden under penalty of excommunication. The same applies to curls, ringlets, false hair or powdered hair. *Fontanges* are forbidden to married and unmarried women under the same penalty.

Women, married and unmarried, are from now on forbidden to have shoes and slippers of any colour except black or with embroidery or coloured braid. But they may wear what they have got already.

Under penalty of excommunication, lace costing more than 1 florin the brabant ell (about 45 inches) is forbidden nor may it be acquired in exchange for other goods. Two kinds of lace may not be bought at the same time, nor lace together with other goods. (The reason for this prohibition is, that women might buy two kinds of lace, one cheap and one expensive or buy cheap material and expensive lace at the same time, in which case their expenditure as a whole would not exceed the permitted amount, but the lace would be of the forbidden kind.) Under the same penalty, not more than two Frankfurt ells may be used for a bonnet.

On kerchiefs and aprons no lace is allowed under the same penalty even if the garments are already made. But women are allowed to use the lace they have cut off kerchiefs and aprons, even if the lace had cost more than 1 florin for their bonnets, but not more than 2 Frankfurt ells may be used for the purpose.

Gold veils are forbidden under the same penalty. Only the mothers of the bridegroom and bride may wear them on the wedding day. But hat pins are completely forbidden under the same penalty.

Gold chains, gold belts and pendants made of precious stones are completely forbidden under the above penalty and still more so are earrings made of pearls or precious stones. Unmarried women are not allowed to wear rings of any kind.

Unmarried women should wear bonnets with black lace only. (Fine 4 thalers).

No maidservant may wear silk clothes on feast-days, Sabbaths or working days. If they transgress this law, they should be immediately removed from our community.

The head of the family and young men may not wear clothes lined with silk on workdays and less still silk clothes or silk coats on penalty of a fine of 20 thalers.

On Sabbaths and feast-days the head of the family should not wear a 'Schabbes-coat' made of silk, even if he already possesses one. Only young men, who own silk coats already may wear them. But no new silk coats may be made to measure for them or bought by them under penalty of excommunication and a fine of 20 thalers. The same applies to married men.

Coloured or white wigs are forbidden to men under penalty of excommunication.

No *Bar Mitzvah* should stand before the *Thora* wearing a wig. He should neither distribute nor send round cakes nor distribute shirts and collars. To the cantor, who has taught him, he may give a collar, but nothing else.

Heads of families and young men should not wear buttons made of spun silver or gold on their clothes. Young men should not wear on Schabbes waistcoats made of *drap d'oren* under penalty of excommunication and a fine of 10 thalers.

Nobody should wear a *tallith* made of silk on workdays (fine 2 thalers) nor may snuff be used in the synagogue. (Fine 4 thalers).

From now on *furbelows* (flounces: pleated borders of skirts) are forbidden on new clothes whether for married women for unmarried women or for small children. Anybody who breaks this regulation will be fined 20 thalers but whoever tries to keep it secret shall be treated as if a sacrilege had been committed.

Married and unmarried women are forbidden to wear—from top to toe—anything made of silver or gold material, anything trimmed with gold or silver, silver or gold braid or lace. They may wear hats and fur caps trimmed with gold or silver which they have already; but it is forbidden to make new hats or fur caps with gold trimmings. Lace on bonnets or breast kerchiefs is allowed.

Women are allowed hats or bonnets with one row of lace only: never a double row of lace nor high bonnets nor Berlin bonnets. The hats may not be ornamented with ribbons made into tassels or bows and no ribbon may be sewn on to the bonnet to tie it under the chin. Only a tape or cord may be used for that purpose.

Silk house-coats (*kuhr*-coats) are forbidden in two colours. Even the sashes with which they are tied must be of the same colour.

Housecoats or dressing gowns trimmed with lace or flounces are forbidden to married and unmarried women.

Velvet for dresses even for linings is forbidden to women and girls with the exception of black velvet. The bride may wear any kind of velvet under the *chupa* during her wedding. But the sashes, facings or cuffs on dresses may be made of velvet.

Bodices and neckerchiefs trimmed with lace are forbidden to women and girls, even to the bride on her wedding day; leg of mutton sleeves bordered with lace are forbidden to all women.

Diamonds, pearls or gold, even if imitation are forbidden to married and unmarried women. Only a ring may be worn. But the bride may wear any type of jewellery for her engagement feast and on her wedding day.

Collars or *palatins* (a kind of stole worn over low cut dresses to hide the *décolleté*) of sable, marten or emine are forbidden to married women and girls.

Dammel-platen are forbidden to married women but allowed to young girls on condition that they are not bordered with silver or gold.

Women and girls are allowed shoes and slippers made of black leather only without any additional ornament. Even the bridegroom must not give any other kind of footwear to his bride on her wedding day.

Polish skirts (short embroidered wide skirts), *cantouches*, boned skirts or crinolines, in short any type of skirt which is stiffened with a hoop of wire or bone or has been made stiff with other devices is forbidden to married and unmarried women. Even small children may not wear skirts of that kind.

Neckerchiefs embroidered with gold or silver are forbidden to married and unmarried women.

Married and unmarried women should not go from one place to the other, not even to Altona and not even on a working-day and definitely not to the market without top coats. They must not walk in the street or go to the synagogue on a Sabbath or feast-day without top coats; they are allowed however to walk as far as three doors away from their home without it, but not further.

Beauty-plasters on the face are forbidden to married women and girls, but they may be worn in the *dünne* (inside the arm).

Palatins (stoles which were often made of transparent material) are forbidden to married and unmarried women with one exception, that is, if they are made of black velvet without tassels or

---

[8] Original in Yiddish. Translated from the German version in *Mittheilungen des Vereins für Hamburgische Geschichte*, Hamburg, 1903 Part I, Nos. 3–4 (1902), 37–44.

silk fringes and definitely without silver or gold which must not be embroidered on the material or added to it in the form of a braid or border.

Gold and silver ribbons on *fontanges* and *flegen* are forbidden even to young girls.

It is forbidden for unmarried men and women to learn to dance. (Fine 20 thalers). Whoever breaks this law openly or in secret will be excommunicated as if he had committed a sacrilege.

No three women, married or unmarried and still less more than that number, should take a walk in the evening without rainwear; on Sabbath or feast-days no women, married or unmarried should sit in big groups in front of the door.

Hats ornamented with tassels or feathers, hats made of gold material even without tassels and lastly hats trimmed with silver or gold braid or lace are forbidden to girls and small children.

Women or girls who wear silk house coats of one colour, or simple dressing gowns in the house or put on wraps of gold material, or fur capes trimmed with gold or silver which they have acquired earlier (before the regulations) should under no circumstances go out in the street in them without top coats and without special covers for their caps. It is forbidden too to sit in any of these clothes in front of the door.

Topcoats with lace or braid are forbidden to married and unmarried women. New clothes of silk are also forbidden. It is forbidden to introduce any new fashion whatever it may be.

The godmother should bring the child to the synagogue with only two other women and they should wear topcoats even on a working day. They should not go to the synagogue in carriages except when it is raining very hard. They should not give any presents with the exception of swaddling clothes which must not be trimmed with silver or gold, because that has been forbidden since olden times.

No maid servant should wear gold or silver lace on her cap, nor shawls of silver or gold threaded material (*drap d'or*) nor bows or head-dress made of ribbons. She should not wear silk dresses and should not have any new embroidered skirts made for her. (Fine one thaler).

Wives and children of doctors are also subject to the laws and regulations cited above.

Silver and gold trimmings on coats and waistcoats, buttons made of silver and gold wire, gold materials (*drap d'or*) and velvet even for linings are forbidden to married and unmarried men. Only waistcoats of black velvet are allowed.

In all cases of death in the family which may God prevent women are not allowed to follow the coffin without a topcoat.

It is not permitted to travel in a carriage to a wedding. Only the bride and three bridesmaids may do so; all other guests are only allowed to use one if it is raining hard. Neither married nor unmarried women should go to a wedding without topcoats. This applies both ways to and from the synagogue. Neither the coachman nor the horses of the bridal carriage should be adorned with ribbons.

Anyone who breaks one of the above laws in which no fine is mentioned should pay the first time two thalers the second time four thalers. But if the law concerning diamonds, pearls and gold is broken the offender should pay the first time four thalers, the second time double the amount and the third time it will be left to the discretion of the people who administer the law to punish the offender according to their own judgement.

From to-day until further notice no silk dresses of two colours should be made for women with the exception of dark grey and brown. (Fine 20 thalers). Whoever offends openly or in secret will be excommunicated and treated as somebody who has sinned against God.

Moreover, nobody is allowed to make a crown or wreath for the bridegroom (not even as a present) to put on top of his *tallith* with which he covers his head. The *tallith* may be made only of white mohair with a four finger wide golden braid at the borders. The cap too must be made of silver white mohair and trimmed with a narrow silver braid or lace. In case the bride's dowry however amounts to 5000 thalers or more the bridegroom is allowed to wear whatever he pleases.

Whoever gives to his daughter 400 thaler or less for a dowry may not give her silk dresses. But if the parents of a girl who is betrothed have bought such clothes already they have to declare in public on their conscience that they have bought these things before the regulations came into force. Otherwise they will be fined ten thalers.

The presents from the bridegroom to the bride should be of the following value from now on. If the dowry is under 5000 thalers the bridegroom may not give any presents worth more than 5% of the dowry. The bride may not give anything worth more than 2% of this amount. If the dowry amounts to 5000 thalers or more the bridegroom may give as much as he likes. Whoever breaks this law will be fined 100 thalers. But whoever employs cunning or trickery in these matters will be excommunicated as if he had sinned against God.

Given in the year 1715

Sumptuary Laws of Carpentras, 26 Heshvan 5499 (9 November 1738)[9]

We, the undersigned, observing the envy of people, how everyone strives to outdo his friend, so that rich and poor cannot be distinguished and all want to look important and wealthy, both in their clothes and their jewellery, and women who cannot afford it, borrow money from Gentiles and become impoverished . . . we have fasted for three days to mend our ways . . . On Saturday night, Parashat Leikh Lekha, on the 12th day of the month of Marcheshvan, there were gathered the elders and members of the community, and others, apart from Moshe Drukomoartino, who is ill, and Jacob Nakit, who was not in the synagogue because of his age, and it was decided to appoint seven representatives of the community who decreed the following changes against which there will be no appeal.

No man, whether married or single, may wear a wig which is not completely round and it may not have a ribbon, curl, a bag enclosing the tail or powder. But the first powder, which is needed for combing it is allowed. Also, no man, whether married or single is allowed to wear any garment apart from an *elbuf* and over it a *carcassonne*. For summer clothes, they are allowed to wear only a *camelot de boursal,* an *estamina,* an *estimina de bougin* and a *camelot* of hair over it and no other *samura* of wool and silk. No garments of silk or lined with silk are allowed and above all, no silver nor gold, whether on the buttons or the buttonholes. Those who already have garments which we have forbidden, will be allowed to wear them as long as they last, but they may not have on them gold or silver and the silk cuff or facing must be removed. Garments made of silk or lined with silk may be worn as long as they last.

A man, whether married or single, may buy secondhand garments of the kind forbidden provided there is neither gold nor silver on them.

No short decorative waistcoat may be made called *coureuse* and no waistcoat for girls called *basin de flandres*, whether short or long. *Justaucorps* may not be lined with muslin and the short waistcoats called *curosoa* may be worn provided the silk facing is taken off.

No man, married or single, may wear decorated cuffs on his garments or on his hands made of any kind of lace. Also, he is not allowed to wear a ring on his fingers, except a round golden one and if it has a stone it may not be a diamond or a stone of great value. Also it is forbidden to buy any new stockings of silk and shoes called *escarpins* (i.e. without heels) but those who have them already may wear them as long as they last. On no account may a silver buckle be worn on shoes or on garters but a silver button on cuffs is allowed. If a man is able to buy old silk stockings he may wear them.

[9] Translated from the Hebrew in C. Roth, *Sumptuary Laws of the Community of Carpentras,* in *Jewish Quarterly Review* 1928 xviii: No. 4.

No woman, whether married or single, is allowed to wear a garment of velvet with silk braid with a floral design or multi-coloured, whether new or old, and also no garment made of silk with flower designs in various colours. The *agagnau* (a divided mantle) and the *camisole* may be made of damask, of silk or any other material apart from velvet with flower designs without any silver or gold on them. Those who have cuffs or facings of silver or gold without plaits or lace may wear them but from now on may not pay more than one *écu* and three francs for each piece, and those who have laced bodices of velvet with silk braid or of a silk material with silver and gold flowers, may wear them provided there are no plaits or silver or gold lace on them and they must not be made of damask. Those bodices that are still permitted may not be worn without one camisole or robe. Unmarried girls who wear a band in their hair, whether of gold or silver may continue to wear one so long as it lasts but they may not buy any more bands of silver or gold. On no account are silk slippers allowed but those who have them already may wear them provided they take off the silver and gold.

No woman, whether married or single, is allowed more than two lace scarves nor may they make new ones until they are worn out, unless they wish to use them as a coif, in which case they may make two others. And those who already have more than two, may only use two until they are worn out, or unless they make a coif as mentioned above. But they may have as many other scarves with borders as they desire also two aprons with lace. They are also allowed to make *cubertas* and handkerchiefs with lace as they choose.

Unmarried girls are not allowed to wear a coif called *jouinessa* with a ribbon attached nor a ribbon in front of the bodice called *escala*.

A man's wife and daughters may not between them wear ornaments of silver or gold, diamond or other precious stones, on their neck, or on their arms or fingers exceeding 20 *écus* in value or pearls exceeding 100 *écus* in value.

They are allowed to wear a belt of silver and a *cornet* and three rings with not more than one diamond apart from the wedding ring which is called *signet* which is not included in the three. A gold clasp is allowed round the neck as well as golden earrings and a velvet collar. Boys and girls up to five years may wear all kinds of lace but garments with silver and gold on them are allowed only until they are worn out.

DRESS REGULATIONS OF THE JEWISH COMMUNITY AT FÜRTH[1]

1. It is forbidden for the head of the house, or a student or a young man, whether a resident or otherwise who has free meals or gets free board, to wear a tunic made of cloth of gold or brocade with silver or golden flowers, either on the Sabbath or a feast day, or a working day. Those who already possess such garments may not go out in them, nor are they permitted to have new ones made. Anyone breaking this law, must pay two Imperial thalers for alms. If he refuses to pay, it will be possible to enforce the penalty.

[*The author comments:* Rules and regulations about clothes to be worn by the Jewish people are indeed necessary, for splendour and wantonness in clothing among them are increasing daily. He who truly knows this people also knows that they, like others, are keen on new fashions. It is scarcely conceivable that it is necessary to forbid the Jews to wear cloth of gold and brocades, since these precious materials are being worn only by the most distinguished people. But experience shows that it is necessary to curb their excessive pride. The Dress Regulations described here

---

[1] Translated from the German. From Wurfel part 2 '*Takanoth* of the Jews of Fürth. Instructions by the Jewish elders in connection with ordinary and ritual meals, the presentation of [bridal] belts, wedding feasts, the pouring of wine, wedding presents, dress etc. and how much they may spend. Translated into German [from Yiddish?] and annotated'. Notes on rabbinic literature kindly supplied by Mr Raphael Loewe.

frequently serve to show how the Jews love extravagant clothes. True, they forbid many things which are too magnificent but they still permit other things which are meretricious. It will not be superfluous for me to quote from a number of clothes regulations contained in the Talmud p. 11: 'Thus Moses when he had to sacrifice for seven days when Aaron was elected priest wore an un-seamed dress, a dress woven in one piece'.[2]]

2. It is forbidden to have a synagogue cloak or other top coats newly made of damask. Those, however, who already possess such a cloak may wear it for circumcision in their family, or as godfathers, or at a wedding of one of their children.

[*The author comments*: The synagogue cloak is not dissimilar to a man's ordinary coat. They are obliged to wear these black cloaks when going to *shul* on the Sabbath day, also when they attend a circumcision, when they are godfathers, or have a wedding in their house. On the other hand, cloaks worn by women usually have collars and other ornaments made of velvet. They use them to hang over their most beautiful Sabbath dresses but so that they are covering only their backs.]

3. No unmarried person should wear a silk cloak, but those who already possess one may use it on Sabbath and feast days. However, on the Sabbath when the bridegroom gives presents to his bride he may wear a newly made silk cloak but no housefather may wear a silk cloak on a working day.

4. No head of a family should wear a velvet jacket newly made or bought secondhand but if he already owns one he may wear it. On the Sabbath day, he must cover it with his *shul* cloak, so that it cannot be seen. In the same way those who wear a jacket made of damask on a feast day must wear their *shul* cloak over it.

5. Neither the head of the family nor an unmarried man may wear silk stockings on working days but he may wear them on Sabbath and feast days. They may not have gold or silver clocks on their stockings, nor wear *bonnets* embroidered with silver or gold, nor *contouchen*, nor dressing gowns made of silk to wear in the street. Fur *bonnets* with some embroidery may be allowed.

6. Heads of families and unmarried men shall also not wear in the street silk coats or coats lined with *chagrin*[3] or silk of other kinds even if they already own such articles, and even more strictly is it forbidden to have them newly made or to buy them secondhand.

[*The author comments*: These rules often prove that Jews are required to dress more beautifully on Sabbath and feast days. It is true that this is caused by prosperity but among Jews, there is another reason. They believe that the Sabbath and feast days must be honoured through beautiful clothes and that God will be pleased by them. This once more confirms the saying that the Jews, on their Sabbath days, are striving only for carnal lust by giving pleasure to the eyes, and for a life of worldly pride, but never think of a proper rest from their sins. Clothing made of silk and velvet is much too sumptuous for the Jews, and their pride ought to be restricted even more than it is done by the regulations. What the Jews under paragraph (5) call *contouchen* for men means in their corrupted jargon, *casagiuns*.[4]]

7. People who wear wigs and are also obliged to wear them for *shul* must not have them powdered.

[*The author comments*: *Derech baijoscher*, p. 73, expressly forbids the saying of prayers in a wig.[5]

---

[2] T.B. *Ta'anith* 11b as interpreted by Rashi.

[3] Taffeta imitating shagreen.

[4] The *contouche*, which became very fashionable at the beginning of the eighteenth century, was a long cloak with sleeves worn by women as an over-dress both indoors and out. There was a short version popular in Germany known as *cossäcklein* which is probably the garment referred to here.

[5] *Derekh Hayashar* a popular moralistic work in Yiddish by Abraham Halevi Epstein (d. 1706). In the Frankfurt ed. wrongly dated 1685 in fact *c.* 1725 f.73a it is stated that false hair should not be worn during prayer or at any rate during the *Amidah* and that if worn at table it should be covered with a *kapele*. The Zohar (iii, 293a) is cited as ultimate authority for this but has in fact been misunderstood.

The regulations discussed here are not quite so strict, as they only forbid the powdering of wigs. Old Jews who want to appear devout only rarely pray in a wig but younger ones, without a feeling of shame, go to *shul* in their powdered wigs to pray, even on the most holy days.]

8. From now on no father of a family may wear on his *shul* cloak a clasp or buckle made of silver and whoever does not, within four days, remove such clasp from his *shul* cloak must pay three Imperial thalers to the alms fund, as a penalty.

9. In future, the *talles* should have no other ornament except white satin, damask, silver embroidery, or cloth of gold; everything else must be white. Also, on the holy Sabbath day, no *talles* made of silk should be worn, not even by the boy who has come of age, and the *talles* of such a boy must be white in the middle, including the ornaments but those who already have such a *talles* may wear it.

[*The author comments*: *Talles* is a shawl which the Jews place over their head when they pray in *shul*. The middle part covering the head is called *atira*, the crown, which is made of precious material, e.g. of cloth of gold or encrusted in addition with expensive pearls. Jews, in general, have two or three *talles*, of which the simplest is worn during the week, the next one on the Sabbath and the best on feast days.]

10. People must be recognised by their dress and therefore those who study must be distinguishable from other people and from servants. For that reason, the children of our community who study and strangers who study here, should wear collars. Those of our children who fail to observe this rule must not apply for a 'title' (diploma), and students who are strangers lose their free board.

[*The author comments*: There is no lack of clothing regulations for learned Jews, and the rabbis of the Talmud have laid down already several rules which I quote here: '. . . The present regulation also contains something about students' dress, viz. that they have to wear collars. All Jews, on the Sabbath, wear large collars on their *shul* cloaks, which reach down to the shoulders. During the week, however, not everybody is permitted to wear a collar. Students wear a small collar on weekdays, no matter whether they have a cloak or a jacket. This collar must always be worn by those who have obtained the title of *chofer*.[6] Those Jews who have obtained the 'Morenubrief',[7] or are in any other way of a learned profession, always wear a large collar. In this way, Jews are recognised by their dress and one can see who among them want to be known as learned men.']

11. It is forbidden to wear a red overcoat or *roquelaure*,[8] even if the latter is of a different colour, both in Fürth and in Nuremberg.

[*The author comments*: This rule proves the repugnance of Jews towards certain articles of clothing for no other reason than their hatred of all Christian customs. They have a general moral commandment to behave differently from Christians, and the hatred they bear the Christians does not allow them to become similar to them. The passage in *Aschle rebobhe*, p. 190, col. 2,[9] bears witness to this. 'You should not dress like Christians, you should not let your hair be cut like that of Christians, your houses should not be built like those of Christians, and the *roquelaure* which is so comfortable is forbidden precisely for this reason because it is being worn by Christians'. As these rules and regulations are no longer in force, we see that travelling Jews also wear *roquelaures*, but red as a colour is still very much avoided by them. I can refer, as proof, to the words contained in *Aschle rebobhe*, p. 168, col. 1[10]: 'should authority command the Jews to wear red laces or thongs in their

---

[6] i.e. *Haber*, a complimentary title sometimes conferred on learned persons who do not have rabbinical authority.

[7] Rabbinical diploma.

[8] Knee-length cloak with a single or double cape-collar buttoned down the front.

[9] *Ashley Ravrevey* i.e. *Shulhan Arukh* with commentaries ed. Fürth 1759f. 190b on *Yoreh De'ah* † 178 (laws against assimilating gentile customs). The basic *Shulhan Arukh* is not specific merely stating that clothing distinctively gentile should be avoided. The gloss of Moses Isserlis cites red as being a colour favoured by the aristocratic classes, to be avoided in favour of black as ought all immodest wear.

[10] Ibid. f. 168a on Y.D. † 157 refers to the extent of permissible conformity to avoid martyrdom. Wurfel's comment exaggerates certain details, in particular the matter of red or black shoelaces.

shoes, Jews should rather choose death, because it is Christians who wear red shoe laces, whilst Jews have black ones'. The fact that Jews believe red to be a cruel colour also contributed to their abhorrence of red. In our time, black as a colour is a favourite with the Jews, and they wear black clothes and cloaks when going to *shul*. Yet we sometimes see that especially women choose red as a colour for their ribbons and skirts.]

12. It is forbidden to take snuff or 'whole Presil' (Brazil tobacco?) either in the old or in the new or any other *shul* on a penalty of 4 Imperial thalers to be paid into the alms box.

[*The author comments*: As the Jews' vanity tolerates many things, it can be seen how they pull out their snuff boxes in *shul* and with frequent sniffing give their beards the most horrible colour, though the beard is the proud ornament both of the Jew and the billygoat.]

Clothes of Women and Girls

13. No woman should have made for herself a golden veil, or any veil studded with stars, or stars threaded through it, or with pearls, nor any fashionable bonnet of cloth or gold, or embroidered with silver or gold, or made out of golden or silver flowers. Those who already have them, are not allowed to wear them on the Sabbath or feast days, let alone during the week, except when they are godmothers, or go with the bride to her wedding, or lead a woman from her childbed to *shul*, or when their sons are thirteen years and one day old. Those who break this rule must pay, as first offenders, a fine of 2 Imperial thalers, the second time 4 thalers, and then 8 thalers.

[*The author comments*: Sumptuous clothing has greatly increased among Jewish women. Because of the hatred of Christian women, Jewish women's clothes are different in many ways. Proof for this is contained in *Kaf Haijoscher*, chapter 81,[11] where it says: 'As redemption of the Jewish people will come through pious women, they may not be dressed like Christian women'. This is why the present regulations speak of articles of dress, which are unknown to Christians.]

14. From now on, no woman, married or unmarried, should wear clothes made of velvet, cloth of gold, or clothes with braid, or with flowers of gold or silver, either woven into the material or embroidered. Of those who already have such clothes, only married women are allowed to wear them under the provisions of paragraph (13). Unmarried women are exempted from this prohibition only at the weddings of their brothers or sisters, but they must not have such clothes made new for them, or buy them.

15. A married woman may wear a cloak of damask on feast days but not on the Sabbath day, under the penalty named above. Those, however, who already own one of this kind and have worn it on Sabbath days, may continue to do so until it is worn out.

16. Crinolines are forbidden to married and unmarried women, as are also night gowns, *fontanges*, pinned up *mantou*,[12] long *contouches* or *andrien* and so are embroidered and trimmed shoes or slippers made of precious or cheap silver or gold or ribbons but they may be made only of black or coloured leather, under the same penalties.

---

[11] *Qav Ha'Yashar* of Sebi Hirsch b. Aaron Samuel Kaidenover, a popular moralistic—practical behaviour work. The author born at Wilna, died at Frankfurt 1712 where the first edition appeared in 1705. Citing the well-known Talmudic passage that one of the three reasons for the redemption from Egypt was the merit of the pious women, he emphasises the consequent importance of modesty in Jewish women even more than for men so that their children may be holy etc. and the exile not even further extended in duration. 'They should not ape gentile fashions as one has recently observed happening, thereby stimulating lascivious interest in [Jewish] men, Jewish women and gentiles being indistinguishable. They also thereby excite the ill-will of the gentile environment when they even out-do gentile women—we ought in exile to wear black, as being in mourning. So far from this, they walk about with fine, proud bearing and décolleté ('naked to their cleavage and nipples'). They moreover run their husbands into heavy expense, in order that their wives may keep up with others or even exasperate them by their importunities to get into debt or to misappropriate funds in order to dress them . . . the men are likewise shaving their beards in imitation of gentile habits . . .'

[12] The *mantua* or *manto* was a loose gown with a long train.

[*The author comments:* These regulations contain various rules about women's clothing, and it is unnecessary to go into more detail, as these things need not be explained further. Only the following I must mention: Not long ago, Jewish women developed a great liking for rain capes which are worn in Nuremberg. There was no objection to this, only the question arose whether such rain capes might be worn on the Sabbath. Some argued that they are a burden and therefore forbidden. Others believed that they could be considered as coats and therefore permitted. The community agreed on the following: a picture was painted of a woman wearing such a cape and this was sent to Poland to obtain the opinion of the Polish rabbis. The decision was that rain capes were forbidden and this resulted in the new fashion among Jewish women being abolished.]

17. Married and unmarried women must not wear necklaces of pearls, cut stones, or pendants and bracelets and buckles of precious stones or golden chains or belts studded with diamonds. From now on, they must not have such jewellery made, but those who already own them may wear them only on the days permitted by paragraph (13).

[*The author comments:* If Jews indulge in ostentation, this is certainly the case with gold and precious stones. Anyone with a slight acquaintance of the Jewish people knows how much they usually spend on such things. Therefore, it is only right and proper that this Set of Rules tries to abolish this excessive pride and it is unfortunate that this prohibition was not maintained.]

18. Married women may wear rings but unmarried women must not do so. Earrings are allowed to both but they must not cost more than 50 Imperial thalers. However, if a bride is given by the bridegroom something precious she may wear it until her wedding day.

19. Neither married nor unmarried women may walk in the street in a dressing gown but it may be worn at home provided it is not trimmed with lace. Even at home it is forbidden to wear a bodice, because it is a shameful habit to wear one without any other clothes over it.

[*The author comments:* It is surprising that this rule tries to make a difference between clothing that may be worn at home and that permitted in the street. Shameless dress must not be tolerated either at home or in the street. Therefore, a good rule is contained in Talmud Sabbath, p. 63, which says: 'What is forbidden in the sight of men is also forbidden in secret'.]

20. No gold belts may be worn, even if they are without precious stones. Belts made of silver are also forbidden, both for married and unmarried women but silver-mounted leather belts are allowed, so that it is possible to hang from them a silver key on the holy Sabbath day. Those, however, who already own the forbidden belts may wear them as set out in paragraph (13).

[*The author comments:* This is a general rule among Jews: What is an ornament to the body may be worn on Sabbath day, but whatever is not of this quality must not be worn. This is why Jewish women do not wear keys made of iron but only silver keys on the Sabbath because the latter are considered an ornament, the former a burden.]

21. No married or unmarried woman should wear a shawl or scarf with white lace trimming. Those who already own them may wear them only according to paragraph (13). From now on, they must not pay for lace more than one guilder for an ell.

22. From now on, neither married nor unmarried men or women should have clothes made for them, even for feast days, which are trimmed with silver or gold, nor should married or unmarried men wear buttons made of gold or silver thread, or of silk and silver and gold mixed. Those who, however, already own such clothes may use them till they wear out. Any breach of this law will be severely punished.

23. Married or unmarried women must not wear embroidered fur gloves, but if the embroidery is not wider than two fingers, it is allowed.

24. It is permitted to wear on the holy Sabbath day, gold or silver embroidered neckerchiefs costing up to two guilders, on feast days those costing up to three guilders. But on the days between two feasts, at new moon and on working days, the wearing of embroidered scarves is forbidden.

25. From now on, no female may wear at the new moon, let alone on working days, clothes made of taffeta or other silken material except petticoats or *contouches*.

26. Short aprons and beauty spots, except those plasters which, for health reasons, are laid upon the temples, are prohibited, and it is also forbidden to learn to dance.

[*The author comments:* Jewish women have a tendency towards any kind of vanity. As the scandalous fashion for short skirts became much too widespread, preventive measures were taken. Nowadays, we see Jewish women and girls walking up and down the streets in such questionable skirts. They patch up their faces with many beauty spots, on their necks they wear all sorts of gilt coins on long ribbons, and they do not care whether they dance with a Jew or a Christian, the main object is to show off and be wanton.]

27. These Clothing Regulations for women do not apply to what is permitted in *shul*. In the streets and on the way to Nuremberg, as well as there, they are allowed to wear silk dresses but no clothing made of damask.

APPENDIX 3 DOCUMENTS RELATING TO THE WEARING OF THE YELLOW HAT IN THE COMTAT VENAISSIN

(From *Revue des Etudes Juives* Vol. 36)

I

Extrait d'une Lettre écrite à Monseigneur Vignoli, évêque de Carpentras (en séjour à Rome.)
Carpentras, 5 juillet 1776.

... Nous vous prions très instamment de faire en sorte, avec votre zèle ordinaire, que Sa Sainteté nous rende justice au sujet de notre administration que Mgr le Cardinal Durini a trouvé bon de critiquer, dans tout le public, sans avoir daigné nous entendre, de l'éclaircir et d'obtenir encore de la bienfaisance de notre souverain qu'il rejette l'instance que les Juifs font pour obtenir le chapeau noir contre les titres les plus sacrés et les plus authentiques dont votre grandeur trouvera ici copie (Suivent les bulles de Clément VII et de Pie V).   *Les élus du pays.*

(Archives de Vaucluse, C. 41, f 1006)

II

Assemblée ordinaire du pays: 12 juillet 1776.

... En laquelle il a été fait lecture du mémoire qui a été dressé, à la suite de la délibération prise par l'assemblée ordinaire du deux du courant, au sujet de la demande faite par les Juifs de pouvoir quitter entièrement le chapeau jaune pour prendre le chapeau noir avec une pièce d'étoffe au-dessus.

Après laquelle lecture, ledit mémoire ayant été approuvé par ladite assemblée, elle a délibéré de l'enregistrer à la suite des présentes et d'en envoyer une copie à M. Celestini, agent du pays en la Cour de Rome, afin qu'il en fasse l'usage convenable en employant même les avocats qu'il croira nécessaires afin d'empêcher l'effet de la demande des Juifs.

(Archives de Vaucluse, C. 42, f11)

III

Extrait du mémoire des Etats du Conseil Venaissin au sujet des Juifs qui y sont établis.

... Comme la tête est la partie la plus apparente du corps, c'est aussi sur la tête qu'on a eu l'attention d'ordonner que soit placé le signe distinctif. Paul IV, dans sa constitution du 12 juillet 1555, ordonne très expressément que les Juifs porteront le bonnet ou chapeau jaune et les Juives une autre marque sur la tête qui ne puisse être cachée en aucune manière. Ce souverain pontife comprenait combien l'obligation imposée aux Juifs de porter le chapeau jaune était nécessaire, puisqu'il défendait à tous les légats, présidents et vice-légats de les en dispenser.

Le saint pape Pie V, confirmant, par sa constitution du 18 avril 1566, celle de Paul IV, ordonne très expressément que, pour ôter toute équivoque, le bonnet ou chapeau des Juifs doit être en couleur jaune.

Le premier concile de Milan, rapporté dans le volume XV des conciles généraux part. IV, page 332, *De Judeis*, fit la même ordonnance sur le chapeau jaune. Nous pourrions citer bien d'autres lois générales également précises et respectables par lesquelles il est ordonné que les Juifs seront obligés de porter le chapeau jaune, mais, pour raison de brièveté, nous nous attacherons surtout a celles qui ont été expressément et particulièrement faites pour les Juifs d'Avignon et du Comté Venaissin.

Nous voyons dans le statut d'Avignon que, conformément à la disposition des constitutions apostoliques, il est ordonné que pour que les Juifs puissent être distingués des chrétiens, ils seront obligés de porter le chapeau de couleur jaune et les Juives un signe sur la tête de même couleur

(Livre I, Rubric. 34, art. V). Ce qui est disposé à cet égard par les souverains pontifes relativement aux Juifs établis a Carpentras et dans le Comté Vanaissin n'est pas moins clair. Pie II, dans sa bulle datée de Mantoue du 5ᵉ janvier 1459, voulant pourvoir aux avantages des habitants de Carpentras et à ceux du Comté Venaissin, daigna confirmer ce qu'il avait établi dans une autre de ses constitutions, que les Juifs de Carpentras et du comté Venaissin osaient enfreindre, et il ordonnait en même temps que les Juifs porteraient une raie ou un autre signe de couleur jaune si grand et d'une telle largeur qu'il dût être vu du dedans et du dehors de l'habit.

Mais les Juifs de Carpentras et d'Avignon ne tardèrent pas d'éluder des ordres aussi précis et aussi nécessaires; ils s'appliquèrent aussitôt à cacher le signe prescrit par Pie II, et a trouver par là le moyen d'être moins distingués des chrétiens. Les habitants du pays furent obligés de recourir de nouveau au Saint-Siège.

Le pape Clément VII ne tarda pas d'avoir égard à des plaintes aussi justes; il fit une constitution datée de Rome du 13 juin 1525. On voit dans cette bulle: 1º que les Juifs établis dans Avignon, Carpentras et dans les autres villes du Comté Venaissin, poussés par leur propre témérité et enflés d'orgueil, affectaient de porter les habits des chrétiens et de marcher comme les chrétiens eux-mêmes et qu'ils osaient quitter ou cacher la marque qu'ils devaient porter sur la poitrine; 2º le souverain pontife, voulant réprimer un pareil attentat, et croyant nécessaire d'employer des précautions propices pour que les Juifs fussent parfaitement distingués de tous les chrétiens, ordonne que, sans exception ni retard et sous peine de cent ducats d'or, payables à chaque con-trevenant, et en cas d'insolvabilité par la communauté des Juifs, les mêmes Juifs établis dans Avignon, Carpentras et le Comté Venaissin eussent à prendre le chapeau jaune ou bonnet jaune sans oser le quitter.

A la vue de titres aussi clairs du souverain lui-même, qui aurait pu croire que les Juifs d'Avignon et du Comté eussent la présomption de s'y soustraire? C'est pourtant ce qu'on vient de voir au très grand scandale des chrétiens et surtout des gens de bien.

D'abord, comme ils ont en horreur la couleur jaune, sans doute par cela seul qu'il leur est ordonné précisément de la porter, quelques-uns des Juifs avaient commencé à porter le chapeau d'une couleur tirant sur le rouge de sorte qu'on voyait une partie des Juifs, c'est-a-dire les riches et les jeunes fanfarons, portant des chapeaux rougeâtres très élégamment ajustés, tandis que les pauvres et quelques vieux tant seulement conservaient le chapeau de couleur totalement jaune. Nous savons que dès lors, les supérieurs animés d'un saint zèle contre un pareil abus avaient pris le moyen de le faire cesser et de remettre les constitutions apostoliques dans leur parfaite et étroite exécution. Mais la prise du Comtat et d'Avignon qui survint, dans ces circonstances, empêcha l'heureux effet d'un dessein aussi juste et aussi louable.

Les Juifs n'ont pas laissé échapper le temps de la domination française pour tâcher de la mettre à profit et se soustraire au chapeau jaune, sinon en tout du moins en partie, mais grâce au zéle des administrateurs publics, ils n'ont rien pu obtenir.

On se flattait qu'enfin le pays étant retourné sous la domination du saint siège, tout reviendrait dans l'ordre primitif, mais combien les chrétiens ont été trompés dans leurs espérances! Ce retour si désiré n'a pas été plutôt arrivé que l'on a vu les Juifs quitter totalement le chapeau jaune et prendre le chapeau noir comme les chrétiens, se contentant seulement de mettre un morceau d'étoffe sur la forme du chapeau, et, qui plus est, les chrétiens ont la douleur d'apprendre que les Juifs remplis comme à l'ordinaire d'espérances les plus flatteuses, comptant sur des protecteurs qu'ils n'ont que trop souvent l'art de surprendre, font à Rome les plus grands efforts pour obtenir cette fatale permission qu'ils désirent avec tant d'ardeur de quitter le chapeau jaune et de prendre le chapeau noir avec la seule pièce d'étoffe sur la forme du chapeau, affectant d'insinuer que la pièce d'étoffe est une marque suffisante pour les faire distinguer des chrétiens (Suit une série de compliments au pape et l'énumération des raisons nécessitant le maintien du chapeau jaune).

. . . Il est difficile d'imaginer quels sont les motifs sur lesquels les Juifs peuvent se fonder pour oser se flatter qu'ils pourront réussir a obtenir le renversement de tant de constitutions apostoliques. Nous apprenons que ces prétextes sont au nombre de deux.

En premier lieu, ils disent que la pièce d'étoffe appliquée sur la forme du chapeau noir est une marque suffisante pour les faire distinguer du chrétien ; ils n'ignorent pas que le statut d'Avignon les oblige à porter le chapeau jaune, et par cela, ils insinuent quel la fin pour laquelle le chapeau jaune a été ordonné aux Juifs qu'ils puissent être distingués des chrétiens. Ce sont les paroles du statut, et ils ajoutent que le pièce d'étoffe étant suffisante pour remplir cet objet, la disposition du statut en reste accomplie, sans qu'il soit nécessaire de recouvrir un chapeau jaune, lequel est non la fin du statut mais un simple moyen pour y parvenir qui peut très bien être rempli par equipotens, c'est-à-dire par la simple pièce d'étoffe. C'est donc ainsi que, pour la première fois, les Juifs découvrent l'esprit de la loi, prétendent se soustraire à la lettre qui véritablement est meurtrière pour eux, ou pour mieux dire, c'est ainsi que, par le secours d'un simple sophisme, ils prétendent, éluder l'esprit et la lettre de la loi la plus claire. . .

. . . Mais on serait encore bien plus indigné contre les Juifs, si l'on avait vu la manière avec laquelle ils portent cette pièce.

1. En élevant les ailes du chapeau qui sont totalement noires, ils viennent à bout de cacher, dans sa plus grande partie ou même dans sa totalité, la pièce d'étoffe qui couvre à peine le dessus de la forme du chapeau.

2. Quand le Juif est grand et qu'il a son chapeau sur la tête il est impossible à ceux des chrétiens qui sont petits de stature de voir la pièce qui n'est que sur la partie supérieure de la forme du chapeau noir.

3. Les Juifs dédaignent même de porter cette pièce d'étoffe de couleur jaune ; ils la portent impunément de couleur grise ou blanche, il y en a même qui se contentent d'y mettre un morceau de papier.

4. Ils ont l'adresse d'attacher cette pièce d'étoffe quelquefois avec de simples épingles, mais toujours si facile à pouvoir la détacher qu'ils l'ôtent quand ils veulent.

5. Il est aisé de concevoir que le chapeau jaune en tout temps et toute occasion est aperçu, mais que le chapeau noir, avec une simple pièce d'étoffe, ne l'est point, surtout lorsque le jour commence à faire place à la nuit. . .

. . . Nous savons bien, et nous ne le nions pas, que le port du chapeau jaune a été ordonné par la bulle de Clément VII, comme un distinctif qui doit exister entre les Juifs et les chrétiens, mais il faut convenir, en même temps, qu'il a été ordonné comme un distinctif seul suffisant pour un objet d'une aussi grande considération.

Il faut convenir encore que le chapeau jaune a été ordonné dans la bulle de Clément VII, comme une punition de leur infraction à la bulle de Pie II, en cachant malicieusement ou en cessant de porter la roue ou le signe jaune sur l'habit comme Pie II leur avait enjoint.

En second lieu, les Juifs d'Avignon et du Comtat, pour obtenir les fins d'une prétention aussi inouïe et à laquelle on n'aurait jamais dû s'attendre, ne manqueront pas d'alléguer l'exemple des Juifs de Rome, d'Ancône et d'autres états d'Italie qui tous ont le seul distinctif du chapeau noir avec la pièce d'étoffe. Nous respectons certainement tout ce que les princes trouvent bon d'ordonner dans leur état, à plus forte raison respectons-nous ce que les papes, nos augustes souverains, ordonnent dans le leur ; mais il nous sera permis de dire si quelque raison, quelque usage particulier rend suffisant à Rome le seul distinctif de la pièce d'étoffe, cette raison et cet usage n'existant pas dans le Comtat, on ne doit pas se servir de·ce qui se pratique à Rome pour en faire une loi pour Avignon et le Comtat.

Nous dirons plus, nous ajoutons qu'il y a dans Avignon et le Comtat, des raisons et des usages particuliers qui font que ce qui s'observe à Rome ne doit point affecter le Comtat et même que tout doit concourir à empêcher que la tolérance que l'on a à Rome pour les Juifs relativement au chapeau jaune ne soit admise dans le Comtat.

A Rome, les Juifs, en général, sont pauvres, avilis ; ils n'exercent point la mercature publiquement, ils sont bornés à la friperie, ils ne cherchent pas à se confondre, à se mêler avec les chrétiens, rien ne les engage à supprimer et à cacher leur distinctif, ils ne peuvent faire au chrétien aucune émulation, aucune jalousie.

Il en est tout autrement à Avignon et dans le Comtat, ils s'y sont emparés de tout le négoce, Leurs richesses, leur opulence sont passées au plus haut point. Non contents de rivaliser avec les chrétiens, ils s'efforcent même de les surpasser dans leurs parures, dans leurs bijoux et toute sorte de luxe ; ils affectent d'avoir des servantes et des valets chrétiens qu'ils emploient aux offices les plus bas ; ils abordent dans les villes sur les plus beaux chevaux ou dans des voitures dorées, le commerce et certains arts qu'ils exercent ne leur fournissent que trop d'occasions de fréquenter les maisons chrétiennes et d'y aller, même la nuit, contre la teneur des ordres les plus précis. Comblés de tant d'avantages, il n'y a qu'un seul objet qui les tienne en respect, les inquiète et les humilie : c'est le chapeau jaune. Leur grand but est donc de le secouer. Ils n'ont que trop facilement trouvé le moyen d'en venir à bout, depuis environ deux ans, en substituant au chapeau jaune le chapeau noir avec une pièce d'étoffe.

Mais ils n'ont pas tardé d'abuser d'une pareille permission, non seulement, ainsi qu'il a été ci-dessus observé, ils trouvent le moyen de cacher, en tout ou en partie, ce distinctif équivoque et de le rendre illusoire, mais il y en a qui par la qualité et la couleur de l'étoffe et par la manière dont ils la portent, paraissent vouloir en faire comme un ornement...

Nous ne croyons pas que les Juifs du Comtat et d'Avignon veuillent citer l'exemple des Juifs qui se trouvent en France et qui y portent publiquement le chapeau noir, car il suffirait d'observer qu'en France, non seulement les Juifs n'y vivent pas en communauté avec l'exercice libre et public de leur religion, mains encore, suivant les lois du royaume, ils ne peuvent et ne doivent y être tolérés en aucune manière. Si donc, contre la teneur de ces lois, il paraît quelques Juifs dans le royaume de France, ils doivent y paraître nécessairement à l'égal des chrétiens, comme n'y étant point connus, sans quoi ils devraient être soumis à toute la rigueur des lois. Ainsi il n'y a aucune comparaison à faire entre les communautés des Juifs dans le Comtat et les quelques Juifs qui peuvent être éparpillés en France.

(Archives de Vaucluse, C. 42, f 11.)

IV.

Assemblée ordinaire du pays.

L'an mil sept cent septante-six et le vingt novembre.

Le syndic a exposé qu'enfin le renouvellement de l'édit du Saint-Office touchant les Juifs vient d'arriver et d'être publié dans cette ville, qu'il est porté par l'article XX dudit Edit que Sa Sainteté adhère non seulement à la bulle de Paul IV, renouvelée par Pie V, mais spécialement au bref de Clément VII en date du 13 juin 1525, soit directement pour l'Etat d'Avignon et selon le statut de la même ville, Livre I, titre *De Judaeis*, Rubric 34, article 5, ordonne et commande que les Juifs de l'un et l'autre sexe qui habitent à présent ou habiteront dans les villes d'Avignon et Carpentras et dans le Comtat Venaissin soient obligés de porter la marque de couleur jaune, c'est-à dire que les hommes doivent porter le *chapeau tout de couleur jaune*, sans aucun voile ou bande par-dessus, et que les femmes doivent pareillement porter la marque de couleur jaune à découvert sur leur tête ; qu'il est porté par l'article XXI qu'à l'avenir on n'aura nul égard à aucune permission émanée de quelque tribunal que ce soit, ou de personnes de quelque dignité, grade ou office qu'ils puissent être, quoique vice-légat même d'Avignon, évêques, majordomes, cardinal, légat ou camerlingue de la Sainte Église. M. le syndic a ajouté en conséquence : les Juifs sont obligés de quitter le chapeau noir avec pièce d'étoffe et de reprendre le chapeau entièrement jaune.

(C. 42, f 81.)

V

Assemblée ordinaire du pays.

L'an mil sept cent septante sept et le second janvier.

. . . M. le syndic a encore exposé, à cette occasion, qu'il est venu à sa notice que les Juifs du Comté Venaissin et de la ville d'Avignon renouvellent leurs efforts à Rome pour obtenir la révocation du susdit édit et, en conséquence, qu'il leur soit permis de reprendre le chapeau de couleur noire avec le seul distinctif d'une pièce d'étoffe et qu'ils font même les offres les plus spécieuses pour obtenir cette grâce. M. le syndic croit inutile de remettre sous les yeux de cette assemblée les justes et puissants motifs qui l'ont engagé de faire à Rome, avec son zèle ordinaire, les représentations convenables. L'assemblée décide d'écrire des lettres à Mgr le cardinal Pallavicini, ministre et secrétaire d'État, et à son Eminence le cardinal Torrigiani, secrétaire de la sacrée congrégation du Saint-Office à Rome.

(C. 42, f 97)

VI

Assemblée générale des seigneurs et messieurs les élus, syndic et procureur général des trois états du Comté Venaissin.

. . . Suit un nouveau vote pour le maintien rigoureux du chapeau jaune.

(C. 42, f 136)

VII

Proclamation.

Nous, maire et officiers municipaux, en suite de la pétition faite par la société des Amis de la Constitution, à la demande de M. le Maire de Courthezon et de M. le commandant des Gardes nationales françaises, au nom desdits Gardes qui ont volé à notre secours en vertu de la délibération du Conseil général du jour d'hier et ensuite des principes de la sublime constitution française ordonnons aux Juifs de porter le chapeau noir, à peine de douze livres d'amende, faisons très expresse inhibition et défense à toutes personnes de les insulter, sous peine de douze livres d'amende, et déclarons que les pères seront responsables des insultes que pourront faire les enfants.

A Carpentras, dans la maison commune, ce 25 janvier 1791.

Signés: D'Aurel, *maire,* Damian, Barjavel, Flandrin, J. Escoffier, Allie l'ainé, Durand, J.-J. Esclargon, Ayme, Barjavel, *officiers municipaux.*

Notes

PART I

1 A striking example is the translation of 2 Samuel 15.30. According to the Authorised and Revised Versions David prayed with his head covered, while the New English Bible makes him bare-headed. All agree that he was bare-foot.

2 Exodus xxii:27

3 Exodus xii:34

4 Jeremiah xiii:2

5 Isaiah xx:2

6 Job xii:18

7 Genesis iii:21

8 Illustrated in *Anatolian Studies*, vi, London 1956

9 British Museum 118908

10 Deuteronomy xxii:5

11 Ezekiel xxiii:40

12 Isaiah iii: 18–23

13 Isaiah lxi:10. Jeremiah ii:32

14 Babylonian *gidlu* = a string.

15 See Isaiah xxvii:6 and xxviii:1, 4

16 The Septuagint renders it *huakinthos* i.e. hyacinth or blue

17 For a detailed study of Assyrian dress see T. A. Madhloom, *The Chronology of Neo-Assyrian Art*, London, 1970

18 Talmud B. Menahoth 41b–43b and see pp. 24–5

19 Talmud B. Menahoth 43a

20 See Parkes, 119 and 274

21 *A History of Jewish Costume*, 1967 ed. pl. 17. Other examples are to be found in the fifth century mosaics of the Church of S. Pudenziana, Rome.

22 Talmud B. Menahoth 6a and 39b

23 Compare also the specific statement by Josephus: 'let none of you wear raiment of wool and linen for that is reserved for the priests alone' (Josephus, Jewish Antiquities iv:211).

24 Terracotta prophylactic masks dating from about 500 B.C., with frontlets between the eyes, have been found in graves at Tharros in North Africa. There is an example in the British Museum and several are illustrated in Cintas.

25 Josephus, Jewish Antiquities iv:213. For a detailed study of the nature and history of *tefillin* see *The Jewish Encyclopaedia* s.v. 'Phylacteries'.

26 A. Scharf, *Byzantine Jewry*, London, 1971, 33.

27 Mishnah, Kethuboth vii:6

28 Talmud B. Kethuboth 72b

29 Talmud B. Berakoth 24a; Mishnah, Kethuboth ii: 10

30 'Apud Judaeos tam solenne est feminis eorum velamen capitis ut inde noscantur' *De Corona Militis*, iv.

31 Talmud B. Nazir 28b; Sanhedrin 112a; Arakin 7b

32 Isaiah iii:17

33 T. H. Gaster, 106

34 Nedarim iii:8

35 Talmud B. Berakoth 60b, referring to a *sudarium*.

36 1 Corinthians xi: 4–7

37 I. Abrahams, *Jewish Life*, 300–2; S. Krauss 'The Jewish rite of covering the head' in *Hebrew Union College Annual*, Vol. xix, 1945–46, pp. 121–168 and J. Z. Lauterbach 'Should one cover the head when participating in divine worship?' in *Year Book, Central Conference of American Rabbis*, Vol. xxxviii, 1928, pp. 589–603.

38 E. Paroda, *Ancient Iran*, London, 1965, pl. 12.

39 Ecclesiasticus 45:12

40 1 Maccabees 1:22

41 The general appearance of the High Priest including his hair and beard and the tailoring details of his dress are based on stone reliefs and steles of Shamshi-Adad V (823–810 B.C.), Sargon II (721–705 B.C.) and Ashur-Bani-Pal (668–624 B.C.) from Nimrud, Khorsabad and Nineveh. (See Parrot pls. 15, 43; Pritchard pl. 442 etc.). For gold chains see Ghirshman pl. 151. For *fibulae* and *bracteae* see Ghirshman pls. 373–380. For bell in shape of pomegranate see Ghirshman pl. 501.

42 Exodus 28:42

43 Exodus 28:39: 'the chequered tunic . . . of fine linen'.

44 Exodus 28:39. The high priest's sash was worn underneath the mantle of the *ephod* except when he entered the sanctuary (Leviticus 16:4). However, as according to Josephus both the *chiton* and its sash reached the ankles the extremities would have been visible and are shown on the drawing.

45 Exodus 28:31. If woven in one piece as described, the garment was a *colobium*.

46 Exodus 28:6. For shape and waistband of *ephod* cf. relief of Ashur-Bani-Pal (pls. 15–16).

47 In the Septuagint it is actually called an *epomis* which was a woman's bodice with a brooch fixed on each shoulder strap.

48 Exodus 28:15. The breastplate was folded to form a pouch in which were inserted the *urim* and *thummim*. For examples of gold pectorals see Ghirshman pls, 137, 360, 373–380.

49 Exodus 28: 36–39: 'the turban of fine linen' to which was attached a gold plate engraved 'Holy to the Lord'. The beginning of the inscription, engraved according to Josephus in ancient Hebrew characters, can be seen on the drawing.
The general form of the crown is based on that worn by King Mithridates Callicinus (1st century B.C.). R. N. Frye, *The Heritage of Persia*, London, 1962, pl. 87.

50 Zephaniah 1:8

51 Leviticus xviii:3

52 2 Maccabees iv:12

53 Josephus, Jewish Antiquities xx:216–8
54 1 Timothy ii:9. See also 1 Peter iii:3
55 Daniel iii:21
56 Jastrow also gives the alternative translation 'Persian trousers' but generally a cloak is indicated, e.g. 'Abaye went out in a worn *sarbal*'. (Talmud B. Mo'ed Katan 23a)
57 Talmud B. *Mo'ed Katan* 23a
58 Talmud B. Berakoth 60b
59 Yadin, 70–1
60 Talmud B. Shabbat 120a. Talmud J. Shabbat xvi:5. The essential garments numbered eighteen, counting pairs as two. The two lists vary slightly and are here combined.
61 John xix:23
62 John xx:7
63 A long *colobium* or *chiton* i.e. the *tunica talaris* was a sign of wealth.
64 Matthew ix:20; xiv:36; xxiii:5. Mark vi:56. Luke viii:44
65 i.e. *tsitsith*
66 Cloaks of great size distinguished in some way from the *himation*
67 See Goodenough, ix:171
68 Krauss 1, 143–7
69 Ecclesiastes ix:8, Revelation iv:4
70 Talmud B. Menahoth 41b–43b
71 Illustrated in Fakhry
72 See Kybalova, 141. There is also a fragment of the roundel illustrated here in the Victoria & Albert Museum and remnants of the tunic to which it belongs have a few symbols similar to Hebrew letters.
73 Yadin, 72 ff.
74 Talmud B. Kelim, Mishnah 7
75 Goodenough ix, 162–4 and figs. 132, 135, 145 and 151.
76 Talmud J. Shabbat 1:3
77 Talmud B. Sukkah 51b
78 Talmud B. Berakoth 60b
79 Although this conclusion seems inescapable to me it is not apparently accepted by Church historians. See *The Catholic Encyclopaedia*, New York, 1912, xiv:302.
80 In some communities it is worn only after marriage.
81 No medieval *tallith* has survived but most Jewish museums can show examples of more modern ones, some of them richly embroidered. The Victoria & Albert Museum has pieces of seventeenth century Italian needlepoint silk lace from a *tallith* (V & A 187–1874 etc.).

PART 2

1 2 Corinthians iii:14
2 According to Tritton the word in its plural form, *zunnarat*, which came into Arabic from Aramaic and Greek, became so closely identified with non-Moslems that it is used in modern Arabic to describe the Jews' side locks *(peoth)*.
3 Blue and black were regarded as the same colour.
4 Graetz iv:272. *Jewish Encyclopaedia* xii:280
5 Quoted by Marcus
6 Sandys, 7, 114–116
7 *Jewish Encyclopaedia* xii: s.v. 'Turkey'
8 De Thevenot, 264
9 Dandini, 282
10 Victoria & Albert Museum, Print Room. Ms. D. 374. 1890.93 B9. Green turbans were reserved for Moslems who had made the pilgrimage to Mecca.

11 Garnett, 13 ff.
12 Bartlett, 192–3
13 Finn, 190–1
14 Quoted by kind permission of Dr Phyllis Abrahams
15 Woodcock, 306–312
16 Woodcock, 43
17 Burnes, ii, 235
18 *Jewish Encyclopaedia* iii, 294
19 Krafft, 154–8
20 See *Jewish Chronicle* 1 September 1961
21 See A. Lancet 'Costumes de Mariage des Juifs de Sa'ana et leurs survivances en Israël' in *Actes du VIe Congrès International . . .* Paris, 1960,
22 Bacher, 262
23 Von Harff, 113
24 Benjamin, 283
25 Benjamin, 287–8
26 Noah, 311–2
27 Henry, 3rd Earl Bathurst (1762–1834), who was then secretary for war and the colonies, was active in the suppression of the slave trade and in the same year instructed the Mediterranean fleet to sail to Tunis in order to force the Bey to release Christian slaves. This action has in some accounts been confused with the 'European hat affair'.
28 Public Record Office F.O. 339/33 and F.O. 8/8.
29 Benjamin, 302
30 De Hesse-Warteg, 117–18, 129
31 Cohen, plates opposite pp. 56 and, 152
32 D'Arvieux, v, 285, 288
33 Lord, 98 ff. 127–8
34 The Victoria & Albert Museum possesses a *çârma* and other examples of Jewish North African dress.
35 Addison, 10–11
36 *A letter concerning the . . . the countries of Muley Arxid*, 1671. Quoted by Mendelssohn.
37 Lempriere, 185–6
38 Goulven, 32–3
39 Lawson, 120

PART 3

1 Strauss, 61. From the context the garment was evidently a head-dress.
2 Grayzel, 335
3 The decree ran as follows: 'Noi, Isabella Clara, arciduchessa d'Austria, duchessa di Mantova, Monferrato, ecc. ecc. . . Siano tenuti tutti gli Ebrei, niuno eccettuato, benche avesse particolare privilegio, ecc. ecc. a portare in questa citta e stato una *lista di filosello rancio sopra il capello*, non aggropata, ma unita di sopra e di sotto, si que resti in ogni parte in circonferenza senza potersi abbassare o piegare della medesima altezza . . . e si dovere in oltre portare sempre una beretta o capello rancio . . . Di Mantova, li 30 dicembre 1665,' (Robert, 78)
4 *Encyc. Judaica* IV 71–4
5 Lindo, 199 ff.
6 *Monumenta Judaica* B.313
7 Probably the same as the *viereckiger schleier* mentioned below. At Speyer and Frankfurt a/M in the fifteenth century the regulations required Jewish women to wear two blue stripes on their clothing as at Rome and veils were not mentioned (see *Monumenta Judaica*, B. 315, 319).
8 Platter, 81
9 Cf. illustrations from the fourteenth-century Persian

Ms., the Demotte *Shahnama*, in *The Times*, 2 December 1969 and an article by E. Schroeder in *Ars Islamica*, University of Michigan Press, Vol. VI, 1939, pp. 113–142.

10 This is in the later form. See R. Grunfeld, *Ein Gang Durch die Geschichte der Juden in Augsburg*, Augsburg, 1917.

11 Sibmacher. Cf. the arms of the English family of *Jew*: 'Argent a chevron between 3 Jews' heads couped at the shoulder proper' (B. Burke, *The General Armory*, London, 1878). A coat of arms on which the charges are 3 Jews' hats appears in a German fourteenth-century *machsor* in the Ambrosian Library, Milan.

12 Wurfel, 24, 31

The *gugel* (Lat. *cucullus*), otherwise *chaperon*, was the fashionable head-dress in Germany from the commencement of the thirteenth-century until the early part of the fifteenth century. Sometimes it had a long tail (liripipe) which was allowed to hang or could be wound round the head like a turban. The *kappe* was presumably a simpler version.

13 *Revue des Etudes Juives* xxxvi, 53 ff.

14 *Revue des Etudes Juives* xxxvii, 30 ff. *Jewish Encyclopaedia*

15 The *Shulhan Aruch*, the most important code of rabbinic Judaism, was written in the sixteenth century.

16 The Christian Church also had its Sumptuary Laws, which were designed to curb luxurious living and, particularly, feminine extravagance. As early as the thirteenth century in Venice special magistrates, *Provveditori Sopra Le Pompe*, were appointed to enforce the regulations while in England, under Edward III, offenders were dealt with by Act of Parliament. In Italy during the eighteenth century the dress restrictions framed by the Church were almost as severe as those issued by the synagogue authorities. (See M. Vaussard, *Daily Life in 18th century Italy*, London, 1962, 36 ff.)

In Germany there were frequent complaints that rich and poor dressed alike and the sumptuary laws of Bremen, Leipzig, Nuremberg and Augsburg and other cities were continually being re-enacted apparently with little success. (Max von Boehn, Vol. 2. English ed. 192 ff.)

17 Finkelstein, 233 ff.

18 Milano, 563–6

19 It was customary at this time for women to wear cloaks for church.

20 *Prammatica . . . Dall 'Ebrei Di Roma*, Rome, 1726. (Mocatta Library).

21 *Prammatica . . . Degli Ebrei D'Ancona*, Ancona, 1766. (Roth Collection).

22 *Prammatica . . . Degli Ebrei Di Modena*, Modena, 1790. (Author's collection).

23 Latin *sericum* = fine woven cotton; German *kittel* = smock or blouse.

24 Segal, 146–7

25 A kind of blouse with fur hem and long sleeves which were turned back to show the silk lining.

26 Buxtorf, 641, 648. Kirchner, 175, 184

PART 4

1 Dubnow, I, 77–8

2 *Jewish Encyclopaedia* viii, 126

3 As seen on an engraving of the Russian ambassadors and their staff at the Regensburg Congress of 1576. There is a framed copy in the London Library. Illustrations of medieval Polish costume are given in Eljasz.

4 For illustrations see Goldstein & Dresdner.

5 Similar attempts to compel Jews to adopt Western dress were made in Austrian Poland. The author has in his possession a Permission from the Austrian police at Lemberg dated 8th July 1840 for a Jewish oculist to live outside the ghetto provided he did not wear Jewish dress.

6 Hollaenderski, 224–5

7 Illustrations of both these items of dress appear in Goldstein & Dresdner and there are actual examples in the Museum of Ethnography, Tel-Aviv.

8 Johnson, 376–8

9 Macmichael, 44–7

10 Henderson, 325–6

PART 5

1 *The History of the Rites, Customs and Manner of Life of the Present Jews . . .* translated into English by Edmund Chilmead, London, 1650, 12–17.

2 Picart, 1733 ed., 246

3 Talmud B. *Hagigah* 14b

4 Skippon, 442

5 Schudt ii:241 ff. The author generally is completely unreliable but presumably in the case of Frankfurt he spoke from personal knowledge.

6 Ulrichs, 49–53

7 M. Grunwald, *Mattersdorf in Jahrbuch für jüdische Volkskunde*, Berlin–Wien, 1925, ii:477–8.

8 Hertzberg, 161, 164–5, 181, 212–3

9 Rubens (ii), pl. 1008

10 Rubens (ii), 2013

11 Hyamson, 19

12 See L. Hershkowitz and I. S. Meyer, *Letters of the Franks Family*, Waltham, Mass. 1968.

PART 6

1 *A History of Jewish Costume*, 1967 ed. pl. 123

2 Hyamson pl. facing p. 113

Bibliography

Abrahams, I. *Jewish Life in the Middle Ages*, London, 1932

Abrahams, Israel & Cook, S.A. in *Encyclopaedia Biblica*, 1899. s.v. Dress, Fringes, Mitre, Shoes, Tunic, Turban

Addison, L. *The Present State of the Jews*, London, 1675

Adler, E. N. *Jews in Many Lands*, London, 1905

Amira, K. von, *Die Dresdener Bilderhandschrift des Sachsenspiegels*, facsimile. Leipzig, 1902

Amira, K. von, *Die Dresdener Bilderhandschrift des Sachsenspiegels*, II: *Erläuterungen*, Part I. Leipzig, 1925

Aronius, J. *Regesten zur Geschichte der Juden in Fränkischen und Deutschen Reiche bis zum jahr 1273*, Berlin, 1887–1902

D'Arvieux, *Memoires du Chevalier D'Arvieux*, Paris, 1735

Bacher, W. *Un Episode de l'histoire des Juifs de Perse* in *Revue des Etudes Juives* XLVII

Barnett, R. D. *Four Sculptures from Amman* in *Annual of the Department of Antiquities of Jordan*, I, 1951

Baron, S. W. *A Social and Religious History of the Jews*. Vol. III. New York, 1957

Bartlett, W. H. *Walks about Jerusalem*, London, 1844

Bauer, J. *Le Chapeau Jaune Chez les Juifs Comtadins* in *Revue des Etudes Juives* XXXVI

Beauclerk, G. *Journey to Morocco*, London, 1828

Beck, J. J. *Tractatus de Juribus Judaeorum*, Nuremberg, 1731

Benjamin, J. J. *Eight Years in Asia and Africa from 1846 to 1855*, Hanover, 1863

Ben-Zvi, I. *The Exiled and The Redeemed*, Philadelphia, 1957

Berliner, A. *Aus Dem Leben Der Deutschen Juden im Mittelalter*, Berlin, 1900

Bertman, S. *Tasseled Garments in the Ancient East Mediterranean* in *The Bible Archaeologist*, Dec. 1961. Vol. XXIV, No. 4

Besancenot, J. *Costumes du Maroc*, Paris, 1942

Boeckler, A. *Die frühmittelalterlichen Bronzetüren*. Vol. III: *Die Bronzetür von Verona*. Marburg a.L., 1931

Boehn, M. von, *Die Mode. Menschen und Moden im Mittelalter . . .* Munich, 1925

Boener, J. A. *Kurze Bericht von dem Alterthum und Freyheiten des freyen Hof-Markts Furth*, 1705

Botta, M. P. E. *Monument de Ninive*, Paris, 1849

Bratton, F. G. *A History of the Bible*, London, 1961

British Museum. *Catalogue of the Ivory Carvings of the Christian Era*, London, 1919

British Museum. *Guide to the Early Christian and Byzantine Antiquities*, London, 1921

Brüll, A. *Trachten der Juden im Nachbiblischen Alterthume*, Frankfurt A/M, 1873

Bruyn, C. de, *Reizen*, Delft, 1698

Budge, E. A. W. *Amulets and Superstitions*, London, 1930

Burnes, A. *Travels in Bokhara in 1830*, London, 1837

Buxtorf, J. *Synagoga Judaica*, Basle, 1661 and Frankfurt, 1728

Cahen, A. *Règlements Somptuaires de la Communauté Juive de Metz a la Fin Du XVIIe Siècle* in *Annuaire de la Société des Etudes Juives* I, 1881

Chappelle, G. de La, *Recueil de divers Portraits* (Paris, 1650?)

Charles-Roux, J. *Le Costume en Provence*, Paris, 1907

Chishull, E. *Travels in Turkey and back to England*, London, 1747

Cintas, P. *Amulettes Puniques*, 1946, Pubs. de l'Institut Des Hautes Etudes de Tunis

Cohen, M. *Gli Ebrei in Libia*, Rome, 1932

Corson, R. *Fashions in Hair*, London, 1965

Coryat, T. *Coryat's Crudities*, Glasgow, 1905

Cunnington, C. W. & P. *Handbook of English Mediaeval Costume*, London, 1952. *Handbook of English Costume in the Eighteenth Century*, London, 1957. *A Dictionary of English Costume*, London, 1960

Curzon, G. N. *Persia and the Persian Question*, London, 1892

Dandini, J. *A Voyage to Mount Libanus*, London, 1811

Danon, A. *La Communauté Juive de Salonique Au XVIe Siècle* in *Revue des Etudes Juives* XL

Davenport, M. *The Book of Costume*, New York, 1948

Demidov, A. N. *Voyage dans la Russie Méridionale et la Crimée . . . Execute en 1837*, Paris, 1840. (Album of Plates . . . drawn and lithographed by Raffet, Paris, 1848)

Dodwell, C. R. *The Great Lambeth Bible*, London, 1959

Dubnow, S. M. *History of the Jews in Russia and Poland*, Philadelphia, 1916

Dubnow, S. *History of the Jews*, Vol. IV, New York, 1971

Dumas, A. *Tangier to Tunis*, Trans, and ed. A. E. Murch, London, 1959

Ehrenstein, T. *Das Alte Testament im Bilde*, Vienna, 1923

Eljasz, W. *Ubiory w Polsce*, Cracow, 1879 (on medieval Polish costume)

Encyclopaedia Biblica, London, 1899

Encyclopaedia of Islam, s.v. Kalansuwa

Encyclopaedia Judaica, Berlin, 1928–34

Encyclopaedia Judaica, Jerusalem, 1971

Evans, J. *Dress in Mediaeval France*, London, 1952

Ewald, P. *Reise . . . Von Tunis Nach Tripolis*, Nuremberg, 1842

Fakhry, Ahmed, *The Necropolis of El-Bagwat in Kharga Oasis*, Cairo, 1951

Ferriol, M. de, *Recueil de cent estampes . . .* Paris, 1714

Finkelstein, L. *Jewish Self-Government in the Middle Ages*, New York, 1964

Finn, E. A. *Home in the Holy Land*, London, 1866

Finn, J. *The Jews in China*, London, 1843

Flügel, J. C. *The Psychology of Clothes*, London, 1930

Fox-Davies, A. C. *A Complete Guide to Heraldry*, London, 1925

Friedberg, C. B. *Bet Eked Sepharim*, 2nd ed. Tel-Aviv, 1952. (Bibliography of Hebrew books.)

Garnett, L. M. J. *The Women of Turkey*, London, 1891

Garrucci, P. R. *Storia della Arte Cristiana*, Prato, 1873–81

Gaster, M. *Samaritan Phylacteries and Amulets*, in *Studies and Texts*, London, 1925–28

Gaster, M. *The Samaritans*, London, 1925

Gaster, T. H. *The Holy and the Profane*, New York, 1955

Gebhardt, O. von. *The Miniatures of the Ashburnham Pentateuch*, London, 1883

Gilyarovskaya, N. *Russkii Istorich Kostyum*, Moscow, 1945

Godbey, A. H. *The Lost Tribes A Myth*, Durham, N. C., 1930. Chap XIII 'Persian, Turkoman, Mongol and Chinese Jews.'

Goetz, H. *The History of Persian Costume*, in Pope III

Gold, H. *Die Juden und Judengemeinden Mährens*, Brünn, 1929

Goldschmidt, A. *Die Elfenbeinskulpturen aus der zeit der Karolingischen und Sächsischen Kaiser VIII–XI jahrhundert*, Berlin, 1914

Goldstein, M. & Dresdner, K. *Kultura i sztuka ludu zydowskiego na ziemiach polskich*, Lwow, 1935 (The Culture and Art of the Jewish People in Poland)

Goodenough, E. R. *Jewish Symbols in the Graeco-Roman Period*, Vols. I–XI, New York, 1953–64

Gordon, C. H. *Before the Bible*, London, 1962

Goulven, J. *Les Mellahs de Rabat-Salé*, Paris, 1927

Graetz, H. *History of the Jews*, London, 1901

Grandidier, A. *Voyage dans les Provinces Méridionales de l'Inde*, Paris, 1870

Grayzel, S. *The Church and the Jews in the XIIIth century*, Philadelphia, 1933

Grunwald, M. *Trachten der Juden* in *Jüdisches Lexikon* V (Eng. translation in *Universal Jewish Encyc.* III *s.v. Costumes*)

Gurney, O. R. *The Hittites*, London, 1961

Haedo, Diego de, *Topographia E Historia General de Argel*, Valladolid, 1612

Hahn, Joseph Nordlingen, *Sefer Yosef Ometz*, Frankfurt A/M, 1723 (new ed. 1928), Secs. 3 and 592 on the *Sarbal*

Hamdy-Bey & Launay, M. de, *Les Costumes Populaires de La Turquie en 1873*, Constantinople, 1873

Hamerton, J. A., Ed. *Peoples of All Nations*, London, 1922–24

Harff, Arnold von, *The Pilgrimage of* . . . translated from the German, London, Hakluyt Society, 1946

Hargreaves-Mawdsley, W. N. *A History of Academical Dress in Europe*, Oxford, 1963

Hargreaves-Mawdsley, W. N. *A History of Legal Dress in Europe*, Oxford, 1963

Harrison, M. *The History of the Hat*, London, 1960

Heaton, E. W. *Everyday Life in Old Testament Times*, London, 1956

Henderson, E. *Biblical Researches and Travels in Russia including a Tour in the Crimea . . . with observations on the state of the Rabbinical and Karaite Jews . . .* London, 1826

Hentze, C. *Chinese Tomb Figures*, London, 1928

Hertzberg, A. *The French Enlightenment and the Jews*, New York and London, 1968

Hesse-Warteg, de, *Tunis, the Land and the People*, London, 1882

Heuzey, L. & J. *Histoire du Costume dans l'Antiquité Classique—L'Orient*, Paris, 1935

Hiler, H. *From Nudity to Raiment*, London, 1929

Hobson, R. L., *Art of the Chinese Potter*, London, 1923

Hobson, R. L. *The George Eumorfopoulous Collection Catalogue*, London, 1925

Hollaenderski, L. *Les Israélites de Pologne*, Paris, 1846

Hölscher, U. *The Excavation of Medinet Habu*—Vol. IV. *The Mortuary Temple of Ramses III* Part 2, Chicago, 1951

Höst, G. *Nachrichten von Marokos und Fes*, Copenhagen, 1781

Hottenroth, F. *Le Costume . . . des peuples anciens et modernes*, Paris, 1883–92

Hottenroth, F. *Handbuch der Deutschen Tracht*, Stuttgart, 1895–96

Hottenroth, F. *Deutsche Volkstrachten*, Frankfurt Am Main, 1898

Hottenroth, F. *Altfrankfurter Trachten*, Frankfurt Am Main, 1912

Houston, M. G. *Ancient Egyptian Mesopotamian and Persian Costume*, London, 1954. *Mediaeval costume in England and France*, London, 1939

Hughes, P. *The Church in Crisis. A History of the Twenty Great Councils*, London, 1961

Hyamson, A. M. *The Sephardim of England*, London, 1951

International Standard Bible Encyclopaedia, Chicago, 1930. *s.v.* Dress

The Interpreter's Bible, New York, 1952

Jastrow, M. *A Dictionary of the Targum, the Talmud Babli and Yerushalmi*, New York, 1950

The Jewish Encyclopaedia, New York, 1902

Johnson, R. *Travels through part of the Russian Empire and the country of Poland along the southern shores of the Baltic*, London, 1815

Josephus, *Loeb Classical Library* ed. 1926

Jouin, J. *Le Costume de la Femme Israélite au Maroc* in *Journal de la Société des Africanistes*, Paris, 1936

Jüdisches Lexikon, Berlin, 1930

Kendrick, A. F. *Victoria and Albert Museum. Catalogue of Textiles from Burying-Grounds in Egypt.* Vol. I Graeco-Roman Period. London, 1920

Kirchner, P. C., *Jüdisches Ceremonial*, Nuremberg, 1734

Kisch, B. *History of the Jewish Pharmacy (Judenapothek) in Prague* in *Historia Judaica* VIII, New York, 1946

Kisch, G. *The Jews in Medieval Germany*, Chicago, 1949

Kisch, G. *The Yellow Badge in History* in *Historia Judaica* XIX No. 2. New York, 1957

Kraeling, E. G. *The Synagogue. The Excavations at Dura-Europos*, New Haven, 1956

Krafft, H. *A Travers Le Turkestan Russe*, Paris, 1902

Krauss, S. *Griechische und Lateinische Lehnwörter im Talmud, Midrasch und Targum*, Berlin, 1899

Krauss, S. *Kleidung im Mittelalter* in *Encyc. Judaica* X

Krauss, S. *Talmudisch Archäologie*, Leipzig, 1910 Vol. I 'Kleidung und Schmuck'.

Kretschmer, A. & Rohrbach, C. *Die Trachten der Volker*, Leipzig, 1860–4

Kybalova, L. *Coptic Textiles*, London, 1967

Lane, E. W. *Manners and Customs of the Modern Egyptians*, Everyman ed. London, 1954

Lancet-Müller, A. *Bokhara*, Israel Museum Catalogue, Jerusalem, 1967

Lawson, C. A. *British and Native Cochin*, Cochin, 1860

Leloir, M. *Dictionnaire du Costume*, Paris, 1951

Lempriere, W. *A Tour through the Dominions of the Emperor of Morocco*, Newport, 1813

Lenz, O. *Timbuktu. Reise Durch Marokko, Die Sahara Und Den Sudan . . . in Den Jahren 1879 Und 1880*, Leipzig, 1892

Letts, M. *The Sachsenspiegel and its Illustrators*, London, 1933

Levy, Moritz, *Die Sephardim in Bosnien*, Sarajevo, 1911

Levy, R. *A Baghdad Chronicle*, Cambridge, 1929

Levy, R. *Notes on Costume from Arabic Sources* in *Journal of the Royal Asiatic Society*, London, 1935, pp. 319–38

Lichtenstadter, I. *The Distinctive Dress of Non-Muslims in Islamic Countries* in *Historia Judaica*, New York, 1943, V, No. 1

Lilien, E. M. *List of the original etchings*, Berlin-Vienna, 1922

Lindo, E. H. *The History of the Jews of Spain and Portugal*, London, 1848

Lord, P. B. *Algiers with Notices of the Neighbouring States of Barbary*, London, 1835

Lortet, L. *La Syrie D'Aujourdhui. Voyages dans La Phénicie, Le Liban et La Judée*, 1875–1880, Paris, 1884

Lovillo, J. Guerrero, *Las Cantigas*, Madrid, 1949

Lutz, H. F. *Textiles and Costumes among the Peoples of the Ancient Near East*, Leipzig, 1923

Lyon, G. F. *A Narrative of Travels in North Africa*, London, 1821

Macdonald, J. *Palestinian Dress* in *Palestine Exploration Quarterly*, London, Jan.-April, 1951

Macmichael, W. *Journey from Moscow to Constantinople*, London, 1819

Madhloom, T. A. *The Chronology of Neo-Assyrian Art*, London, 1970

Mahler, J. G. *The Westerners Among The Figurines of the T'Ang Dynasty of China*, Rome, 1959

Marcais, G. *Le Costume Musulman D'Alger*, Paris, 1930

Marcus, J. R. *The Jew in the Mediaeval World*, Cincinnati, 1938

Mayer, L. A. *Mamluk Costume*, Geneva, 1952

Mayer, N. *The Jews of Turkey*, London, 1913

Mendelsohn, S. *The Jews of Africa*, London, 1920

Milano, A. *Storia degli ebrei in Italia*, Turin, 1963

Minorsky, V. *The Chester Beatty Library. A Catalogue of the Turkish Manuscripts and Miniatures*, Dublin, 1958

Monumenta Judaica, Cologne, 1963

Morey, C. F. *Early Christian Art*, Princeton New Jersey, 1953

Muller, D. H. & Schlosser, J.v. *Die Haggadah von Sarajevo*, Vienna, 1898

New Schaff-Herzog Encyclopaedia of Religious Knowledge, New York, 1909, *s.v.* Dress

Nicolay, N. de, *Les Quatre Premiers Livres des Navigations . . . Orientales*, Lyons, 1568

Noah, M. M. *Travels . . . in the Years 1813–15*, New York and London, 1819

Norblin, J. P. *Collection de Costumes Polonais*, Paris, 1817

Norris, H. *Costume and Fashion*, London, 1924

Norris, H. *Church Vestments*, London, 1949

Oppenheim, M. *Bilder aus dem Altjüdischen Familienleben*, Frankfurt A/M, 1886 (Drawings dated 1866–69)

Padover, S. K. *The Revolutionary Emperor: Joseph II of Austria*, London, 1967

Pahlen, K. K. *Mission to Turkestan*, ed. R. A. Pierce, London, 1964

Parkes, J. *The Conflict of the Church and the Synagogue*, Philadelphia, 1961

Parrot, A. *Nineveh and Babylon*, London, 1961

Parrot, A. *Nineveh and the Old Testament*, London, 1955

Parrot, A. *Samaria. The Capital of the Kingdom of Israel*, London, 1958.

Pfister, R. *Les Débuts du Vêtement Copte* in *Etudes D'Orientalisme . . . Le Musée Guimet II*, Paris, 1932

Pfister, R. *Textiles de Palmyre*, Paris, 1934

Pfister, R. & Bellinger, L. *The Excavations at Dura-Europos*. Final Report IV. Part II. The Textiles. New Haven, 1945

Picart, B. *Ceremonies et Coutumes Religieuses de tous les Peuples du Monde*, Amsterdam, 1723–43. First English edition, 1731

Picken, M. B. *The Fashion Dictionary*, New York, 1957

Pignatti, T., *Pietro Longhi*, London, 1969

Planché, J. R. *A Cyclopaedia of Costume*, London, 1876

Platter, Thomas, *Journal of a Younger Brother*, transl. and ed. by S, Jennett, London, 1963

Pocknee, C. E. *Liturgical Vesture*, London, 1960

Pope, A. U. *A Survey of Persian Art*, London and New York, 1938–9

Prilutsky, N. *Dos Gevet*, Warsaw, 1923

Pritchard, J. B. *The Ancient Near East in Pictures*, Princeton, New Jersey, 1954

Prodan, M. *The Art of the Tang Potter*, London, 1960

Purchas, S. *Purchas His Pilgrimes*, Glasgow, 1905

Racinet, M. A. *Le Costume Historique*, Paris, 1888

Réau, L. *Iconographie de l'Art Chrétien*, II, Paris, 1956

Richardson, H. G. *The English Jewry under Angevin Kings*, London, 1960

Rice, D. Talbot, *The Beginnings of Christian Art*, London, 1957

Rice, D. Talbot, *Art of the Byzantine Era*, London, 1963

Richter, J. P. & Taylor, A. C. *The Golden Age of Classic Christian Art*, London, 1904

Robert, Ulysse, *Les Signes D'Infamie Au Moyen Age*, Paris, 1891

Roger, E. *La Terre Sainte*, Paris, 1664

Rosenzweig, A. *Kleidung Und Schmuck Im Biblischen Und Talmudischen Schriftum*, Berlin, 1905

Roth, C. *The History of the Jews of Italy*, Philadelphia, 1946

Rubens, A. (i) *Anglo-Jewish Portraits*, London, 1935; (ii) *A Jewish Iconography*, London, 1954

Rünsberg, E. von, *Der Sachsenspiegel. Bilder aus der Heidelberger Handschrift*, Leipzig, 1934

Salamé, A. *A Narrative of the Expedition to Algiers in the Year 1816*, London, 1819

Sandys, G. *Sandys Travailes*, 5th Ed. London, 1652

Sassoon, D. S. *A History of the Jews in Baghdad*, Letchworth, 1949

Schemel, S. *Die Kleidung der Juden im Zeitalter der Mischnah*, Berlin, 1912

Schipper, I. *Kultur Geschichte*, Warsaw, 1926

Schudt, J. K. *Jüdische Merkwürdigkeiten*, Frankfurt and Leipzig, 1714–18

Segal, J. B. *The Hebrew Passover. From the earliest time to A.D. 70*, London, 1963

Seyrig, H. *Armes et Costumes Iraniens de Palmyre* in *Syria XVIII*, Paris, 1937

Sibmacher, J. *Wappenbuch*, Nuremberg, 1856–1936

Skippon, P. *An Account of a Journey*, London, 1746

Stern, S. *The Court Jew*, Philadelphia, 1950

Straus, R. *The Jewish Hat as an aspect of Social History* in *Jewish Social Studies IV*, New York, 1942

Strauss, E. *The Social Isolation of Ahl Adh-Dhimma* in *Etudes Orientales à la Mémoire de Paul Hirschler*, Budapest, 1950

Sukenik, E. L. *The Ancient Synagogue of Beth Alpha*, Jerusalem, 1932

Tcherikover, V. *Hellenistic Civilization and the Jews*, Philadelphia, 1961

Thevenot, M. de, *Voyages*, Amsterdam, 1727

Tobar, J. *Les Inscriptions Juives de K'ai-Fong-Fou*, Shanghai, 1900

Tristram, E. W. *English Mediaeval Wall Painting . . . The 13th century*, Oxford, 1950

Tritton, A. S. *Islam and the Protected Religions* in *Journal of the Royal Asiatic Society*, London, 1927

Ulrichs, J. C. *Sammlung Jüdischer Geschichten . . . in der Schweiz*, Basel, 1768

The Universal Jewish Encyclopaedia, New York, 1948

Van Lennep, H. J. *The Oriental Album*, New York, 1862

Vaux, R. de, *Ancient Israel*, London, 1961

Vinaver, S. *Spomenica*, Belgrade, 1924

Wellesz, E. *The Vienna Genesis*, London, 1960

White, W. C. *Chinese Jews*, Toronto, 1942

Wilpert, J. *Die Römischen Mosaiken und Malereien der Kirchlichen Bauten vom IV bis XIII Jahrhundert*, Frieburg im Breisgau, 1917

Wilson, J. *The Lands of the Bible*, Edinburgh, 1847

Wischnitzer-Bernstein, R. *Symbole und Gestalten der Jüdischen Kunst*, 1935

Woodcock, W. J. *Scripture Lands . . .*, London, 1849

Woolley, C. L. *Ur of the Chaldees*, London, 1929

Woolley, C. L. *Mesopotamia and the Middle East*, London, 1961

Yadin, Y. *Bar-Kokhba*, London, 1971

Zwarts, J. *The Significance of Rembrandt's The Jewish Bride*, Amsterdam, 1929

List of Illustrations

(Subjects set in quotation marks are actual inscriptions on the original illustrations)

Glossarial Index